OXFORD ENGLISH MONOGRAPHS

General Editors

D0169205

Society and Politics
in the Plays of
Thomas Middleton

SWAPAN CHAKRAVORTY

CLARENDON PRESS · OXFORD
1996

Oxford University Press, Walton Street, Oxford OX2 6DP
Oxford New York
Athens Auckland Bangkok Bombay
Calcutta Cape Town Dar es Salaam Delhi
Florence Hong Kong Istanbul Karachi
Kuala Lumpur Madras Madrid Melbourne
Mexico City Nairobi Paris Singapore
Taipei Tokyo Toronto
and associated companies in
Berlin Ibadan

Oxford is a trade mark of Oxford University Press

Published in the United States
by Oxford University Press Inc., New York

British Library Cataloguing in Publication Data
Data available

Library of Congress Cataloging in Publication Data
Chakravorty, Swapan.
Society and politics in the plays of Thomas Middleton/Swapan Chakravorty
p. cm.— (Oxford English monographs)
Based on the author's thesis (doctoral)—Oxford, 1991
Includes bibliographical references and index.
1. Middleton, Thomas, d. 1627—Political and social views.
2. Politics and literature—England—History—17th century.
3. Literature and society—England—History—17th century
4. Political plays, English—History and criticism. 5. Social problems in literature.
I. Title. II. Series.   PR2718.P6C43 1996   822'.3—dc20   95–10647
ISBN 0–19–818266–X

1 3 5 7 9 10 8 6 4 2

Typeset by Pure Tech Corporation, Pondicherry, India
Printed in Great Britain
on acid free paper by
Bookcraft Ltd.
Midsomer Norton, Bath

Preface

This book is on Thomas Middleton's plays. His non-dramatic corpus hence receives less sustained treatment than I should have otherwise wished. The earlier poems and prose tracts are valuable evidence for the conditions under which Middleton took up a career in the theatre, and are given more attention than the later pageants and masques. The use made of the biographical material is equally discriminatory, and for the same reason.

The last collection of Middleton's works was edited by A. H. Bullen over a century ago. The Oxford *Collected Works*, which will replace Bullen's dated texts, is nearing completion. At the moment, one has to rely on modern critical editions of single plays. Their editorial conventions are not uniform, and I have retained the spellings of source editions in quotations while modernizing play titles and character names. This has been my rule with other works of Middleton, and with plays by other dramatists. Bullen, however, has been preferred to more recent editions not easily available.

The *Textual Companion* to the Oxford *Collected Works* will deal authoritatively with issues relating to Middleton's canon and chronology. I have, therefore, avoided referring readers to authorship and dating controversies, providing instead a summary chart of the extant canon.

The Bibliography excludes forthcoming titles and those quoted from mediate texts. It does not itemize multiple titles cited from collections. In all such cases, the notes give fuller details. Pre-1800 texts are cited by signatures because of frequent errors in pagination. Unless mentioned, the place of publication for pre-1800 titles is London.

The doctoral thesis which led to this monograph was written at Oxford between Michaelmas 1988 and Trinity 1991. As the notes will show, a number of books and articles published since then have coincided with my interests. An important few I was unable to obtain at the time of delivering the manuscript. An earlier draft of Chapter 6 will appear in *Renaissance Essays for Kitty Scoular Datta*, ed. Sukanta Chaudhuri, to be published by Oxford University Press, India.

Research for the thesis was funded by a Commonwealth Academic Staff Award, for which I wish to thank the Commonwealth Scholarship Commission in the UK, Jadavpur University and the University Grants Commission in India, and British Council officials in both countries. At Jadavpur, Jasodhara Bagchi made sure that I had neither problems nor excuses.

I was fortunate to have been writing on Middleton when so much work was under way in connection with the Oxford *Collected Works*, although this book comes too early to make use of its texts and editorial contributions. To its general editor, Gary Taylor, I am grateful for many courtesies, including making available photocopies of early printed editions and a draft text of his own general introduction.

Unchanging structure and changing event have remained inseparable dimensions of the text in my awareness since my early training under two extraordinary though unlike teachers, Arun Kumar Das Gupta and the late Ranajay Karlekar. Kitty Scoular Datta guided my initial studies in Calcutta, and I continued to profit from her kindness and learning at Oxford. Dennis Kay's supervision of the thesis, and comments on it from Julia Briggs, Andrew Gurr, Emrys Jones, and the anonymous publisher's reader saved me from many indiscretions. Stephen Gill of the Oxford English Monographs Committee, and Andrew Lockett and Jason Freeman of the Oxford University Press were patient with my unprofessional anxieties. So were the staff of the Bodleian and the English Faculty Libraries at Oxford, and of the University Library at Jadavpur.

This book would have taken longer to write but for some timely help from Kantik Ghosh, Martine Grice, Indraneel Mukherjee, and Kate Teltscher.

S. C.

Calcutta
December 1993

Contents

Abbreviations

Bullen	A. H. Bullen (ed.), *The Works of Thomas Middleton*, 8 vols. (London, 1885– 7)
CD	*Comparative Drama*
CI	*Critical Inquiry*
CLA Journal	*College Language Association Journal*
CQ	*Critical Quarterly*
CSP Dom.	*Calendar of State Papers, Domestic*
CSP Ven.	*Calendar of State Papers, Venetian*
EC	*Essays in Criticism*
EETS	Early English Text Society
ELH	*English Literary History*
ELN	*English Language Notes*
ELR	*English Literary Renaissance*
ES	*English Studies*
E & S	*Essays and Studies*
HLQ	*Huntington Library Quarterly*
JEGP	*Journal of English and Germanic Philology*
JMRS	*Journal of Medieval and Renaissance Studies*
L & P	*Literature and Psychology*
MLN	*Modern Language Notes*
MLQ	*Modern Language Quarterly*
MLR	*Modern Language Review*
MP	*Modern Philology*
MRDE	*Medieval and Renaissance Drama in England*
MSR	Malone Society Reprints
NLH	*New Literary History*
N & Q	*Notes and Queries*
PBSA	*Papers of the Bibliographical Society of America*
PLL	*Papers on Language and Literature*
PMLA	*Publication of the Modern Language Association*
PQ	*Philological Quarterly*
RD	*Renaissance Drama*
RES	*Review of English Studies*
RORD	*Research Opportunities in Renaissance Drama*
RQ	*Renaissance Quarterly*

Ren. & Ref.	Renaissance and Reformation
SB	Studies in Bibliography
SEL	Studies in English Literature 1500-1900
SP	Studies in Philology
SQ	Shakespeare Quarterly
SR	Sewanee Review
SS	Shakespeare Survey
TLS	Times Literary Supplement
TSLL	Texas Studies in Literature and Language
UTQ	University of Toronto Quarterly
YES	Yearbook of English Studies

Abbreviations of Middleton Titles

Ant	The Ant and the Nightingale
Chaste Maid	A Chaste Maid in Cheapside
Dissemblers	More Dissemblers besides Women
Family	The Family of Love
Five Gallants	Your Five Gallants
Hengist	Hengist, King of Kent
Heroes	The Inner Temple Masque, or The Masque of Heroes
Lady	The Lady's Tragedy
Lucrece	The Ghost of Lucrece
Mad World	A Mad World, My Masters
Michaelmas	Michaelmas Term
No Wit	No Wit, No Help Like a Woman's
Penniless	The Penniless Parliament of Threadbare Poets
Plato	Plato's Cap
Quarrel	A Fair Quarrel
Quiet Life	Anything for a Quiet Life
Revenger	The Revenger's Tragedy
Solomon	The Wisdom of Solomon Paraphrased
Timon	Timon of Athens
Trick	A Trick to Catch the Old One
Truth	The Triumph of Truth
1 Whore	The Honest Whore, Part 1
Women Beware	Women Beware Women
Yorkshire	A Yorkshire Tragedy

The Extant Canon of Thomas Middleton

Square brackets enclose abbreviations used; co-authors are named in paren-
theses. The earliest probable dates of composition are given, and these do not
always coincide with the years of publication or performance. All dates are
new-style.

1597:	The Wisdom of Solomon Paraphrased [Solomon]
1599:	Microcynicon
1600:	The Ghost of Lucrece [Lucrece]
1601:	The Penniless Parliament of Threadbare Poets (revision of Smellknave) [Penniless]
1603:	The Magnificent Entertainment (Dekker)
1603:	The Family of Love (Dekker; revised by Barry, 1607) [Family]
1603:	The Phoenix
1604:	Plato's Cap [Plato]
1604:	The Black Book
1604:	The Ant and the Nightingale [Ant]
1604:	The Meeting of Gallants at an Ordinary
1604:	The Honest Whore, Part 1 (Dekker) [1 Whore]
1604-7:	Your Five Gallants [Five Gallants]
1605:	Michaelmas Term [Michaelmas]
1605:	A Yorkshire Tragedy [Yorkshire]
1605:	Timon of Athens (Shakespeare) [Timon]
1605:	A Mad World, My Masters [Mad World]
1605:	A Trick to Catch the Old One [Trick]
1606:	The Puritan
1606:	The Revenger's Tragedy [Revenger]
1609:	Sir Robert Sherley . . . his Royal Entertainment
1609:	The Two Gates of Salvation
1609-21:	Macbeth (additions to Shakespeare)
1611:	The Roaring Girl (Dekker)
1611:	The Lady's Tragedy [Lady]
1611:	No Wit, No Help Like a Woman's [No Wit]
1613:	A Chaste Maid in Cheapside [Chaste Maid]
1613:	Entertainment at the Opening of the New River
1613:	Wit at Several Weapons (Rowley)
1613:	The Triumphs of Truth [Truth]
1613:	The Witch

1615-16:   *A Fair Quarrel* (Rowley) [*Quarrel*]
1615-16:   *The Nice Valour* (?revision of Fletcher)
1616:   *The Widow*
1616:   *Civitatis Amor*
1617:   *The Triumphs of Honour and Industry*
1618:   *The Peacemaker*
1618:   *The Old Law* (Rowley)
1618:   *The Owl's Almanac*
1619:   *The Inner Temple Masque, or The Masque of Heroes* [*Heroes*]
1619:   *More Dissemblers besides Women* [*Dissemblers*]
1619:   'On the Death of Richard Burbage'
1619:   *The World Tossed at Tennis* (Rowley)
1619:   *The Triumphs of Love and Antiquity*
1620-21:   *Honourable Entertainments*
1620-22:   *Hengist, King of Kent* [*Hengist*]
1621:   *The Sun in Aries* (?Munday)
1621:   *Women Beware Women* [*Women Beware*]
1621:   *Anything for a Quiet Life* (Webster) [*Quiet Life*]
1621:   *Measure for Measure* (adaptation of Shakespeare)
1622:   *An Invention Performed for the Service of the Right Honourable Edward
            Barkham*
1622:   *The Triumphs of Honour and Virtue*
1622:   *The Changeling* (Rowley)
1623:   *The Triumphs of Integrity*
1623:   'Upon this Masterpiece of Tragedy' (prefixed to Webster's *Duchess
            of Malfi*)
1624:   *A Game at Chess*
1624:   'A harmless game, made only for delight'
1626:   *The Triumphs of Health and Prosperity*

Introduction

Thomas Middleton's reputation rides a curious paradox. Among the major dramatists of his time, we know him least, although we feel he knew us best. Surmounting over three centuries of neglect, Middleton is more our contemporary today than any other Jacobean playwright. Dickens, Balzac, Baudelaire, Ibsen, Chekhov, Strindberg, Giraudoux, Brecht, Albee, and Pinter are only a few of the later authors Middleton has reminded his readers of.[1] Peter Barnes, Edward Bond, and Howard Barker have written their own versions of *A Trick to Catch the Old One*, *A Mad World, My Masters*, and *A Chaste Maid in Cheapside*.[2] Brian Meeson staged a few scenes 'with Wesker in mind' for the 1967 University Alumnae Club production of *Women Beware Women* in Toronto. The all-women cast of the 1979 University of California production of *The Roaring Girl* staged two parallel scripts: the one Middleton and Dekker's; the other, airing feminist issues raised at rehearsals, by the director Sue-Ellen Case. The ending of *Women Beware*, which many consider too tame for a strikingly unorthodox

---

[1] See Una Ellis-Fermor, *The Jacobean Drama: An Interpretation* (London, 1936), 152; G. R. Hibbard, 'The Tragedies of Thomas Middleton and the Decadence of Drama', *Renaissance and Modern Studies*, 1 (1957), 54; Richard Hindry Barker, *Thomas Middleton* (New York, 1958), 109–10, 131, 141; T. B. Tomlinson, *A Study of Elizabethan and Jacobean Tragedy* (Cambridge, 1964), 158, 171, 186, 191–2, 197; Robert Brustein, *Seasons of Discontent: Dramatic Opinions 1959–1965* (London, 1966), 253; Brian Gibbons, *Jacobean City Comedy* (1968; 2nd edn., London, 1980), 3; Dorothea Krook, *Elements of Tragedy* (New Haven, Conn., 1969), 150, 180; Inga-Stina Ewbank, 'Realism and Morality in *Women Beware Women*', *E & S* 22 (1969), 58–9; Dorothy Farr, *Thomas Middleton and the Drama of Realism: A Study of Some Representative Plays* (Edinburgh, 1973), 77, 83–4; S. Gorley Putt, 'The Tormented World of Middleton', *TLS*, 2 Aug. 1974, 833; Charles A. Hallett, *Middleton's Cynics: A Study of Middleton's Insight into the Moral Psychology of the Mediocre Mind* (Salzburg, 1975), 13, 126, 198–208; Raymond J. Pentzell, '*The Changeling*: Notes on Mannerism in Dramatic Form', *CD* 9 (1975), 25; Margot Heinemann, *Puritanism and Theatre: Thomas Middleton and Opposition Drama under the Early Stuarts* (Cambridge, 1980), 185; Kenneth Muir, 'The Role of Livia in *Women Beware Women*', in Antony Coleman and Antony Hammond (eds.), *Poetry and Drama 1570–1700: Essays in Honour of Harold F. Brooks* (London, 1981), 79; G. B. Shand, 'Middleton's *Phoenix* and the Opening of *Bleak House*', *Dickensian*, 78 (1982), 93–5; Roma Gill, 'The World of Middleton', in Kenneth Friedenreich (ed.), *'Accompaninge the Players': Essays Celebrating Thomas Middleton, 1580–1980* (New York, 1983), 32, 36–7; and Kenneth Friedenreich, 'Introduction: How to Read Middleton', ibid. 1, for such comparisons.

[2] See Bryan Loughrey and Neil Taylor (eds.), *Thomas Middleton: Five Plays* (London, 1988), p. xxiv.

text, was rewritten by Howard Barker for the 1986 production at the Royal Court Theatre in London.[3]

And yet, as Margot Heinemann said not so long ago, 'we are still none too sure how to take him'.[4] Although T. S. Eliot led the revival of academic interest in Middleton, his judgement that Middleton is 'merely the name which associates six or seven great plays' has had a distracting influence, setting critics on the hunt for his missing 'personality' and 'point of view'.[5] Such pursuits share a common three-point strategy: tease out Middleton's latent moral and political sympathies through thematic analysis, trace the sorted themes down the canon to establish its coherence, use the inferred authorial bias to prove his partisan religion and politics.

The strategy has yielded several persuasive versions of Middleton, but they very often fail to explain the greatness of the plays. Critics reacting against Eliot's morally noncommittal Middleton fit together the portrait of a sombre Calvinist,[6] and we lose sight of the artist whom Nicholas Brooke called 'the subtlest moral intelligence of the Jacobeans'.[7] More important, we lose the playwright whose bleak laughter continues to worry and provoke our own theatres, and whose carnal wisdom made Kenneth Tynan declare that in matters of sex, there was

---

[3] See J. R. Mulryne's Introduction to the Revels Plays edition of *Women Beware* (London, 1975), p. lxxviii; Paul Mulholland's Introduction to the Revels Plays edition of *Roaring Girl* (Manchester, 1987), 50–1; id., 'Let Her Roar Again: *The Roaring Girl* Revived', *RORD* 28 (1985), 17–18; and Thomas Middleton and Howard Barker, *Women Beware Women* (London, 1986). See also the account of the 1966 Royal Court production of *Chaste Maid* in R. B. Parker's Revels Plays edition (London, 1969), 147–54.

[4] Heinemann, *Puritanism and Theatre*, 1.

[5] T. S. Eliot, *Selected Essays 1917–1932* (London, 1932), 162. On Middleton's reputation, see Sara Jayne Steen, 'The Response to Middleton: His Own Time to Eliot', and Geraldo U. de Sousa, 'Thomas Middleton: Criticism since T. S. Eliot', *RORD* 28 (1985), 63–71, 73–85. For a fuller treatment of the earlier response, see Sara Jayne Steen, *Ambrosia in an Earthen Vessel: Three Centuries of Audience and Reader Response to the Works of Thomas Middleton* (New York, 1993).

[6] The classic statement of the problem is R. B. Parker, 'Middleton's Experiments with Comedy and Judgment', in J. R. Brown and B. Harris (eds.), *Jacobean Theatre* (London, 1960), 178–99. For moralist readings, see Robert Ornstein, *The Moral Vision of Jacobean Tragedy* (Madison, Wis., 1960), 170–99; Irving Ribner, *Jacobean Tragedy: The Quest for Moral Order* (London, 1962), 123–52; David M. Holmes, *The Art of Thomas Middleton: A Critical Study* (Oxford, 1970); Arthur C. Kirsch, *Jacobean Dramatic Perspectives* (Charlottesville, Va., 1972), 75–96; and David Farley-Hills, *Jacobean Drama: A Critical Study of the Professional Drama, 1600–25* (London, 1988), 112–31. On Middleton's Calvinism, see John Stachniewski, 'Calvinist Psychology in Middleton's Tragedies', in R. V. Holdsworth (ed.), *Three Jacobean Revenge Tragedies: A Casebook* (Basingstoke, 1990), 226–47.

[7] Nicholas Brooke, *Horrid Laughter in Jacobean Tragedy* (New York, 1979), 110.

more 'authentic reportage' in *Women Beware* and *The Changeling* 'than in the whole of the First Folio'.[8] An equally unadventurous academicism seeks to answer L. C. Knights, who accused Middleton of social and political orthodoxy.[9] Knights's critics demonstrate Middleton's sympathies for the city and the middling ranks, and his political tilt towards the pro-Parliamentary 'left'.[10] Again, we may well wonder if they are not selling short a dramatist who consistently laid bare the symbiosis of country and city, culture and power, desire and domination. We have several manifestly reductive versions of Middleton—the clinical realist, the cynic, the Calvinist, the pro-Puritan author of the city—but all of these versions, pushed beyond a point, impoverish the many-sidedness of his texts. In 'uncovering' the author, they confine his works.

Some dissenters, it is true, have kept up what may be called an 'open-Middleton' campaign. They stress Middleton's suspicion of dogma, his subversive use of irony and burlesque, his trick of reversing perspectives and withholding judgement.[11] The trouble with these positions is that they may easily shade off into critical quietism, if not

---

[8] Kenneth Tynan, in *Observer*, 8 July 1963, quoted in Kathleen McLuskie, *Renaissance Dramatists* (Atlantic Highlands, NJ, 1989), 18–19.

[9] See L. C. Knights, *Drama and Society in the Age of Jonson* (London, 1937), 256–69. See also Louis B. Wright, *Middle-Class Culture in Elizabethan England* (Chapel Hill, NC, 1935), 652–3.

[10] The most thorough argument for this view is Heinemann, *Puritanism and Theatre*. See also, W. Power, 'Thomas Middleton vs. King James I', *N & Q* 202 (1957), 526–34; A. A. Bromham, 'The Date of *The Witch* and the Essex Divorce Case', *N & Q* 225 (1980), 149–52; id., 'The Contemporary Significance of *The Old Law*' *SEL* 24 (1984), 327–39; id., 'The Tragedy of Peace: Political Meaning in *Women Beware Women*', *SEL* 26 (1986), 309–29; Anne Lancashire, '*The Witch*: Stage Flop or Political Mistake?', in Friedenreich (ed.), '*Accompaninge the Players*', 161–81; G. B. Shand, 'The Elizabethan Aim of *The Wisdom of Solomon Paraphrased*', ibid. 67–77; Annabel Patterson, *Censorship and Interpretation: The Conditions of Writing and Reading in Early Modern England* (Madison, Wis., 1984), 73–9; Jerzy Limon, *Dangerous Matter: English Drama and Politics in 1623/4* (Cambridge, 1986), 98–129; Albert H. Tricomi, *Anticourt Drama in England, 1603–1642* (Charlottesville, Va., 1989), 121–30, 142–52; A. A. Bromham and Zara Bruzzi, *The Changeling and the Years of Crisis, 1619–1624: A Hieroglyph of Britain* (London, 1990); and Julia Briggs, 'Middleton's Forgotten Tragedy: *Hengist, King of Kent*', *RES*, ns 41 (1990), 479–95.

[11] A few examples are Richard Levin, *The Multiple Plot in English Renaissance Drama* (Chicago, 1971), 25–48, 59–75, 124–37, 168–83, 194–202; Parker, Introduction to the Revels Plays edition of *Chaste Maid*, pp. lvi–lix; John F. McElroy, *Parody and Burlesque in the Tragicomedies of Thomas Middleton* (Salzburg, 1972); Anthony Covatta, *Thomas Middleton's City Comedies* (Lewisburg, Pa., 1973); R. V. Holdsworth, Introduction to the New Mermaids edition of *A Fair Quarrel* (London, 1974), pp. xxxii–xxxiv; Pentzell, '*Changeling*: Notes on Mannerism', 3–28; Brooke, *Horrid Laughter*, 70–110; Michael E. Mooney, ' "The Common Sight" and Dramatic Form: Rowley's Embedded Jig in *A Faire Quarrel*', *SEL* 20 (1980), 305–23; Neil Taylor and Bryan Loughrey, 'Middleton's Chess Strategies in *Women*

superior nescience. A recent apologist of the 'open–Middleton' school writes: 'Where did Middleton stand? It's not a question you can answer by appealing to party loyalties of one kind or another, because Middleton had the courage to stand stubbornly on his own ground.'[12] The critic does allow Middleton moral and political opinions, but claims that these are impossible to name. The artist who was merely a name produced an art that was 'nameless'.

One reason for our undecidedness about Middleton is the sparse evidence we have for his biography. We know something of early lawsuits and family squabbles, a truncated career at Oxford, his marriage, his association with a few companies and patrons, his appointment as City Chronologer, and the political flak drawn by *A Game at Chess*. Middleton's precise role in any of these, however, is scholarly guesswork.[13]

Scholarship is on surer grounds in matters of authorship and dating, and the Oxford *Collected Works* is certain to provide the canon with a more secure basis.[14] But there are lost plays, collaborations, and revisions in which Middleton's share is imprecisely known, and scanty

Beware Women', SEL 24 (1984), 341–54; P. K. Ayers, 'Plot, Subplot, and the Uses of Dramatic Discord in A Mad World, My Masters and A Trick to Catch the Old One', MLQ 47 (1986), 3–18; Viviana Comensoli, 'Play-Making, Domestic Conduct, and the Multiple Plot in The Roaring Girl', SEL 27 (1987), 249–66; Paul Yachnin, 'A Game at Chess: Thomas Middleton's "Praise of Folly" ', MLQ 48 (1987), 105–23; and Martin White, Middleton and Tourneur (Basingstoke, 1992), 18.

[12] Ronald Huebert, 'Middleton's Nameless Art', SR 95 (1987), 591–2.

[13] The fullest treatment of the evidence is Gary Taylor, 'Thomas Middleton: Lives and Afterlives', the general introduction to the forthcoming Oxford *Collected Works*. See also Barker, *Middleton*, 1–25; Harold N. Hillebrand, 'Thomas Middleton's *The Viper's Brood*', MLN 42 (1927), 35–8; R. C. Bald (ed.), *A Game at Chesse* (Cambridge, 1929), 19–25; id., 'Middleton's Civic Employments', MP 31 (1933), 65–78; Mark Eccles, 'Middleton's Birth and Education', RES 7 (1931), 431–41; id., 'Thomas Middleton: A Poett', SP 54 (1957), 516–36; John Robert Moore, 'The Contemporary Significance of Middleton's *Game at Chesse*', PMLA 50 (1935), 761–8; M. G. Christian, 'Middleton's Residence at Oxford', MLN 61 (1946), 90–1; ead., 'A Sidelight on the Family History of Thomas Middleton', SP 44 (1947), 490–6; Edward M. Wilson and Olga Turner, 'The Spanish Protest against *A Game at Chesse*', MLR 44 (1949), 476–82; Geoffrey Bullough, ' "The Game at Chesse": How it Struck a Contemporary', MLR 49 (1954), 156–8; P. G. Phialas, 'Middleton's Early Contact with the Law', SP 52 (1955), 186–94; Samuel Schoenbaum, 'A New Middleton Record', MLR 55 (1960), 82–4; John B. Brooks, 'Middleton's Stepfather and the Captain of *The Phoenix*', N & Q 206 (1961), 382–4; David George, 'Thomas Middleton at Oxford', MLR 65 (1970), 734–6; Heinemann, *Puritanism and Theatre*, 258–83; and Thomas Cogswell, 'Thomas Middleton and the Court, 1624: *A Game at Chess* in Context', HLQ 47 (1984), 273–88.

[14] See David J. Lake, *The Canon of Thomas Middleton's Plays: Internal Evidence for the Major Problems of Authorship* (Cambridge, 1975); and MacD. P. Jackson, *Studies in Attribution: Middleton and Shakespeare* (Salzburg, 1979).

evidence for deciding which of the two major tragedies, *Changeling* and *Women Beware*, came first. A surprising few still doubt his authorship of *The Revenger's Tragedy*. The current story of Middleton's growth as a playwright has, as a result, been divided into dubious generic segments. This is a narrative which I wish to question, and which, I am sure, the Oxford *Works* will discredit for good.

Another difficulty is the daunting range of Middleton's professional output. He wrote poetry, prose satire, journalistic pamphlets, comic almanacs, masques, civic pageants, political allegory, history plays, comedy, tragicomedy, and tragedy. Within each of these, he mixed genres and modes, imitation and parody, prose and verse. His plays were staged by adult and boy actors, at the court and in the city. He shared writing plays with dramatists as divergent as Dekker, Rowley, and Webster, and borrowed freely from Shakespeare, Marston, Jonson, and Fletcher. The problem is further complicated by Middleton's equal flair for repetition and innovation. Scholars have noted his 'self-cannibalizing tendencies',[15] his habit of recycling the same materials and devices. At the other extreme, if one compares the civic pageant, *The Triumphs of Truth*, to the play, *Chaste Maid*, both written in 1613, one might derive some idea of the radically dissimilar texts Middleton could fashion out of similar ingredients at the same point in his career.[16] Like Diotima's Eros, Middleton thus appears a paradoxical union of poverty and plenty. The most repetitive of Jacobean playwrights, and also the writer of the sparest dramatic verse, seems possessed of the most prodigious invention.

HISTORY, TEXT, INTERPRETATION

A deeper source of the trouble are the restrictive notions of the relationship of history, text, and interpretation at work behind most studies of Middleton's plays. Fredric Jameson is right: 'One does not need to argue the reality of history: necessity, like Dr. Johnson's stone, does that for us.'[17] It is not enough to say that writer and reader are

---

[15] R. V. Holdsworth, '*The Revenger's Tragedy* as a Middleton Play', in id. (ed.), *Three Jacobean Revenge Tragedies*, 80.

[16] David M. Bergeron, 'Middleton's Moral Landscape: *A Chaste Maid in Cheapside* and *The Triumphs of Truth*', in Friedenreich (ed.), '*Accompaninge the Players*', 13–46, studies elements common to the two works.

[17] Fredric Jameson, *The Political Unconscious: Narrative as a Socially Symbolic Act* (London, 1981), 82.

both historically situated, they are writer and reader by virtue of their historical situation. But to limit situatedness to the immediate conditions of genesis and impact is to endorse a sociological functionalism which, while it may recover the contextual dimension of a work, fails to account for the continued historical validity of the text.[18]

A narrow understanding of context was never an offence exclusive to academic crtics. When Howard Barker rewrote *Women Beware*, his declared purpose was to destroy the Jacobean opposition of lust and kingship by making sexual knowledge the key to political freedom. 'Middleton knew the body was the source of politics,' wrote Barker. 'He did not know it was also the source of hope.'[19] It would indeed be over-zealous to expect Middleton to hold Reichian views on sex and politics. Nevertheless, if he saw the relationship of lust to death, he also sensed, as Barker in fact acknowledges, the mutual implication of sex and power. When Livia explains why it is easier for husbands to remain faithful, she talks of the 'many sundry dishes' that women never lay their lips to. The menu that compensates male sexual abstinence is a political one, 'As obedience forsooth, subjection, duty, and such kickshaws' (1.2.40–2). Later, in Leantio's comparison of 'government in love' to that in a kingdom, popular revolt is imagined as phallic insurrection, 'That raised in self-will wars against all reason' (1.3.43–6). The Cardinal's final line, 'So where lust reigns, that prince cannot reign long' (5.2.225), asserts the moral pretext of power in Church and State, but cannot erase the play's disclosure of the tacit pact between desire and violence. Middleton had destroyed the Jacobean opposition of lust and political rule long before Barker's intervention.

For an author as culturally precocious as Middleton, context is best conceived as a liberating condition of the text. '*Being situated* is an essential and necessary characteristic of freedom.'[20] We need to situate Middleton not to reduce him to a 'point of view', but to relate the continued appeal of his text to the initial moment of its engagement with, and disengagement from, received cultural images. Only by virtue of this initial gesture is language placed in what Heidegger called 'the Open'[21]—situated yet responsive to changing interpretations, implacable yet contingent.

[18] See Wolfgang Iser, 'The Current Situation of Literary Theory: Key Concepts and the Imaginary', *NLH* 11 (1979), 13.
[19] Programme note to William Gaskill's production at the Royal Court Theatre, London, 1986; quoted in Loughrey and Taylor (eds.), *Five Plays*, p. xxiv.
[20] Jean-Paul Sartre, *What is Literature?*, trans. Bernard Frechtman (London, 1950), 112.
[21] See Martin Heidegger, *Poetry, Language, Thought*, trans. Albert Hofstadter (New York, 1971), 17–87.

A stress on context is destined to limit our perception of the text's vitality if writing is not, at the same time, allowed an inaugural function, the status of a constitutive act in which the author is 'himself a kind of new idiom, constructing itself'.[22] This is all the more important in view of the social and exigent nature of Jacobean play-making and plural authorship. A contrary assumption which haunts much critical industry is that the author can say things in a new way provided he has, before saying them, decisively freed himself from the 'false consciousness' governing his old ones. Such a positivist sequence underlies, for instance, Althusser's statement that Brecht could break with the formal conditions of the theatre since he had by then broken with its material conditions.[23] You rewrite the ideological subtext if you have already burnt the false bridges, you merely write it if you have not.

It is true that Althusser claims that 'real' art makes us see *from the inside*, by an *internal distance*, the very ideology in which they are held'.[24] That internal distance, however, is already real and material before it is conscious, and 'knowledge', he cannot help implying, does not belong to this immanent critique, but to its interpretation. 'Like all knowledge,' Althusser writes, 'the knowledge of art presupposes a preliminary *rupture* with the language of *ideological spontaneity* and the constitution of a body of scientific knowledge to replace it.'[25] Since its modalities are not propositional, art, it would seem, may only achieve the 'rupture'. The task of constituting 'scientific knowledge' is left to criticism, which is asked to measure the distance the artist has travelled from his ideological base. Even the most daring, however, can achieve only an 'allusive' proximity to 'reality'. This is because the road from ideology to 'knowledge' is not a measurable distance. It is an ontological divide, and you cannot clear the abyss in two jumps.

Althusser's is merely a better-known instance of a variety of mono-logical schemes which assume a Kantian definition of 'knowledge' and deny it to expressive uses of language. The value of a literary text in any such scheme will depend on the price one is prepared to put on ideology. The moment of rupture with ideological consciousness in art

[22] Maurice Merleau-Ponty, *The Primacy of Perception and Other Essays on Phenomenological Psychology, and Philosophy of Art, History and Politics*, ed. James M. Edie (Evanston, Ill., 1964), 9.
[23] Louis Althusser, *For Marx*, trans. Ben Brewster (1969; London, 1979), 144.
[24] Louis Althusser, *Lenin and Philosophy and Other Essays*, trans. Ben Brewster (London, 1971), 204.
[25] Ibid. 207.

is variously accounted for,[26] but all such schemes ultimately appeal to a pre-ontological (for literature, a pre-verbal) cognizance and critique of ideology.

It would perhaps be easier to reconcile a historicized reading of Middleton with an argument for his continued cultural importance if we agreed that the cognitive dimension of his plays, as that of all creative work of significance, lies more in 'an addition to the reality from which it begins' than in 'the discovery or reconstruction of latent meaning'.[27] Certainty of consensus is not what one might expect of such 'knowledge'. It only promises the possibilty of shared cultural experience, implicit in what Clifford Geertz has described as the 'social history of the imagination'.[28]

It could be argued that a reinterpretation of Middleton or of any other past writer will necessarily employ methods of academic reading which assume a reader-spectator who is either transcendental or a rigid historical abstraction. These are instances of the two 'faulty perspectives' which E. D. Hirsch calls 'subjectivist' distortions and 'objectivist' reconstructions.[29] Both appear to be consequences of equally homogeneous notions of the past and present. Any simple model of homology between structures of literature and of social reality is weakened by Gadamer's point that the questions we ask of a past text, and the questions to which we imagine the text is an answer, reflect our situation in the present, the presuppositions directing our own reading. What we think a text says must be what it is saying to us; interpretation is, in a certain sense, self-encounter.[30] The self which encounters the work, and the self we encounter in our experience of it, are fashioned by history, but history understood in a dialogical sense.

The pursuit of context may be aligned with new readings of Middleton if, instead of trying to recover a univocal account of his

---

[26] Two examples are Bloch's stress on the utopian dimension in all ideology, and Goldmann's theory of art's ability to maximize the potential consciousness of privileged social groups. See Ernst Bloch, *The Utopian Function of Art and Literature: Selected Essays*, trans. Jack Zipes and Frank Mecklenburg (Cambridge, Mass., 1988), 78–155; and Lucien Goldmann, *The Hidden God: A Study of Tragic Vision in the* Pensées *of Pascal and the Tragedies of Racine*, trans. Philip Thody (London, 1964), 12–21.

[27] See Pierre Macherey, *A Theory of Literary Production*, trans. Geoffrey Wall (London, 1978), 6.

[28] Clifford Geertz, *Local Knowledge: Further Essays in Interpretive Anthropology* (New York, 1983), 102, 119.

[29] See E. D. Hirsch, Jr., *The Aims of Interpretation* (Chicago, 1976), 36–49.

[30] See Hans-Georg Gadamer, *Philosophical Hermeneutics*, trans. and ed. David E. Linge (Berkeley, Calif., 1976), 100–1.

past reception, it turns to the modes of representation from which the texts break free. This could also justify the use of the term 'literary' in talking of his play-texts. Waking up to the form of representation is inseparable from waking up to its object; to transform 'the received cultural imagination' of an object is to alter its received cultural forms.[31] It is this '*differential* quality',[32] the sense that form in a text is history committed, that enables us to speak of its 'literary' function, even if we were to agree that 'there is no literary object strictly speaking'.[33]

This study of society and politics in Middleton's plays attempts to historicize the texts as a condition for understanding the source of their undiminished vitality. It shares with New Historicism the desire for basing interpretation on a dialogical understanding of history, for reading changing event into the text's changeless structure. That desire, I wish to stress, is rooted in a purposive view of writing, and in the conviction that formal and historical concerns in cultural analysis are inseparable.[34] The study of what Stephen Greenblatt calls the '*circulation of mimetic capital*' is justified by the insight it provides into the intervention of the artist's mimetic labour.[35]

PURITANISM

My brief comment on Barker's revision of *Women Beware* had implied that it was possible to consider Middleton 'the first great secular playwright in English drama',[36] even when placing him in the context of the religious idiom of Jacobean political discourse. The most sustained attempt in recent years to recover that context has been Margot Heinemann's portrayal of Middleton as a playwright of 'Parliamentary-Puritan' loyalties. One need not labour the political sympathies of the

---

[31] Robert Pinsky, 'Responsibilities of the Poet', *CI* 13 (1987), 423.

[32] See Jurij Tynjanov, 'On Literary Evolution', in Ladislav Matejka and Krystyna Pomorska (eds.), *Readings in Russian Poetics: Formalist and Structuralist Views* (Cambridge, Mass., 1971), 69.

[33] Gérard Genette, *Figures of Literary Discourse*, trans. Alan Sheridan (Oxford, 1982), 4.

[34] Louis A. Montrose emphasizes the need for this awareness in New Historicism. See 'Professing the Renaissance: The Poetics and Politics of Culture', in H. Aram Veeser (ed.), *The New Historicism* (New York, 1989), 17.

[35] Stephen Greenblatt, *Marvelous Possessions: The Wonder of the New World* (Oxford, 1991), 6.

[36] Huebert, 'Middleton's Nameless Art', 608. See also J. A. Bryant, Jr., 'Middleton as a Modern Instance', *SR* 84 (1976), 584, 593–4.

author of *Game at Chess*, and these coincide with the ones Julia Gasper has recently called 'militant Protestant'.[37] But there are difficulties with Heinemann's description of Middleton as 'Puritan', and an early look at these problems might be useful.

In a survey of the idea of 'Puritanism' in historians since Hobbes, Michael Finlayson finds three reasons why the concept has remained slippery and confusing. First, scholars have not always distinguished between contemporary and later applications of the word 'Puritan'; secondly, its connotations between 1560 and 1660 were not constant; and, thirdly, the abstraction 'Puritanism' has come to acquire a spurious autonomy comparable to 'biological or other natural phenomena'.[38] These same problems bedevil discussions of Middleton's 'Puritanism'.

For most of the period Finlayson surveys, 'Puritan' was an enemy word everyone disowned. Thomas Wood, a Marian exile who later returned to England, complained to the Earl of Warwick on 20 August 1576 that the 'true professors' of God's glory, anti-vestiarians among them, were being 'falsly termed Puritanes' by 'wicked worldlings and vaine courtiers'.[39] Such complaints continue beyond Middleton's time, the term being applied to describe people of all shades, including Jesuits.[40]

Until the 1620s, however, it was used chiefly to brand Nonconformists and sectaries, as was pointed out by Fuller in his *Church History* (1655).[41] As late as in 1630, Giles Widdowes defined the 'Puritan' as a 'Non-Conformist' rejecting the Articles, Canons, and Prayer Book, and then lumped him with Brownists and separatists.[42] Nicholas Tyacke maintains that it was only after the Arminian ascendancy, which began around 1626 and culminated in Laud's appointment to the

---

[37] See Julia Gasper, *The Dragon and the Dove: The Plays of Thomas Dekker* (Oxford, 1990), 2–9.

[38] Michael G. Finlayson, *Historians, Puritanism, and the English Revolution: The Religious Factor in English Politics before and after the Interregnum* (Toronto, 1983), 3–12, 42–76.

[39] See Patrick Collinson, *Godly People: Essays in English Protestantism and Puritanism* (London, 1983), 98.

[40] King James followed precedents in calling Jesuits '*Puritan-papists*'; see Charles Howard McIlwain (ed.), *The Political Works of James I* (1918; New York, 1965), 126; Thomas H. Clancy, 'Papist-Protestant-Puritan: English Religious Taxonomy, 1565–1665', *Recusant History*, 13 (1976), 243; and Peter Milward, *Religious Controversies of the Elizabethan Age: A Survey of Printed Sources* (London, 1977), 58–9.

[41] Thomas Fuller, *The Church History of Britain*, ed. J. S. Brewer, 6 vols. (Oxford, 1845), v. 529.

[42] Giles Widdowes, *The Schismatical Puritan* (Oxford, 1630), A3ᵛ, quoted in John Morgan, *Godly Learning: Puritan Attitudes towards Reason, Learning and Education, 1560–1640* (Cambridge, 1986), 12.

primacy of Canterbury in 1633, that the word was used to label all
reforming Protestants and Calvinists.[43] Christopher Hill has sub-
sequently challenged the thesis of a dramatic Arminian or Laudian
coup, shifting the burden of historical causation from personalities and
theology to long-term economic and political factors. The effect either
way was the extension of the term 'Puritan' to those who had long
been defenders of the reformed English Church. There were, as Hill
says, 'no great innovations in policy': 'Only now there were more
"Puritans".'[44] 'Puritan' thereafter was an epithet used increasingly to
designate secular loyalties. Henry Parker wrote of this 'new enlarge-
ment of the name' in A Discourse Concerning Puritans (1641): 'besides
the Puritans in Church policy, there are now added Puritans in
Religion, Puritans in state, and Puritans in morality.'[45]

With hindsight, one could perhaps see the religio-political alliance
as a convergence of movements for church reform and against royal
absolutism. It still remains hard to distil an essential 'Puritanism' from
the unevenly mixed ingredients within the movements. Nor can a
stable description of a 'Puritan' be based on the opportunism of
contemporary branding. There is some truth in Lucy Hutchinson's
partisan exaggeration that 'whatever was odious or dreadfull to the
king', his flatterers 'fixt that upon the Puritane'.[46] To call 'Puritans' all
who, prior to the Laudian ascendancy, shared any of the mixed
concerns of Hutchinson's heroes would be to risk persistent confusion
between contemporary and later usage.

Even before the Arminian assault, when James's pro-Spanish bias
was incensing zealous Protestants, the term 'Puritan' was increasingly
used to divide them from the loyal moderates. An anonymous 1622
verse pamphlet, The Interpreter, complained that the 'Protestant' was
now one who could flirt with 'all faiths', while the 'sound Protestant',
who spoke his mind in Parliament, was being nicknamed a 'Puritan'.[47]

---

[43] Nicholas Tyacke, 'Puritanism, Arminianism and Counter-Revolution', in Conrad
Russell (ed.), The Origins of the English Civil War (London, 1973), 119–43. Tyacke develops
his argument in Anti-Calvinists: The Rise of English Arminianism c.1590–1640 (Oxford, 1987);
see esp. 7–8, 137–9, 185–8.

[44] Christopher Hill, A Nation of Change and Novelty: Radical Politics, Religion and Literature
in Seventeenth-Century England (London, 1990), 73; see also 56–81.

[45] Henry Parker, A Discourse Concerning Puritans (1641), as quoted in Finlayson, Historians,
Puritanism, and the English Revolution, 47.

[46] Lucy Hutchinson, Memoirs of the Life of Colonel Hutchinson with the Fragment of an
Autobiography of Mrs Hutchinson, ed. James Sutherland (Oxford, 1973), 43. The memoirs were
written between 1664 and 1671.

[47] C. H. Firth (ed.), Stuart Tracts 1603–1693 (Westminster, 1903), 235, 237, 243.

During the 1621 Parliament, John Pym objected to 'that odious and factious name of Puritan' which a member had used for the promoters of a Sabbatarian bill.[48] Isaac Bargrave, in a sermon to the Commons in 1624, warned patriotic Protestants that there was 'no meanes so prompt to make a Protestant a Papist, as by the opposition of a Puritane'.[49] In the same year, Francis Bacon advised the Duke of Buckingham not to withdraw his favour 'from such as are honest and religious men' simply because Papists 'traduced' them as 'Puritans'.[50] Thomas Scott's *Vox Populi* (1620), on which Middleton relied heavily for *Game at Chess*, has the Spanish ambassador Gondomar boast of his success in laying the blame for Catholic plots on 'Puritans', 'Which very name and shadovv the King hates, it being a sufficien aspertiõ to disgrace any person, to say he is such'.[51]

A plagiarist who put together the mock-almanac *Vox Graculi* (1622) predicted for the year 1623 that 'Holinesse shall be faine to hide its head, for feare of being branded with that irreligious Nick-name of Puritan'.[52] The prophecy was not quite accurate. Buckingham returned with Charles from Madrid without a Spanish bride later in the year to drum up popular support for war with Spain. The 1624 Parliament voted supplies for war with Spain and expelled the Jesuits. As the godly rejoiced at the fall of Babylon, *Game at Chess* ran at the Globe with stunning success, and it endeared Middleton, William Hemminge was to write later, to the 'Puritans'.[53] But then followed another Catholic match for the prince, the suspension of the recusancy laws, English aid to Richelieu against French Protestants, the disaster of the English mission under Count Mansfeld to Germany, the accession of Charles, and the Arminian ascendancy. The three virtually silent years Middleton lived after the success of *Game at Chess* saw that expansion of the meaning of 'Puritan' and that convergence of oppositional movements in Church and State described by Parker.

From the date of *The Family of Love* to that of *Game at Chess*, most Englishmen concerned to banish popery would have resented the label 'Puritan' as a ploy to club them with 'Brownists, Anabaptists, Familists,

---

[48] Quoted in Tyacke, 'Puritanism, Arminianism and Counter-Revolution', 129.

[49] Isaac Bargrave, *A Sermon Preached before the Honorable Assembly of Knights, Cittizens, and Burgesses of the Lower House of Parliament, February the Last 1623* [1624] (1624), F2.

[50] J. Spedding et al., *The Works of Francis Bacon*, 14 vols. (London, 1857–74), xiv. 448–9.

[51] [Thomas Scott], *Vox Populi or Newes from Spayne* (1620), B3–3ᵛ.

[52] *Vox Graculi, or Iacke Dawes Prognostication* (1622), F4ᵛ.

[53] See William Hemminge, *Elegy on Randolph's Finger Containing Well-Known Lines 'On the Time-Poets'*, ed. G.C. Moore Smith (Oxford, 1923), ll. 185–6.

and all the rabble of such schismaticall Sectaries'.[54] Heinemann follows
Hill in defining 'Puritans' as those who desired reform from within,
although she finds some place for the separatists and sects, alongside
'Parliamentary Puritans', within a 'broad movement'.[55] Heinemann
distinguishes between the two strands of the movement, but selectively
blends the components of the package in discussing the plays. Thus the
'anti-Puritan' satire in *Family of Love* is explained as gentle ribbing of
extremist cranks, *The Puritan* is considered too intolerant of the moderates to have been by Middleton, the 'popular feminism' of *Roaring Girl*
is compared to the views of 'Ranters and sectaries after 1640', and
Game at Chess is seen as voicing the 'radical, sceptical, plebeian
opposition of ordinary Londoners'.[56] This is to blur all semantic shades
within and outside contemporary usage.

Another trouble with 'Parliamentary Puritanism' is that it implies a
precise correlation between Middleton's 'Puritanism' and his 'par-
liamentarism', a correlation which is neither necessary nor demon-
strable. A 'Puritan' in religion might sort strangely with a 'Puritan' in
politics, as the royalist allegiance of 'Puritans' such as Sir Ralph
Hopton, Sir Bevil Grenville, and Samuel Ward testifies.[57] Since
Middleton's sympathy for causes Heinemann identifies as 'Puritan' is
social and political in its stress, he does not even fit the psychological
definition of 'Puritans' as the 'hotter sort' of Protestants, fired by a
godly zeal following the experience of conversion.[58] I do not wish to
claim that differences more fundamental than those of 'theological
temperament' between the 'hotter sort' and the conformists did not
surface at critical moments.[59] But Middleton's political and religious
sympathies cannot be judged 'Puritan' on the basis of such differences.
His 'Puritanism', like his 'radicalism', makes more sense as a relational
marker than as a commitment to a stable religious or political sect.

[54] C[ornelius] Burges, *The Fire of the Sanctuarie Newly Vncouered, or, A Compleat Tract of
Zeale* (1625), E5^v.
[55] Heinemann, *Puritanism and Theatre*, 2–6. Christopher Hill's view is summarized in
Society and Puritanism in Pre-Revolutionary England (1964; Harmondsworth, 1986), 15–30.
[56] Heinemann, *Puritanism and Theatre*, 75 n., 77–8, 100, 170, 284–6.
[57] See Hill, *Society and Puritanism*, 27.
[58] See Charles Lloyd Cohen, *God's Caress: The Psychology of Puritan Religious Experience*
(New York, 1986), 4 and *passim*. The definition of 'Puritans' as the 'hotter sort of protestants'
is from Percival Wiburn, *A Checke or Reproofe of M. Howlet's Untimely Screeching* (1581), as
quoted in Patrick Collinson, *The Elizabethan Puritan Movement* (1967;255MI repr. Oxford,
1990), 27.
[59] On this point, see Collinson, *Elizabethan Puritan Movement*, 26–8.

COMPLICIT PREMISES

One can admit Middleton's support for the religio-political causes Julia Gasper has termed 'militant Protestant'—opposition to Rome, political alliance with Protestant states, armed support for Protestant minorities in Europe, belief in an apocalyptic theology with a Calvinist slant, and distrust of royal absolutism—without having to call him a 'Parliamentary Puritan'.[60] That Gasper leaves Middleton out of her list of 'militant Protestant' dramatists (which includes Marlowe, Chapman, Dekker, Heywood, Webster, Fletcher, and Massinger) may point to a more fundamental problem about docketing Middleton, one which is related to what I have already said concerning the study of his context.

I choose to interpret the omission as an unwitting recognition of the fact that Middleton eludes even Gasper's label because it does not say enough. The 'militant Protestant' views Gasper discusses were not confined to high or low, court or city, educated or uneducated. In Middleton, on the contrary, political commitment and betrayal are inalienable from questions of rank, place, and gender. Religio-political causes in themselves hold very little of Middleton's significant attention. What interests him are the vital links of the institutions which enshrine or betray these causes with the cultural practices on which they are founded. Politics in Middleton is, therefore, sexual; and sex, political. Localizing Middleton's sympathies only begins to reveal the text's engagement with such historical rudiments often obscured by the political choices of the moment.

Instead of looking for the controlling presence of an author who has his mind made up, this study will focus on the context and career of a playwright whose response to the events, images, and professional demands of his time generated disturbing insights into the structures of social and political authority. These insights were not always explicit or uniform. They were often incipient and discontinuous, and the contradictions they encountered remain visible in the generic puzzles of Middleton's plays, in the startling paradoxes of his dramaturgy.

Middleton, it has been said often, resists summary description. This is different from saying that his art was 'nameless'. Certain preoccupations will emerge from examining a body of texts joined by his name, and it may help to signal the leading ones. One theme likely to unite

---

[60] Gasper, *Dragon and the Dove*, 2–9.

a study of society and politics in the plays is their repeated discovery of the indivisibility of culture and power. Stuart absolutist ambitions and the anomalies of late feudal culture sharpened Middleton's unusual instinct for the concealed mechanics of power, the interests which underlie its pretexts, and the contingent nature of the cultural institutions and values which sustain its structures.

Such a concern could perhaps be described as one with power as the 'ruse of history'. The phrase is Foucault's, although it is not quite how he would characterize power.[61] Nevertheless, it is in Foucault's analysis of power that one finds an approximation to a crucial discovery in Middleton's plays. 'Relations of power are not in a position of exteriority with respect to other types of relationships (economic processes, knowledge relationships, sexual relations)', writes Foucault, 'but are immanent in the latter'.[62] A similar immanence in Middleton's plays joins public heights to subliminal depths, politics to sex, money to morals, families to kingdoms. The ideological separation of these spheres would reflect for Foucault the way a culture proposed to divide and rule its discursive formations. Middleton too seemed to have glimpsed the complicit premises on which these domains were founded.

Foucault has explained for us the intentional yet non-subjective nature of all power, and 'its ability to hide its mechanisms'.[63] In Middleton, we repeatedly witness the stereotypes and self-definitions of social groups, subjection to which is a condition for the exercise and acceptance of domination, running into intolerable contradictions. Middleton's celebrated 'irony' is less a matter of clinical sang-froid than of a committed search into the linked premises and hidden mechanisms which condition the self-understanding of sexual desire, social interest, and political ambition.

The Jacobean theatre provided Middleton with a strategic site for exploring the roles social exigencies fashioned for individuals, and the network of interests which required political control of these roles. From the early comedies to *Game at Chess*, his work displays a readiness to use role-playing and cross-dressing on the stage to suggest the fictionality of social identities. Added to this was his alertness to the

---

[61] Michel Foucault, *The History of Sexuality:i. An Introduction*, trans. Robert Hurley (1978; Harmondsworth, 1984), 95.

[62] Ibid. 94.

[63] Ibid.

ambiguous social place of the theatre.⁶⁴ Even while making the best professional use of the conditions of patronage, censorship, and the market, Middleton was able to exploit the subversive potencies of the ludic and to reflect upon the theatricality of political representations. The man whom King James was prepared to accept as his ghost-writer, and several of whose plays were produced at court, could thus not infrequently be a political nuisance.⁶⁵ Middleton's ambivalent relation to political authority was mistaken in the past for cynical opportunism; his ability to bring into simultaneous view the shifts of history and art, for bland dispassion. It is easier for our times to recognize in these traits a great precursor of politically self-conscious theatre.

⁶⁴ This ambiguity is best discussed in Steven Mullaney, *The Place of the Stage: License, Play, and Power in Renaissance England* (Chicago, 1988). Douglas Bruster has recently claimed a more focal place for the theatre in *Drama and the Market in the Age of Shakespeare* (Cambridge, 1992). For a sceptical view of the subversive potential of the ludic, see Paul Yachnin, 'The Powerless Theater', *ELR* 21 (1991), 49–74.

⁶⁵ *Peacemaker*, thought to have been by the king, was authorized by James in 1619. *Phoenix, Trick, No Wit, Quarrel, Old Law, Widow, Dissemblers,* and *Changeling* were performed at the court.

The Press and the Playhouse: Early Trials

Two truths are told by the sparse narrative of Thomas Middleton's early life: his roots lay almost entirely in London, and he entered the theatre as a blue-collar journeyman. The son of William Middleton, 'cittizen and Bricklayer',[1] Thomas was christened on 18 April 1580 at St Lawrence in the Old Jewry, the well-off part of town where the Middletons lived. When William died on 24 January 1586, he had earned a coat of arms, and was worth over £335, leaving property in Limehouse and in Shoreditch, adjoining the Curtain theatre. Anne, his wife, was the daughter of another Londoner, William Snow. Ten months after William's death, Anne married Thomas Harvey, 'Cittizen and grocer of London',[2] who was one of Ralegh's colonists rescued by Drake from the Roanoke Island. At the time of her second marriage, Anne was 48, a year younger than the wealthy widow Livia in *Women Beware*. Harvey was about the age of Leantio, perhaps in his twenties.

Middleton, like De Flores in *Changeling*, 'tumbled into th'world a gentleman' (2.1.49), but a series of legal squabbles between Anne and Harvey over William's bequest soon robbed him of his social place. In 1590, some tenants of the Curtain property complained to the Lord Chancellor that Harvey was squandering the fortune he had gained by the marriage, and that he was planning to travel overseas leaving Anne and her children with no maintenance. In 1586 Anne had herself arrested on purpose for the children's share of the estate so that Harvey too would be gaoled unless he discharged the debt, which he did by auctioning his goods. Harvey was again arrested for debt in 1592, and he left England to dodge his creditors after 1595, the year in which, Anne later claimed, he had tried to poison her.

---

[1] William Middleton was thus described in the 1601 Close Roll extract recording the sale of Thomas's share of the Curtain property; see Christian, 'Middleton's Residence', 90. The sources for Middleton's biography are listed in n. 13 to the Introduction.

[2] Christian, 'Sidelight', 496.

In 1598, Allan Waterer, yeoman of Shoreditch and husband of Anne's daughter Avis, brought a writ of attachment against Anne, Thomas Harvey, Thomas Middleton, and one John Knapp, to whom Harvey had conveyed some leases. It seems that Anne soon placated Waterer, since their names appear together as defendants in the two suits brought on 10 June and 6 December 1600 by Harvey, who had returned to England in 1599. It was Harvey's last effort to wrest William Middleton's estate which Anne, like the 'wise widdowes' Truewit describes in *Epicoene* (2.2.142–3), or the 'old cozening widows' Moll mentions in *Roaring Girl* (2.2.61–3), had conveyed in trust to three lawyers of the Inner Temple soon after William's death. He never gained control over this property, since a Close Roll extract sealed on 28 June 1600 records Thomas Middleton selling his share to Waterer.

On 7 April 1598 Middleton was matriculated from Queen's College, Oxford, the 'continuing estate' of which he wished 'all happiness' in the 1619 mayoral pageant *The Triumphs of Love and Antiquity* (Bullen, vii. 325). Queen's was a stronghold of Oxford Calvinists, although it is doubtful if Middleton developed any great admiration for Oxbridge 'Puritanism'. In the christening scene in *Chaste Maid*, drunken 'Puritan' women drool over an unappetizing moron since he is from politically correct Cambridge.

It was probably Waterer's 1598 writ of attachment which first dragged Middleton into the lawsuits. John Kyrby, a deponent in the first of Harvey's two 1600 suits, told the court on 8 February 1601:

Thomas Middleton was forced by reason of some controversies betweene his mother and Allen Waterer to come from Oxenforde to helpe his mother Anne Harvie when her husbonde was at Sea whereby he thinkethe he loste his Fellowshipp at Oxenforde.[3]

This testimony was backed by two other deponents, Thomas Dawson and Anthony Snode. Middleton was a co-defendant in both the suits brought by Harvey in 1600, and could not possibly have avoided hearings in London. Kyrby was wrong, however, in saying that Middleton had stayed away from Oxford since coming down to assist his mother in 1598, for on 28 June 1600 he sold his share of the Curtain property to Waterer to pay for his studies at Oxford. Severe inflation

---

[3] Phialas, 'Middleton's Early Contact', 191. John D. Reeves suggested in 'Thomas Middleton and Lily's *Grammar*: Some Parallels', *N & Q* 197 (1952), 75–6, that Middleton had a grammar school education before Oxford.

hit England in the middle 1590s, and the sale indicates that lawsuits at such a time had drained away Middleton's resources. There is little reason to doubt that when Anthony Snode made his deposition in February 1601 Middleton had left Oxford. Snode thought that the suits had cost Middleton his studentship, 'for nowe he remaynethe heare in London daylie accompaninge the players'.[4] Middleton, 'his studies amazed' like the poor university scholar's in *A Yorkshire Tragedy* (4.14), fell at least three terms short of the sixteen required for his degree.

The litigations, involving property and marriage, allowed Middleton an early glimpse into the entwined mechanics of money and sex. He was thus later able to see the law as the institutional hinge and ideological guarantor of economic and sexual power. Debts and lawsuits dogged the rest of Middleton's life. He was defendant in another Chancery suit brought in 1600 by a Limehouse tenant. In 1609, Robert Keysar, manager of the Revels children, sued him for a debt of £16. Middleton answered that he had handed over to Keysar a tragedy called *The Viper and her Brood* in full discharge of the bond.[5] We know of two other occasions when he was sued for debts, once for £5 to one Richard Harper, and again for owing an innkeeper £7. Success as a playwright, regular comissions since 1617 for the annual Lord Mayor's shows (he wrote his first one in 1613), and appointment as City Chronologer in 1620 may have steadied Middleton's finances, but *Game at Chess* fetched him a summons only three years before his death.

The financial slide must have brought to the young Middleton insecurity, possibly disenchantment, about his place in society. In the Close Roll extract of 1600 recording the sale of his share of the Curtain property, the son of the armigerant bricklayer declared himself 'Thomas midleton of london gent'.[6] The 1598 matriculation entry in the University Register at Oxford had, on the contrary, described him as *plebei filius*. It is symptomatic of the uncertainty of the young Middleton's class identity that he was first designated *generosi fis*, but this was crossed out and replaced with *plebei filius*.[7] The alteration may reflect the nature of the studentship he held at Oxford. The scholar in *The*

[4] Phialas, 'Middleton's Early Contact', 192.

[5] W. D. Dunkel, 'The Authorship of *The Revenger's Tragedy*', *PMLA* 46 (1931), 781–5, suggested that the play is the same as *Revenger*. See Samuel Schoenbaum, *Internal Evidence and Elizabethan Dramatic Authorship: An Essay in Literary History and Method* (London, 1966), 208–9, for a discussion.

[6] Christian, 'Middleton's Residence', 90.

[7] See Eccles, 'Thomas Middleton a Poett', 524.

Ant and the Nightingale, possibly a self-portrait, goes up to the university as 'a poor scholar and servitor to some Londoner's son . . . by whose peevish service I crept into an old battler's gown' (Bullen, viii. 102). The discrepancy of social designation, however, is not peculiar to the University Register. The prefatory verse to *Microcynicon* (1599) and the title-page of *The Ghost of Lucrece* (1600) are signed 'T.M. Gent', while in 1604 *Ant* and *The Black Book* were published simply under the initials 'T.M.'.

PATRONS AND POEMS

For the adolescent writer, the only route to security left was patronage, and Middleton made a bid for it even before he went up to Oxford. In 1597, he dedicated to the Earl of Essex *The Wisdom of Solomon Paraphrased*, a poem of 706 six-line stanzas which moralizes on The Wisdom of Solomon in the Apocrypha. It was probably influenced by Henry Lok's verse paraphrase of Ecclesiastes, published the same year but licensed on 11 November 1596.[8] Essex was at this time deemed a saviour of Protestant letters.[9] G. B. Shand reads the poem as 'a statement of patriotic Elizabethan protestantism, Calvinistically tinged'.[10] The reliance on the Geneva version of the Apocrypha, the implicit equation of Solomon and Queen Elizabeth, the attacks on idolatry, the introduction of Astraea, and the praise of chastity and barrenness (cf. Bullen, viii. 162, 182–90, 164–5, 167–8) support Shand's reading. There is no evidence, however, that either the queen or the earl took any notice of the work. Nor did the poem merit much fuss, although it is obsessed with the opposition of substance and shadow, sin and shame, insight and blindness—contrasts which take many forms in his plays.

Despite the evidence in the poem of Middleton's acquaintance with Marlowe,[11] there is as yet no sign of his desire to write for the theatre. It was into the 'unprofitable sweetness' of poetry that the poor scholar in *Ant* was lured (Bullen, viii. 104), and Middleton's own college years produced two published poems: *Microcynicon: Six Snarling Satires*, a

---

[8] See Shand, 'Elizabethan Aim', in Friedenreich (ed.), *'Accompanige the Players'*, 67.

[9] See Heinemann, *Puritanism and Theatre*, 52.

[10] Shand, 'Elizabethan Aim', in Friedenreich (ed.), *'Accompaninge the Players'*, 75.

[11] The debt of 16.12 to *Edward II*, ll. 1997–2000, was noted by Bullen, viii. 266 n. See also John Bakeless, *The Tragicall History of Christopher Marlowe*, 2 vols. (Cambridge, Mass., 1942), ii. 37–8.

formal satire; and *Ghost of Lucrece*, a complaint modelled on those in *The Mirror for Magistrates*.

Microcynicon followed in the wake of Hall's *Virgidemiarum* (1597), which set a vogue for the savage Juvenalian persona.[12] Each of the six satires in heroic couplets attacks an urban stereotype—the usurer, the prodigal, the proud lady, the con man, the 'ingle' or male bawd, and the fool. *Microcynicon* is the first known work of Middleton to make contemporary London its setting. Its 'Troynovant' is a mixture of Juvenalian and medieval nightmares, and is yet to acquire the vivid presence or the ironic complexity of his London plays. Nevertheless, he finds in the poem the fictional voice in which to rail at urban vices. In the sixth satire, in which the fool finds the satirist a bigger fool— 'Twenty to one this fool's some satirist' (Bullen, viii. 134)—Middleton even doffs the fictionality and strained idiom of his adopted persona, a quick-change trick he would play with increasing dexterity on the presenter-satirists of his city comedies.[13]

Along with the satires of Hall and Marston, *Microcynicon* was burnt following the bishops' edict of 1599. This event may have finally driven Middleton to the theatre, and if J. Q. Adams is right in thinking that *Lucrece* was written earlier, Middleton never wrote a long poem after *Microcynicon*.[14] *Lucrece*, however, was published after the ban. It was dedicated to William, second Baron of Compton. Middleton calls him the 'baptizer of mine infant lines | With golden water in a silver font' (Dedication, ll. 5–6), but there is no record of his receiving any favours. Adams thinks that Middleton pinned his hopes on Compton, not renowned for his generosity to poets, because in 1599 he had married the heiress to the fortune of Sir John Spencer. Adams also entertains the possibility of Compton being the model for Sir Christopher Clutchfist, the mock-dedicatee of *Ant*, who dismembered folios presented to him and sent the parchment to his tailor, saving the silk strings for his Spanish-leather shoes (Bullen, viii. 52, 108).[15] A caricature of Compton or not, Clutchfist certainly indicates Middleton's early frustration with the pursuit of aristocratic patronage.

---

[12] See Alvin Kernan, *The Cankered Muse: Satire of the English Renaissance* (New Haven, Conn., 1959), 81–2.

[13] See ibid. 106–7.

[14] J. Q. Adams (ed.), *The Ghost of Lucrece* (New York, 1937), p. xvi.

[15] Ibid. pp. xxiv–xxxi. See the discussion of mock-dedications in Sandra Clark, *The Elizabethan Pamphleteers: Popular Moralistic Pamphlets 1580–1640* (London, 1983), 26–7.

Lucrece borrows freely from Greene's *Ciceronis Amor* and Shakespeare's *Rape of Lucrece*. Although he follows Shakespeare's example in
choosing the rime royal stanza, Middleton's is a very different poem.
His Lucrece curses the 'Iron Age' of the world (l. 306) with a hoarse
vehemence which brings the poem's tone close to satire and revenge
play, and which has reminded at least one critic of Vindice.[16] Rape is
seen as an image of social and political violence, and is personified as a
rack-renting landowner (l. 188). Vesta is a captive of Venus, and Venus
a whore in princely courts (ll. 302–5). To this raucous stress on
corruption, Middleton adds militant Protestant overtones. Collatine is
asleep 'at Rome' while 'a Roman thief' robs him (ll. 216–17), and
Tarquin's 'triple crown and sevenfold head' (l. 114) allude to Protestant
representations of papacy. But Middleton does not write about the
Augustinian Lucrece who is charged with either adultery or suicide.[17]
He cares little for shifting the moral blame for political abuse on to the
victim, and emphasizes instead the outraged helplessness of the disad-
vantaged—'When tigers prey, the silly lambs must yield' (l. 201).

PROFESSION AND PLAYS

Without money, patron, or a university degree, Middleton at the age
of 21 was 'daylie accompaninge the players'. Marriage added to his
financial cares around this time. His wife Mary Marbeck came from a
family of achievers. Her father Edward was one of the Six Clerks in
Chancery, and her uncle Roger was Provost of Oriel at Oxford. John
Marbeck, father of Edward and Roger, was organist at Windsor. He
was tried and sentenced for his radical Protestant views, but was saved
from the stake by his fame as musician. Later in life at least, Middleton
seems to have viewed this social enhancement with unawed scepticism. A character in *The Nice Valour* sneers at his wife's gentry status
derived from a musician (4.1.289–90), and an apprentice in *Anything
for a Quiet Life* ridicules Puritan dislike of organs while referring to his
master's musician father-in-law (5.1.87–92). By 1609, Thomas and
Mary were living in Newington in Surrey. They never seem to have

---

[16] Laura G. Bromley, 'The Lost Lucrece: Middleton's *The Ghost of Lucrece*', *PLL* 21 (1985),
270–4.

[17] On the Augustinian view, see D. C. Allen, 'Some Observations on *The Rape of Lucrece*',
SS 15 (1962), 89–98; and Ian Donaldson, *The Rapes of Lucretia: A Myth and its Transformations*
(Oxford, 1982), 21–39.

moved out, since it was at St Mary's churchyard in Newington that Middleton was buried on 4 July 1627.

In 1601 there could thus be no turning back for the daily companion of players. Perhaps it was because of this early professional commitment that Middleton never, by Jonson's standards, graduated to 'the number of the Faithfull'. With Markham and Day, he remained 'but a base fellow'.[18] This blue-collar status is borne out by the virtual absence of verse eulogies addressed to Middleton, and by the large proportion of his plays printed anonymously during his lifetime. It also explains the arch sales-talk of the signed preface to *Roaring Girl*, which assures 'the Comic Play-readers' that 'play-making' is not much different from up-market tailoring:

Now in the time of spruceness, our plays follow the niceness of our garments: single plots, quaint conceits, lecherous jests, dressed up in hanging sleeves; and those are fit for the times and the termers. Such a kind of light-colour summer stuff, mingled with diverse colours, you shall find this published comedy . . . (ll. 6–11).

The passage may be an ironic allusion to Jonson's description of Dekker, the play's co-author, as 'a dresser of plaies about the towne' in *Poetaster* (3.4.321–2). Middleton also tells his readers that the comedy is a good substitute for 'dice' and 'venery'. This bracketing of the theatre with other forms of low pastime in its vicinity looks back to the more tart analogy used in the unsigned epistle to the 1608 edition of *Family of Love*: 'for plays in this city are wenches new fallen to the trade, only desired of your neatest gallants whiles they're fresh' (Bullen, iii. 7).

The theatre was not respectable, but it was certainly paying. In 1602 Philip Henslowe was offering Middleton up to £6 for a play, almost three times the sum he could hope for from a dedication or a prose pamphlet. On 22 May 1602 Henslowe paid him, along with Munday, Drayton, and Webster, an advance for a play called *Caesar's Fall*. A final instalment was paid after a week to the same playwrights plus Dekker. Later that year, Henslowe paid him for *The Chester Tragedy*, and for a prologue and an epilogue to a court revival of *Friar Bacon and Friar Bungay*. All these commissions were for the Admiral's, while he received an advance on 3 October for an unnamed play pledged to Henslowe's other company, the Earl of Worcester's Men.[19]

---

[18] C. H. Herford, Percy and Evelyn Simpson (eds.), *Ben Jonson*, 11 vols. (Oxford, 1925–52), i. 137.

[19] See R. A. Foakes and R. T. Rickert (eds.), *Henslowe's Diary* (Cambridge, 1961), 201–2, 205–7, 217.

None of Middleton's early work for Henslowe has survived. The earliest group of plays to come down are the comedies he wrote for the children's companies, mostly for Paul's Boys, between 1603 and 1606. Middleton was a freelancer, but during this early phase most of his comedies were written for Paul's. On 14 March 1604 Henslowe records a payment to Dekker and Middleton for the first part of *The Honest Whore*, to be played by the Prince's Men, as the Admiral's were now called.[20] The title-page of the published play (1604), however, mentions only Dekker, and David Lake has traced Middleton's presence in only one scene and in fewer than two hundred lines of another.[21] The major evidence of Middleton's early skills in comedy, therefore, is his work for Paul's.

When Middleton wrote for Paul's, it had lost much of the exclusive character given to it by Lyly during the first phase of its commercial success (1583–9), and by Marston during the earlier part of the second (1599–1603).[22] In *Jack Drum's Entertainment*, played at Paul's in 1600, Planet says that the audience there were spared 'the stench of Garlicke' and 'the barmy Jacket of a Beer-brewer' (Act 5, p. 234). Under the management of Thomas Woodford (1603–4), the company targeted a wider market. The bishops' injunction of 1599 had deflected satire to the stage, and satiric comedy had become a money-spinner in all playhouses.[23] The War of the Theatres saw the song schools and the Globe competing for the same audience using the same resources of personal and topical invective. Marston's influence on Paul's declined after the War of the Theatres, and its plays now were more journalistic. Chapman's *Old Joiner of Aldgate*, produced at Paul's in 1603, sold a local scandal, and confirmed the tabloid notoriety of Paul's under Wood-ford. The praise of law and matrimony in *The Phoenix*, which followed Chapman's play at Paul's after a plague lay-off, may have been aimed at repairing the damaged reputation of the troupe after the *Old Joiner* affair. Middleton was perhaps also exploiting public memory of the scandal, especially in the Captain's auctioning of Castiza and in Falso's

---

[20] R. A. Foakes and R. T. Rickert (eds.), *Henslowe's Diary* (Cambridge, 1961), 209.

[21] Lake, *Canon*, 58. See also Jackson, *Studies in Attribution*, 101–3.

[22] See Reavley Gair, *The Children of Paul's: The Story of a Theatre Company, 1553–1608* (Cambridge, 1982), 147–75.

[23] Oscar James Campbell, in Comicall Satyre *and Shakespeare's* Troilus and Cressida (San Marino, Calif., 1938), 1–3, 135, suggested that Marston turned to writing satiric plays to circumvent the bishops' edict. Campbell's thesis is questioned by Anthony Caputi, *John Marston, Satirist* (Ithaca, NY, 1961), 80–1; and Philip J. Finkelpearl, *John Marston of the Middle Temple: An Elizabethan Dramatist in his Social Setting* (Cambridge, Mass., 1969), 116–19. Whatever Marston's motivation, the edict was followed by an increase in satiric plays.

effort to defraud his niece of her dowry. In the events which occasioned *Old Joiner*, a barber-surgeon had auctioned off his daughter,
breaking her engagement to a bookbinder of Paul's Yard. When the
girl sought the help of a clergyman, the latter promptly married her
himself to corner the huge dowry left by her aunt.[24]

Old Joiner was part of a series of attempts to attract playgoers from a
wider social range to Paul's, especially from its bustling neighbourhood
and from the crowds that daily thronged Paul's Walk. The advantage
of a local clientele was that ease of access could offset the higher rates
of admission. The hodgepodge of classes and occupations which
constituted the crowd on Paul's middle aisle is recorded vividly by
Dekker:

For at one time, in one and the same ranke, yea, foote by foote, and elbow by
elbow, shall you see walking, the Knight, the Gull, the Gallant, the vpstart,
the Gentleman, the Clowne, the Captaine, the Appel-squire, the Lawyer, the
Vsurer, the Cittizen, the Bankerout, the Scholler, the Begger, the Doctor, the
Ideot, the Ruffian, the Cheater, the Puritan, the Cut-throat, the Hye-men,
the Low-men, the True-man, and the Thiefe: of all trades & professions some,
of all Countreyes some . . .[25]

Dekker's account is corroborated by Lucifer in *Black Book*, who walks
in Paul's to observe fashions and to eavesdrop on conspirators. To the
objector who asks how a devil should walk in a cathedral, Lucifer
replies: 'Why not, sir, as well as a sergeant, or a ruffian, or a murderer?'
(Bullen, viii. 32).

In the early years of the seventeenth century, therefore, the audiences at Paul's or at the Blackfriars were not as exclusive, nor performances as infrequent, as they were once believed to have been.[26]
Recent scholarship warns us against a simple adults/children or pub-
lic/private dichotomy for the theatres of the time. Besides, the plays
are not always a guide to the social composition of audiences at
different playhouses, which had more to do with the admission rates

---

[24] See Gair, *Children of Paul's*, 156. C. J. Sisson discusses the affair in *Lost Plays of
Shakespeare's Age* (Cambridge, 1936), 12–79.
[25] Thomas Dekker, *The Dead Tearme, or Westminsters Complaint for Long Vacations and Short
Termes* (1608), in Alexander B. Grosart (ed.), *The Non-Dramatic Works of Thomas Dekker*, 5
vols. (1884–6; New York, 1963), v. 51.
[26] See Alfred Harbage, *Shakespeare and the Rival Traditions* (New York, 1952), 29–57; and
William A. Armstrong, 'The Audience of the Elizabethan Private Theatres', *RES*, NS 10
(1959), 234–49. The theory that the indoor players performed once a week is questioned in
David Farley-Hills, 'How Often did the Eyases Fly?', *N & Q* 236 (1991), 461–6.

than with audience taste.[27] Middleton's comedies for Paul's use the stage conventions of the song school, and allude to earlier plays given by them.[28] But it is necessary to remember that he was at this point favourably placed to write satiric comedy, and yet address a broad cross-section of social groups. Middleton's apprenticeship in both adult and boy companies was in a popular, topical, and marketable medium.

Phoenix (1603), *Michaelmas Term* (1605), *Mad World* (1605), *Trick* (1605; also played at the Blackfriars),[29] and *Puritan* (1606) were all produced at Paul's. The 1607 Stationers' Register entry for *Family of Love* and the title-page of its first edition (1608) mention performances by the King's Revels. The King's Revels did not exist before 1607, and since most scholars settle for an earlier date of composition (1603), it is likely that it was originally a Paul's play.[30] *Your Five Gallants* was acted by the Children of the Chapel Royal sometime between 1604 and 1607. E. K. Chambers suggested that it too was written for Paul's Boys, and, when they ceased playing, was transferred to the Blackfriars.[31] Middleton, however, had sold the lost *Viper and her Brood* to the Chapel Royal troupe around 1606, and might well have written a comedy for them.

Of Middleton's comedies for Paul's, *Family of Love* is the play for which the earliest date of composition has been proposed. The extant text discourages much speculation about early Middleton, since it is a revision involving at least two other contributors, Dekker and Lording Barry. Lake's complicated theory accommodates the evidence for the presence of all three playwrights. Lake believes that Middleton and Dekker wrote the play in 1602–3, Dekker alone revised it in 1605, and Barry put the final touch for the King's Revels revival in 1606–7.[32]

One reason why the play still features prominently in Middleton criticism is that its lampooning of Familists has a crucial place in any

---

[27] See Andrew Gurr, *Playgoing in Shakespeare's London* (Cambridge, 1987), 72–9, 153–64. For the same reason, the preponderance of the 'privileged' in both kinds of theatre, as argued by Ann Jennalie Cook, *The Privileged Playgoers in Shakespeare's London, 1576–1642* (Princeton, NJ, 1981), is not an index of audience preference.

[28] See Gair, *Children of Paul's*, 151–4; and Michael Shapiro, *Children of the Revels: The Boy Companies of Shakespeare's Time and their Plays* (New York, 1977), 54–66, 218–27.

[29] On the stage history of *Trick*, see G. R. Price, 'The Early Editions of *A Trick to Catch the Old One*', *Library*, 5th ser. 22 (1967), 222–3.

[30] See E. K. Chambers, *The Elizabethan Stage*, 4 vols. (Oxford, 1923), iii. 440–1; and Lake, *Canon*, 94.

[31] Chambers, *Elizabethan Stage*, iii. 440.

[32] Lake, *Canon*, 94.

argument for or against his 'Puritanism'. Thus Bertil Johansson and William Holden held that the play was a summary attack on 'Puritans', and Simon Shepherd and Margot Heinemann replied that to mock Familists was not to attack 'Puritanism', and that, at any rate, the Familists came out better in the play than gallants.[33]

The case is a good instance of the confusions which the term 'Puritan' has generated in Middleton criticism. As we have seen, it was usual during Middleton's career to pass on the name to the schismatic fringe. The Familists were especial targets of such branding, and King James, having reviled 'Puritans' in *Basilikon Doron* (1599), stuck the label on their sect: '*Of this speciall sect I principally meane, when I speake of Puritans.*'[34] Although the Familists dissociated themselves from 'erroneous sorts of the anabaptists, Brown, Penry, puritans, and all other proud-minded sects and heresies' in a petition to the king in 1604,[35] the distinction was hardly ever made in popular literature.[36] The English Familists' eagerness to keep property and marriage within the sect indicated to opponents a secret agenda of communism and sexual licence.[37] Familism became virtually synonymous with sexual libertinism, aided by the semantic confusion between Nicolaits, a name for the disciples of Hendrik Niclaes introduced by Lodge, and Nicolaitanes, the sect mentioned in Revelation 2:6, which supposedly held women in common.[38] In Marston's *Dutch Courtesan* (1605) Freewill uses 'Family of Love' to mean a brothel, and the bawd Mary Faugh describes herself as 'one of the Family of Love' (1.1.139–40, 1.2.17). On the other hand, since Niclaes, the founder of Familism, did not oppose existing state churches or every Catholic tenet, preachers in England suspected the sect as crypto-Catholic.[39] In *A Sermon Preached at Pavles*

---

[33] Bertil Johansson, *Religion and Superstition in the Plays of Ben Jonson and Thomas Middleton* (Uppsala, 1950), 102; William P. Holden, *Anti-Puritan Satire 1572–1642* (New Haven, Conn., 1954), 128–31; Simon Shepherd, *Amazons and Warrior Women: Varieties of Feminism in Seventeenth-Century Drama* (Brighton, 1981), 57–62; and Heinemann, *Puritanism and Theatre*, 77–83.

[34] McIlwain (ed.), *Political Works*, 7.

[35] Fuller, *Church History*, v. 329, quoting the Familists' 1604 petition to the king.

[36] See William C. Johnson, 'The Family of Love in Stuart Literature: A Chronology of Name-Crossed Lovers', *JMRS* 7 (1977), 95–112; and Julia G. Ebel, 'The Family of Love: Sources of its History in England', *HLQ* 30 (1967), 331–43.

[37] See Alastair Hamilton, *The Family of Love* (Cambridge, 1981), 119.

[38] Lodge's introduction of the link in *Wits Miserie* (1596) is noted by Johnson, 'Family of Love in Stuart Literature', 98–9.

[39] See Christopher Hill, *Antichrist in Seventeenth-Century England* (London, 1971), 11–12; Lynnewood F. Martin, 'The Family of Love in England: Conforming Millenarians', *Sixteenth Century Journal*, 3 (1972), 99–108; and Jean Dietz Moss, 'The Family of Love and English Critics', *Sixteenth Century Journal*, 6 (1975), 35–52.

Crosse the 13 of Iune, 1602, Francis Marbury alleged that Papists 'behaue themselues so as the Familists in their assemblies: and that company of them which are called Iesuites, may more worthily bee called Adamites, which were the first founders of the Familists'.[40] Thus the argument about whether the authors of *Family of Love* were mocking the sectaries in particular or the 'Puritans' in general is anachronistic. Their audience would have cared little about the difference. The same may be said of the many mocking references to 'Puritans' elsewhere in Middleton's corpus.[41]

It is doubtful, however, if the playwrights cared to learn more about the Familists outside what they seemed to have gathered from popular diatribes such as John Rogers's *The Displaying of an Horrible Secte of Grosse and Wicked Heretiques* (1578), and William Wilkinson's *A Confutation of Certaine Articles Deliuered vnto the Familye of Loue* (1579). The depiction of nocturnal meetings depend on Rogers's account, while the anecdote of the Familist bellows-mender's wife, who extols her husband's trade since men are 'but bellows, for they take wind in at one place and do evaporate at another' (4.1.20–2), parodies the Familists' stress on inspiration, and matches Wilkinson's statement that the Familist elders were weavers, basketmakers, musicians, and other itinerant traders.[42] The hero, when disguised as a porter, calls himself 'Nicholas Nebulo' in what looks like an irreverant reference to Niclaes (4.3.52).[43] There is the overall caricature of Familists as sexual communists, and familiar jibes at sectarian precisianism. It is even possible that the play's many quibbles on 'purging' allude to the Familist belief in the purgatorial nature of earthly suffering.[44] Beyond this, the satire against the sect is neither specific nor sustained.

The work itself is much more than religious satire. In the central romance, Gerardine, a gentleman-gallant, loves Maria, but the match

---

[40] Francis Marbury, *A Sermon Preached at Pavles Crosse the 13 of June, 1602* (1602), as quoted in Hamilton, *Family of Love*, 134.

[41] See e.g. *Mad World*, 1.2.67–8; *Trick*, 4.3.63; *Revenger*, 2.2.32, 2.3.60; *Five Gallants*, 1.1.251–3; *Yorkshire*, 1.15–16; *Roaring Girl*, 3.3.45; *Witch*, 1.1.84–5; *Widow*, 1.2.175–8; *Hengist*, 5.1.184–5; *Heroes*, ll. 31–4; *Quiet Life*, 1.1.86–9, 2.1.98–101, 5.1.87–92. Besides, there is *Puritan*, and the christening scene (3.2) in *Chaste Maid*.

[42] Rogers and Wilkinson are cited in Moss, 'Family of Love and English Critics', 38–41. See also Christopher Hill, *The World Turned Upside Down: Radical Ideas during the English Revolution* (London, 1972), 22–3.

[43] See Clifford Davidson, 'Middleton and the Family of Love', *English Miscellany*, 20 (1969), 87.

[44] On the Familist notion of the purgatorial nature of earthly suffering, see the passage from Niclaes's *Evangelium Regni* quoted in Martin, 'Family of Love in England', 105 n. 28. On the

is opposed by her physician uncle Glister, since Gerardine's lands are mortgaged. Glister detests gallants, but does not mind taking charge of Gerardine's possessions when he wills it to Maria before leaving on a pretended voyage. Gerardine gains access to the locked-up Maria by hiding in the 'trunk' supposedly containing his 'substance' (2.4.270–1)— one of the play's numerous phallic jokes—and he soon gets her pregnant. Gerardine manages to make Glister's wife suspect that Maria is with her husband's child, and then presides in disguise over a fake trial which blackmails Glister into consenting to the wedding and to paying a hefty dowry. A sub-plot has an apothecary named Purge connive at Glister's affair with his Familist wife, but lament the 'misery of married men's estate' (4.4.29) on discovering that she uses the Familist conclaves for extra flings. The two plots are fringed by the antics of two stupid gallants, Lipsalve and Gudgeon, all of whose ploys to seduce Maria, Mrs Purge, and Mrs Glister end in disaster.

In *Jack Drum's Entertainment*, produced at Paul's in 1600, Marston had burlesqued the romantic conventions of popular playhouses, especially in the balcony scenes in Act 2.[45] *Family of Love* follows its example to the extent of reworking the balcony scenes. The lovers' frank pursuit of sex and money make their romantic idealism sound more like a deliberate parody than an inept imitation of *Romeo and Juliet*.[46] Although Gerardine master-minds the denouement and brings everyone to the comic bar, he is a farceur like Follywit, Witgood, and Touchwood Jr. in the later plays, not a moral satirist like Phoenix or Fitsgrave.[47]

many senses of 'purging' in the play, see Arthur F. Marotti, 'The Purgations of Middleton's *The Family of Love*', *PLL* 7 (1971), 80–4. Joanne Altieri, 'Pregnant Puns and Sectarian Rhetoric: Middleton's *Family of Love*', *Mosaic*, 22 (1989), 45–57, studies the play as a satire exploiting the flesh/spirit confusion fostered by sectarian rhetoric. On Familist rhetoric, see Janet Halley, 'Heresy, Orthodoxy, and the Politics of Religious Discourse: The Case of the English Family of Love', *Representations*, 15 (1986), 98–120; and Nigel Smith, *Perfection Proclaimed: Language and Literature in English Radical Religion 1640–1660* (Oxford, 1989), 144–84.

[45] See Michael C. Andrewes, '*Jack Drum's Entertainment* as Burlesque', *RQ* 24 (1971), 226–31.

[46] See David L. Frost, *The School of Shakespeare: The Influence of Shakespeare on English Drama 1600–42* (Cambridge, 1968), 28–33, for a discussion of the play's borrowings from *Romeo and Juliet*. See also W. J. Olive, 'Imitation of Shakespeare in Middleton's *The Family of Love*,' *PQ* 29 (1950), 75–8. On the parodic nature of the imitation, see John F. McElroy, 'Middleton, Entertainer or Moralist? An Interpretation of *The Family of Love* and *Your Five Gallants*', *MLQ* 37 (1976), 37–41.

[47] See George E. Rowe, Jr., *Thomas Middleton and the New Comedy Tradition* (Lincoln, Neb., 1979), 35–7; and Theodore B. Leinwand, *The City Staged: Jacobean Comedy, 1603–1613* (Madison, Wis., 1986), 121–3, for similar views.

The difference between Gerardine and the other gallants in the play is defined by his privileged function in the New Comedy structure. The symmetrical contrasts between his manœuvres and those of Lipsalve and Gudgeon, such as the paired balcony scenes in which Gerardine and Lipsalve woo Maria (1.2 and 3.2), stress this difference rather than mock court gallants in general. Lipsalve and Gudgeon are the stereotypes of the courtier-gentleman the city likes to imagine and hate, and Gerardine, the true gentleman, shows up their 'gallantry' as an upstart attempt to live the fantasy of the court's sexual mastery over the city.

It proves equally difficult to read the play as unambiguously for or against the city. Shepherd thinks that it refuses the obvious joke against Puritan traders by making Dryfat, the merchant, partner Gerardine in the final trick.[48] This is to forget that Dryfat's complicity is gained at the expense of his class role. Gerardine confides in him only after he agrees to 'lay by awhile' his 'city's precise humour' (4.2.34–5). Other citizens too have their functions split. Glister is deceived in the Maria–Gerardine plot, deceiver in the Lipsalve–Gudgeon–Mrs Purge sub-plot. Purge is a most unlikely combination of Allwit in *Chaste Maid* and Harebrain in *Mad World*—the poles of dread and scorn in the courtier's idea of the citizen. He is *mari complaisant* in the beginning, treating his wife as capital investment and preferring city discretion to court machismo: 'I smile to hear our knights and gallants say how they gull us citizens, when indeed, we gull them, or rather they gull themselves' (2.1.12–15). In the end, however, he is a pitied cuckold.

The absence of any righteous class animus in *Family of Love* becomes clear if one compares the episode involving Lipsalve, Gudgeon, Mrs Purge, and Glister with the sub-plot in Massinger's *Parliament of Love* (1624).[49] Lipsalve and Gudgeon approach Glister for a potion to seduce Mrs Purge. Glister advises them separately that a spirit, appearing to each in the likeness of the other, must be whipped for the charm to work. He then spies on them with malicious glee as the pair flog each

[48] Simon Shepherd (ed.), *The Family of Love*, Nottingham Drama Texts (Nottingham, 1979), p. iii.

[49] David George, 'Thomas Middleton's Sources: A Survey', *N & Q* 216 (1971), 18, suggests the last tale in the anonymous *Tarletons Newes out of Purgatorie* (1590) as the probable source of the episode. But a closer version is to be found in *Iacke of Dover, his Quest of Inquirie, or his Priuy Search for the Veriest Foole in England* (1604), the jestbook entered in the Stationers' Register in 1601. The jest concerned begins on C2ᵛ and continues on E1–1ᵛ, the sequence of pages being misidentified. The play's version of the story is retold by Sir Nicholas Le Strange. See H. F. Lippincott (ed.), *'Merry Passages and Jeastes': A Manuscript Jestbook of Sir Nicholas Le Strange (1603–1655)* (Salzburg, 1974), 122–3.

other. In revenge, the gallants move in as Glister's patients and nearly succeed in bedding his wife before Glister's 'purge' knocks them out with diarrhoea. This story seems to be the source for the sub-plot in Massinger's play, in which the court gallants Perigot and Novall are likewise punished by a doctor, helped by a country nobleman. Massinger turns this comic revenge into a moral lesson which an aggrieved city and insulted country unite to teach the court. The occasion is seized upon to argue the case of 'rich merchants, advocates and docters', who 'How ere deservinge from the comon wealth' are looked upon as 'Predestind cuckolds' (4.5.86–9). The plight of Lipsalve and Gudgeon, on the contrary, is dismissed by Gerardine as 'particles in our sport' and 'fit subjects of laughter' (5.3.49–50).

There is, nevertheless, one significant deviation from the seeming trajectory of the New Comedy resolution. The gallants and Dryfat deride the Familists, but the mockers are one with the mocked in using courtesy and religion as a cover for sex. Both are laughed at in the end for not being smart enough: the standard of judgement at the mock-trial is hardly moral.

The law by which the offenders are tried is not simply one of wit and mirth. It is 'club-law' (5.3.452), a phrase that recalls the title of a play staged at Clare Hall sometime between 1597 and 1600. In that work, 'club-law' meant the use of the stick, not argument, to knock down one's opponent, and the action showed how the University used this *argumentum baculinum* against the town administration at Cambridge.[50] The phrase is applied in this sense at first by Dryfat (cf. 5.3.12–15). But he and an apprentice, suitably named Club, soon demonstrate that 'club-law' is to be used to 'wrest this smock-law' (5.3.37), and it makes their knavery 'as near allied as felling of wood and getting of children' (5.3.50–1). The clubs, like Lollio's phallic whip in *Changeling*, are 'commanding pizzles' (*Changeling*, 4.3.62), which must tame women, families, estates, and kingdoms. In the absence of any other moral distinction between classes, the club must arbitrate in its courtroom ending. Club explains the real point of Familist egalitarianism in the light of 'club-law': 'you're above me in flesh, mistress, and there's your boast; but in my t'other part we are all one before God' (3.3.12–14). If social divisions are to be maintained,

---

[50] G. C. Moore Smith (ed.), *Club Law: A Comedy Acted in Clare Hall, Cambridge about 1599–1600* (Cambridge, 1907). 'Clubs' is a battle-cry in Dekker's *Shoemaker's Holiday*, 5.2.28, and Middleton's *Puritan*, 3.1.47.

phallic violence must police the desires of women and inferior ranks. This, and not any moral claim of the privileged, is the safeguard against economic and sexual communism. Dryfat warns that if the Familists are not 'punished and suppressed by our club-law, each man's copy-hold will become freehold' and wives 'will be made common' (5.3.195–201). Gerardine, in his capacity as the judge in the mock-trial, agrees:

Byrlady, these enormities must and shall be redressed, otherwise I see their charter will be infringed, and their ancient staff of government the club, from whence we derive our law of castigation,—this club, I say (they seeming nothing less than men by their fore-part), will be turned upon their own heads. (5.3.203–8)

The denouement of New Comedy demands a release of vital energies from the rigour of the 'club-law'; *Family of Love* ends by calling for its reimposition. Even in its revised form, the play briefly engages a key theme of Middleton's drama, namely, the politics of the libido.

The Phoenix was given a court performance, probably on 20 February 1604, and some scholars think it was commissioned for a royal audience.[51] The early reference to the Duke of Ferrara's reign of forty-five years (1.1.7) coincides with the duration of the late queen's rule, and in *The Magnificent Entertainment* (1604), Dekker's welcome pageant for James to which Middleton contributed a speech, the new king was given Elizabeth's figural identity as the phoenix.[52] In *Ant*, Middleton hails the new monarch as the 'manly lion' who 'now can roar | Thunder more dreaded than the lioness' (Bullen, viii. 61). *Phoenix*, performed the same year as *Ant* was published, could well have been designed to compliment James, although the theory that its action closely shadows Ralegh's alleged sedition strains the evidence.[53] Besides, Middleton

[51] See N. W. Bawcutt, 'Middleton's *The Phoenix* as a Royal Play', *N & Q* 201 (1956), 287–8; Marilyn L. Williamson, '*The Phoenix*: Middleton's Comedy *de Regimine Principum*', *Renaissance News*, 10 (1957), 183–7; W. Power, '*The Phoenix*, Raleigh, and King James', *N & Q* 203 (1958), 57–61; and Daniel Dodson, 'King James and *The Phoenix*—Again', *N & Q* 203 (1958), 434–7.
[52] See Fredson Bowers (ed.) *The Dramatic Works of Thomas Dekker*, 4 vols. (Cambridge, 1953–61), ii. 278–9. On the phoenix in Stuart iconography, see Graham Parry, *The Golden Age Restor'd: The Culture of the Stuart Court 1603–1642* (Manchester, 1981), 10–18.
[53] Phoenix in this reading stands for James, and Proditor, the courtier who plots to assassinate the prince and usurp the throne, for Ralegh. See Power, '*Phoenix*, Raleigh, and King James', 57–61; and id., 'Middleton vs. James I', 526.

does not seem to have written it exclusively for a royal audience. There are two unflattering swipes at James's newly dubbed knights (1.6.150–1, 2.3.3–5), and the allusion to the sign of a Cheapside alehouse in the line 'Pegasus the flying horse yonder' (3.1.48–9) confirms the impression that he wrote the play also for the audience at Paul's.[54]

The structure of *Phoenix* rests on two generic models: the estates morality and the disguised-ruler play.[55] Like the first, it depicts corruption at different social levels; like the second, it redresses all wrongs through the return of the redeeming hero. In estates plays such as *A Knack to Know a Knave* (1592) and *A Knack to Know an Honest Man* (1594), the middle ground between the two conventions was provided by observer figures such as Honesty and Sempronio, who mediated the exposure of social ills. The observer is the prince in disguise in Shakespeare's *Measure for Measure* (1604), a play to which Middleton added a few lines around 1621 for a stage revival.[56] The same device is used in Marston's *Malcontent* (1604) and *Fawn* (1605), Edward Sharpham's *Fleer* (1606), and in two plays by John Day, *Law Tricks* (1604) and *Humour out of Breath* (1607–8). Middleton may have followed the lead of Shakespeare and Marston, or he could have given them the idea—the sequence of composition for *Measure for Measure*, *Malcontent*, and *Phoenix* is difficult to determine.[57]

In Middleton's story, the Duke of Ferrara wants his son Phoenix to travel abroad for political experience. Phoenix decides instead to move incognito among his own people. In the company of a friend named Fidelio, Phoenix searches 'into the heart and bowels of this dukedom' (1.1.100–1). The journey casts him in unexpected roles. He is hired as his own assassin by Proditor, the courtier planning a coup. He stands witness to the deed by which Fidelio's mother Castiza is sold off to

[54] See Paul Yachnin, 'The Significance of Two Allusions in Middleton's *The Phoenix*', *N & Q* 231 (1986), 375–7.

[55] See Alan C. Dessen, 'Middleton's *The Phoenix* and the Allegorical Tradition', *SEL* 6 (1966), 291–308.

[56] The interpolation in *Measure for Measure* occurs at the beginning of 1.2. The case for Middleton's hand has been convincingly argued in Gary Taylor and John Jowett, *Shakespeare Reshaped 1606–1623* (Oxford, 1993), 107–236.

[57] Thomas A. Pendleton, 'Shakespeare's Disguised Duke Play: Middleton, Marston, and the Sources of *Measure for Measure*', in John W. Mahon and Thomas A. Pendleton (eds.), *'Fanned and Winnowed Opinions': Shakespearean Essays Presented to Harold Jenkins* (London, 1987), 77–98, concludes (p. 95) that Shakespeare 'borrowed substantially' from Middleton, without providing for the fact that the extant text of *Measure for Measure* contains additions by Middleton. The evidence suggests that Middleton borrowed from Shakespeare; see R. V. Holdsworth, '*Measure for Measure*, Middleton, and "Brakes of Ice" ', *N & Q* 236 (1991), 66–7.

Proditor by her second husband.[58] He is then plaintiff in a country trial which shows Falso, the magistrate, having highwaymen in his keep.[59] He also fills in for the knight paid to be a gigolo by Falso's married daughter.

The disguised-ruler device reconciles the conflicting demands made on the observer-satirist of drama. He must be intimate with vice and yet feel moral outrage; he must distance himself from the action, and yet be involved in it.[60] One way round the problem is to have two satiric voices in the same play—one genial and native, the other waspish and alien.[61] Carlo Buffone and Asper in *Every Man Out of his Humour*, and Sir Edward Fortune and Planet in *Jack Drum's Entertainment* are examples of the formula, and the pairing of Touchstone and Jaques in *As You Like It* is a sophisticated variant. The disguised observer makes this duplication unnecessary, since his dual identity enables him to be inside and outside the action at the same time. It further allows the prince-observer to move in and out of places and ranks, a necessity which obliged the author of estates plays to appoint 'a plaine man of the country' (*Knack to Know a Knave*, A3) as social investigator. The prince may catch the world off-guard by appearing to it, like Phoenix does, as 'some filthy farmer's son' (2.2.80), and yet not lose, as Shakespeare's Bolingbroke thought his son had lost, his 'princely privilege | With vile participation' (*1 Henry IV*, 3.2.86–7). Sir Amoroso could thus say of the disguised duke in *Fawn*: 'all inward, inward, he lurked in the bosom of us, and yet we know not his profession' (5.1.288–90).

If the disguised-ruler device solves some problems, it also creates others. The separate plots, for instance, are made to revolve round a moral commentator like 'a multi-ringed circus with a single ring-master'.[62] This inhibits the possibility of connecting the plots by the less intrusive logic of irony, and risks stifling the fun with heavy moralizing.

A more serious difficulty is that the royal authority of the disguised presenter validates the very system which his investigations discredit— an anomaly which is basic to social rescue-fantasies. The society to

---

[58] Brooks, 'Middleton's Stepfather and the Captain of *Phoenix*', 382–4, suggests that the episode remembers the disastrous second marriage of Middleton's mother.

[59] The JP-criminal nexus was notorious. Thomas Scott, in *The Proiector* (1623), D3, warns the JPs against protecting and patronizing criminals.

[60] See Kernan, *Cankered Muse*, 219; and R. A. Foakes, *Shakespeare: The Dark Comedies to the Last Plays: From Satire to Celebration* (London, 1971), 33–7.

[61] See Campbell, *Comicall Satyre*, 79.

[62] Parker, 'Middleton's Experiments', 185.

which Phoenix is initiated is one in which everything sells, including the *'beauties of mind, chastity, temperance, and . . . patience'* (2.2.107–8), to name a few of Castiza's marketable merits. Phoenix sings the praise of law (1.4.197–227), but it is no longer 'chaste from sale' (1.4.200). A 'bar of bribes' shields criminals from punishment (1.1.118–19). Falso, the robber-turned-JP, is happy that he is 'a greater thief now, and in no danger' (3.1.70–1). He and the demented term-trotter Tangle fight a duel with law terms instead of with the usual weapons. Phoenix also addresses an ode to holy matrimony (2.2.164–92), but finds it reduced everywhere to a mockery. The Captain marries a rich widow to sell her at a premium. Falso proposes to marry his orphaned niece himself so that he might retain her dowry. The knight and Falso's daughter trade sex for money. She calls him Pleasure, he calls her Revenue. 'Credit' and 'honour' mean just money and class. The knave 'by blood' is a 'lord by birth' (2.2.236–7).

For a society thus denuded of all its legitimating principles, the prince's remedy is the restoration of a more vigilant personal rule. Such politics is the absolutist fantasy of despotism-as-providence, and it is emptied of all social content. The king in such schemes, as Franco Moretti explains, is the only self-determining being, deriving authority from a transcendental order.[63] That order must be symbolically reproduced in social relations to give royal authority a claim to legitimacy. In the Ferrara Phoenix brings to light, lust and greed appear to have eroded that possibility.

The picture of civil society that emerges has implications for political culture which the text seems unable to absorb. Phoenix argues that power is justified by virtue 'More than by birth or blood' (1.1.131), and on the same moral ground Fidelio defends Castiza's marriage to a sea captain (cf. 1.1.165). The action of the play shows that this moral rationale of privilege is a pretext for the operation of money and muscle. Yet, in the final trial, the charge brought by Phoenix against Lussurioso and Infesto, two prodigal heirs, is not simply that they are morally undeserving of their place, but that they upset the social hierarchy determined by birth in *'mortgaging their livings to the merchant ... from whence this abuse comes, that in a short time the son of the merchant has more lordships than the son of the nobleman, which else was never born to inheritance'* (5.1.93–7). Again, the court and the city are both shown to

---

[63] See Franco Moretti, *Signs Taken for Wonders: Essays in the Sociology of Literary Forms*, trans. Susan Fischer *et al.* (1983; rev. edn., London, 1988), 45.

have their own brand of 'ridiculous pride', and the Falso-plot has the country 'preying' upon it (1.1.97). But the formulaic opposition of country and city survives the disclosure of their moral and economic kinship. Quieto, whose patience is mocked as 'A country thing' (5.1.293), gives Tangle an emetic to purge him of law terms, and his lance drains Tangle's poisoned blood, black as lawyer's ink—an episode which harks back to Jonson's *Poetaster*,[64] and to the images of the pen as moral scalpel in Middleton's early poems (cf. also the blood–ink–pen association in *Revenger*, 1.2.1–6, and *Roaring Girl*, 3.2.227–8). Quieto thus redeems the country just as Phoenix redeems the court. The most transparent instance of the play's withdrawal from its own radical implications is Phoenix's ode to law. Although law is no longer 'chaste from sale', Phoenix maintains that its 'upper parts' are still 'incorruptible', 'As noble in their conscience as their birth' (1.4.206–7, 212). Bawcutt's guess that Middleton softened the attack here with an eye to the royal audience is superfluous, for the speech is not inconsistent with the strained dissociation of politics and society in the rest of the play.[65]

The anomaly typical of social rescue-fantasies expresses itself in the conflict between the class angle from which corruption is diagnosed, and that from which order is restored in the routine courtroom climax. Shakespeare exploited this incongruity in *Measure for Measure*, as also in *Henry IV*, to give a deeply disturbing account of the foundations of human polity. *Phoenix*, on the contrary, appears trapped by the paradox.

Swinburne correctly located *Phoenix* 'on the debatable borderland between the old Morality and the new Comedy'.[66] This need not imply that the play's limitation is the consequence of its split lineage. The multiple stage business of the wife-auction scene (2.2) and the metaphoric action of the law-duel (2.3.113–278) prove that Middleton has already learnt to turn generic ambiguities into bold theatre. A deeper uncertainty, a wavering faith in the text's own evidence and resources, marks the unresolved problems of the disguised-prince device in the play. Middeton did not achieve a radical way out of these

---

[64] See Gair, *Children of Paul's*, 151–2.

[65] See Bawcutt, 'Middleton's *Phoenix* as a Royal Play', 288; and also Shapiro, *Children of the Revels*, 55–6. However, see John B. Brooks (ed.), The Phoenix by *Thomas Middleton: A Critical Modernized Edition* (New York, 1980), 234, for the point that in the same scene (1.4.91–7), Tangle advises a suitor to bribe Court of Chancery officials.

[66] Algernon Charles Swinburne, *The Age of Shakespeare* (London, 1908), 153.

problems until *Roaring Girl*, in which the median functions of the disguised male prince were given to a cross-dressed female thief. She was, moreover, an observer-presenter who could herself come to the theatre and watch her fictional double.

PRINT AND PROSE

By 1603 Middleton was a recognized playwright in both adult and children theatres. But a career in show business was risky, and he had to fall back on print when the plague closed the London theatres for almost a year until April 1604. He was now more interested in the paying reader than in rich patrons, and concentrated on prose genres which involved quick production, low costs, and brisk sales.

His earliest work in popular prose was a revision for a sequel to a jestbook entitled *Iacke of Dover, his Quest of Inquirie, or his Priuy Search for the Veriest Foole in England*, published in 1604. It was entered in the Stationers' Register on 3 August 1601, and it appears that an edition was published the same year. The sequel in this last edition seems to have been subtitled 'The Assembly of Fools', and to have been the target of an unsuccessful libel charge brought in the Commons on 16 December 1601.[67]

The extant text is in two parts. The first is a collection of jests, clumsily revised to lead on to the second part, a mock-parliament now called *The Penniless Parliament of Threadbare Poets*. The revision could not hide the discreteness of *Penniless*, and it was published separately in 1608. Two other editions followed in 1615 and 1637, the first with the earlier jests, the second without.

Penniless is itself a revised version of a mock-prognostication written in 1591 by Simon Smellknave, obviously a pseudonym, called *Fearefull and Lamentable Effects of Two Dangerous Comets*. The future tense of the prophecies could easily be turned into the imperative mood of statutes, and Middleton's changes and additions are quantitatively marginal. But the change from the mock-prophecy to a parliament of indigent poets assembled near Duke Humphrey's tomb in Paul's south aisle, or 'Duke Humphrey's Ordinary', the rendezvous of debtors seeking sanctuary in the cathedral, testifies to his early disenchantment with the worldly prospects and social efficacy of verse. It also shows his keen market

---

[67] See F. P. Wilson, *Shakespearian and Other Studies*, ed. Helen Gardner (Oxford, 1969), 316. I argue the case for Middleton's hand in the revision in the introductions and commentary to *Penniless* in the Oxford *Collected Works*.

sense. The change of format converted the relatively obscure text of Smellknave into a work which had at least six editions between 1601 and 1649.

Almanacs, as in all pre-industrial economies, sold well in Jacobean London. Their bogus predictions were the target of many jokes in Middleton's work (*No Wit, No Help Like a Woman's* and *The Masque of Heroes* are obvious instances), and their layout, with prophecies for different professions and ranks, invited his skill in satiric parody. Mock-almanacs followed almanacs and comic forecasts also in their habit of recycling earlier material, and attracted seasonal satirists like Middleton who needed to put together cheap texts quickly for a set readership. Large chunks from Smellknave found their way into at least two contemporary texts, one of them being Middleton's *Plato's Cap*, published anonymously in 1604.[68] Having revised Smellknave's comic prophecy into a mock-parliament in *Penniless*, Middleton in *Plato* reverts to the mock-prognostication format, one which he would use again in *The Owl's Almanac* (1618). Although Middleton did not add to the *Iacke of Dover* jests, he tried the jestbook form in *The Meeting of Gallants at an Ordinary*, published also in 1604. The anecdotes portray London in the grip of the plague, and provide an instance of black humour as the emotional resort of a city where death could be as dramatic as a revenge masque and as swift as a comic denouement.

These early prose works align poetry and poverty with populist criticism of privilege. Smellknave was not complimentary to poets and players, predicting that 'one may lye by authoritie, the other cogge without controle: the one as necessary in a Commonweale, as a candle in a strawbed; the other as famous in idlenes, as dissolute in liuing' (B2). In the opening paragraph of *Iacke of Dover*, which Middleton possibly revised in order to insert a pretext for splicing two disparate works, Smellknave's attack on players is ignored, and the joke on poets is softened into defensive irony, calling penniless poets 'fellowes of a merry disposition, (but as necessary in a Common-wealth as a Candle in a Straw-bed)' (A2). The young playwright already has the clue to the political threat posed by literary and theatrical mirth.

Middleton had reason to speculate on the role of poets in a commonwealth in 1604. That year Thomas Creede, the man who printed *Meeting of Gallants*, produced two more pamphlets by him, *Father*

---

[68] The other text is Anthony Nixon, *The Blacke Yeare* (1606). See Wilson, *Shakespearian and Other Studies*, 266–9.

Hubburd's Tales, or The Ant and the Nightingale and *Black Book. Ant* had two editions the same year, the earlier being a shorter version.[69] The work is cast in the form of a dialogue, in which the ant's prose narration of his former lives as ploughman, soldier, and scholar-poet is punctuated by rhymed exchanges between it and the nightingale. The beast-fable framework as well as the title link it to Spenser's *Mother Hubbard's Tale*, and Middleton informs the reader that he has been careful with the title so as 'not to have them called in again, as the Tale of Mother Hubburd' (Bullen, viii. 53). Spenser's poem may well have invited official suppression owing to its offensive portrayal of Burghley. In fact, there is a reference to Mother Hubbard in *Black Book* which implies such an attempt: 'she that was called in for selling her bottle-ale to bookbinders, and spurting the froth upon courtiers' noses' (Bullen, viii. 31).

The prose narratives move away from the formal style of *Microcynicon* to follow the popular manner of Greene and Nashe, and the nightingale's introductory admonition to the ant takes Nashe's side against the Harveys (Bullen, viii. 62-3). Nashe, who suffered dismal poverty after the bishops banned his books and who died in 1601, had been a model of the 'penniless' poet. Middleton's social attitude, Heinemann points out, is less conservative than Nashe's, and his sympathy for the deprived and hard-working is, like Dekker's, keener. Middleton, however, seizes the subversive possibilities opened up by Nashe's parodic excess and carnal humour, employing his black copiousness in the service of more radical attitudes.[70]

In *Ant*, Middleton uses the insect narrator to unite the ploughman, the soldier, and the scholar-poet as three instances of merit and diligence victimized by social injustice. His choice of the ant, a symbol of industry since antiquity, recalls the example of Thomas Deloney's *Iack of Newbery* (1597), whose eponymous hero had presented himself as a 'Prince of Ants' and had refused knighthood: 'I beseech your Grace let mee live a poore Clothier among my people, in whose maintenance I take more felicity, than in all the vaine titles of Gentility: for these are the labouring Ants whom I seeke to defend'.[71]

---

[69] See G. R. Price, 'The Early Editions of *The Ant and the Nightingale*', PBSA 43 (1949), 179–90. The work may have been written in late 1603.

[70] Heinemann, *Puritanism and Theatre*, 52–7. Nashe's subversion of conservative discourse is stressed in Lorna Hutson, *Thomas Nashe in Context* (Oxford, 1989). See also Neil Rhodes, *Elizabethan Grotesque* (London, 1980), 60–1.

[71] Francis Oscar Mann (ed.), *The Works of Thomas Deloney* (Oxford, 1912), 27, 38.

Middleton's social sympathies are clearest in the story of the plough-man, whose young master sells his estate to city sharks to pay for his city luxuries. The merchant, mercer, and lawyer take over and rack the poor tenants until the word *fines* blows them all back to the shape of little ants. The censure of urban vices is conventional, but the ant's-eye-view is not. The lowly persona allows the satire an unusual proximity to the interests of the labouring poor:

but yet there is a difference between the sweat of a ploughman and the sweat of a gentleman, as much as between your master's apparel and mine, for when we sweat, the land prospers, and the harvest comes in; but when a gentleman sweats, I wot how the gear goes then. (Bullen, viii. 73-4)

Even when the prodigal's whoring is censured, the stress is less on sexual sin than on the economic misfortune it exploits. The prostitutes are either 'discontented and unfortunate gentlewomen, whose parents being lately deceased, the brother ran away with all the land', or 'decayed gentlemen's wives' whose husbands have been arrested for bankruptcy (Bullen, viii. 78-9).

The most remarkable thing about the work is the implied equation of the act of writing satire with the social protest of the deprived. In *Solomon*, Middleton had brandished his pen as a moral scalpel: 'My pen shall be officious in this scene, | To let your hearts blood in a wicked vein' (Bullen, viii. 253). In the verse preface to *Microcynicon*, the 'pens two nebs' were turned 'into a fork' to chase out Envy (Bullen, viii. 114). But the days when 'a virtuous writer . . . might maintain himself better upon poems than many upon ploughs' (Bullen, viii. 104) are past. In the ant's story, it is the ploughmen who turn the pen into a weapon of redress. When the tenants are called upon to witness the deed of transfer, the ploughman

took the pen first of the lawyer, and turning it arsy-versy, like no instrument for a ploughman . . . drew the picture of a knavish emblem, which was a plough with the heels upward, signifying thereby that the world was turned upside down since the decease of my old landlord, all hospitality and good housekeeping kicked out of doors . . . ploughs turned into trunks, and corn into apparel.

The episode plebeianizes the act of writing, turning the implement of high culture 'arsy-versy'. It is then given a self-reflexive turn so that the ploughmen's 'satire' might suggest the narrator's own insectile sub-version:

These marks, set down under the shape of simplicity, were the less marked with the eyes of knavery; for they little dreamed that we ploughmen could have so much satire in us as to bite our young landlord by the elbow. (Bullen, viii. 74-5)

It comes as no surprise after this that in the final episode the ant steps out of the tale to become its teller, Oliver Hubburd. The plebeianizing of authorship is made to signal the satirist's personal career by the rare device of making the work itself and its mock-dedication part of its narrative. Hubburd tells us about his frustrated efforts to win the patronage of Sir Christopher Clutchfist, to whom he had dedicated his first poem. Hubburd and Clutchfist are the author and dedicatee of the tales, and Middleton could not have made the self-reference clearer. The nightingale returns us to the fiction by asking the ant to rest 'From sword, book, or plough', the linked implements of industry and independence. After hearing the ant speak for so long, we are told that the industrious ants 'Fell to their work and held their tongues' (Bullen, viii. 109). Oliver Hubburd, of course, did not hold his tongue, since he was threatening in the dedication to have Sir Christopher arrested 'at the Muses' suit' (Bullen, viii. 51–2) even after this reported silencing.

Black Book was entered in the Stationers' Register two months after Ant, and it too was published twice within a year.[72] Like Dekker's Newes From Hell (1606), it is a reply to Pierce's supplication to the devil in Nashe's Pierce Penilesse (1592), and the description of Pierce's squalid room in Pict-hatch seems a dramatized picture of Nashe's last days (cf. Bullen, viii. 24–5). Middleton's declared intention in the work is, 'under the shadow of the devil's legacies', to 'bare the infectious bulks of craft, cozenage, and panderism, the three bloodhounds of a commonwealth' (Bullen, viii. 6). Lucifer, after reciting a verse prologue to his own play, 'Ascends the dusty theatre of this world' (Bullen, viii. 7; probably hinting at the Globe), and slips successively into the shapes of a constable, a usurer, and a captain. Thus disguised, he makes his way through brothels, the Exchange, a gambling tavern, and Paul's Walk. Finally, changing into the shape of a covetous farmer, he makes his will, bequeathing his legacy to crooks, and appointing a usurer and a pawnbroker as his executors. To Pierce, he leaves a tithe of all brothels so that he would 'never have need to write Supplication again' (Bullen, viii. 44).

[72] See G. B. Shand, 'The Two Editions of Thomas Middleton's The Blacke Booke', PBSA 71 (1977), 325–8.

Black Book shows Middleton emulating Nashe's gutter idiom and grotesque caricature, but he redirects them towards firmer narrative and more audacious social criticism.[73] The most dramatic change is rung by the choice of the devil as satirist-presenter. Alvin Kernan has seen in this choice the 'logical conclusion' to the discrepant status of the 'satyr', who was associated with both beast and writer in the English tradition, and who was hence guilty of the sins he scourged.[74] The decision should also be seen in relation to Middleton's problems with the satiric spokesman on the stage. Lucifer balances the contrary demands of detachment and involvement made on such a figure, and his multiple disguises remove the necessity for a disguised prince or revenger. The only way he can 'share' his 'comic sleek-ey'd villanies', Lucifer confides, is to 'turn actor and join companies' (Bullen, viii. 8). The devil needed Middleton's theatre as much as that theatre needed him, and Allwit in *Chaste Maid* was the diabolic legatee to inherit his dramatic function as satirist-presenter.

The prose tracts of the plague year bear witness to Middleton's increasing ability to command a large and diverse readership. They also show his alertness to the resources of print. The prose narrative of *Black Book*, for instance, is printed in black letter to distinguish it from the roman–italic verse prologue. This awareness of the visual dimension of the book stayed with Middleton. In the theological tract, *The Two Gates of Salvation* (1609), the parallel passages showing the correspondence of the Old and New Testaments are laid out in six columns across the middle. He also made a regular habit of having illustrated title-pages for his published plays, masques, and pageants.[75]

In producing scripts for the press and the playhouse, the young Middleton proved himself a writer who understood the market-place. This was more than just a good instinct for consumer taste. It was also a growing insight into the market-place as the site of exchange and contest between public authority and private desire. And it was here that the professional playwright had to negotiate his social business in the name of pleasure.

---

[73] See Rhodes, *Elizabethan Grotesque*, 58–60; and Heinemann, *Puritanism and Theatre*, 52–7.
[74] Kernan, *Cankered Muse*, 115.
[75] See Taylor, 'Middleton: Lives and Afterlives'.

2

Libido and the Market-Place: The Fools of Paul's

In the major comedies he wrote for Paul's Boys, Middleton chose to make his satiric point through irony and the biter-bit motif. This enabled him to tighten the dramatic structure, connecting multiple episodes in an ironic nexus.[1] The pivotal presenter becomes super-fluous in this lateral scheme, and obtrusive moralizing is replaced by the logic of irony.

The substitution helped impartial criticism of all classes, although that does not explain the social point of Middleton's irony.[2] Such criticism was the concern of the estates drama, and Middleton used the disguised prince to the same purpose in *Phoenix*. Herod Frappatore says in Marston's *Fawn* that inveighing against folly has become a fruitless labour (2.1.19–22). He may have been referring to the bishops' ban on satires, but the comment also raises the problem of shifting the material of non-dramatic satire to the stage. The disguised-prince device was one way of avoiding fruitless invective. Hercules in *Fawn* could lurk in the midst of rogues, and yet win 'more loved reputation of virtue, of learning, of all graces . . . than all your snarling reformers' (2.1.16–18). Another, as we saw, was the use of two satiric voices. Thus alongside Hercules, Marston has Dondolo the buffoon, who calls 'all manner of fools of court, city, or country, of what degree, sex, or nature' aboard the ship of fools (4.1.183–4).

The medieval survey of fools of all ranks thus survives in estates plays and city comedies, and it had no particular need of Middleton's irony or black humour. Fastidius Brisk, Puntarvolo, and Deliro in *Every Man out of his humour* (1599) illustrate the 'humours' of court, city, and country, and similar use is made of Matthew and Stephen, the town

---

[1] See Parker, 'Middleton's Experiments', 178–99.
[2] Social impartiality is deemed the purpose of Middleton's irony in e.g. Kathleen M. Lynch, *The Social Mode of Restoration Comedy* (1926; London, 1967), 25.

and country gulls, in *Every Man in his Humour* (1598). In Dekker and Middleton's *1 Whore*, a Bedlam crank numbers courtiers, gentlemen, merchants, lawyers, puritans, women, and the sons of citizens, aldermen, and farmers among the mad (5.2.121–50). Madness itself he defines as hypertrophy of the class-animus, 'for the Courtier is mad at the Cittizen, the Cittizen is mad at the Country man' (5.2.145–6).

However, what the estates plays, and city comedies derived from them, lack is an immanent principle linking social groups and governing their behaviour. The principles which do link them, such as lust and avarice, are represented as independent of the characters' places in the economy. Deviancy and redress are both derived from transsocial sources, thereby, as in *Phoenix*, emptying structures of moral and political authority of their social marrow. In *The London Prodigal* (1603-5), for instance, the hero is a merchant's son and the heroine a gentleman's daughter, but their prodigality and virtue operate regardless of their social origins.[3] By refusing to connect moral conduct and social role, the playwright conforms to the hegemonic logic which encouraged the social critic and climber to view them as discrete spheres.[4] 'Rule and subiection are matters of outward policy,' argued William Gouge, '. . . but faith, piety, and such graces are inward matters of the soule . . . These being thus different, one that is more excellent in the one, may be inferiour in the other.'[5] Such an argument could rationalize both élite privilege and the exclusion of the deserving outsider from it.

The ironic cross-weave of plots in Middleton's city comedies destroys the separation of power and morality from the dynamics of social life. At their simplest, the comedies establish the drive for money and sex as the motor of human behaviour at all levels. In a less elementary way, they connect desire and power, markets and morals, civil society and political structures. Everyday conduct expresses a hidden solidarity of cultural premises. The so-called 'realism' and 'irony' of Middleton's early comedies are more effects of this causal cohesion than of a fidelity to what the historian might perceive as the 'facts' about Jacobean England.

There is nothing new in money and sex making the comic world go round; they have been the prizes of comic gamblers since Menander.

---

[3] See Leinwand, *City Staged*, 8.

[4] See Frank Whigham, *Ambition and Privilege: The Social Tropes of Elizabethan Courtesy Theory* (Berkeley, Calif., 1984), 82.

[5] William Gouge, *Of Domesticall Duties: Eight Treatises* (1622), 2Q1. On Luther's use of a similar argument to justify slavery, see Stephen Greenblatt, *Learning to Curse: Essays in Early Modern Culture* (New York, 1990), 105.

Nor are the social types strictly specific to the age. 'Our *Scene* is *London*,' announces the Prologue to *The Alchemist* (l. 5), but the whore, bawd, squire, impostor, and others it lists come down from the Introduction to *Menaechmi*.[6] As Jonson acknowledges, their manners 'haue still beene subiect, for the rage | Or spleene of *comick*-writers' (ll.10–11). Middleton is no exception. Familiar gallants, merchants, country heirs, widows, citizens' wives, and whores people his comedies, a fact which incited L. C. Knights's scorn.[7] The crucial point is that Middleton allows the logic of the chase of flesh and profit to destroy the moral and suprasocial claims of privilege. The effect of this subversion is a re-imagining of comic stereotypes as instances of the human determination of social estate. It inaugurates that shift 'from a sense of *kinds* of humans to a sense of humans who *act* variously' which Frank Whigham considers a decisive achievement of the post-Elizabethan age.[8]

A visible result of Middleton's technique is the dissolution of the ideological opposition of country and city, and that of the court to both. Although routinely portraying crooks and fools from all three, the estates plays and their descendants retain the ideological indices of these locations. The equation of the country with innocence and the city and the court with sin depended, as Raymond Williams pointed out, on 'an ideological separation between the processes of rural exploitation . . . and the register of that exploitation, in the law courts, the money markets, the political power and the conspicuous expenditure of the city'.[9] The separation expresses itself in drama as a neo-pastoral contrast. In a pastoral, wrote Thomas Heywood, playwrights 'shew the harmlesse loue of Sheepheards diuersly moralized, distinguishing betwixt the craft of the Citty, and the innocency of the sheep-coat'.[10] In the city comedies we are about to examine, the neo-pastoral opposition between natural order and commercial depredation gives way to an image of social corruption in which court, city, and country are locked in a symbiotic nexus. In the country men become beasts, wrote Donne; in the city, blocks; and in a lewd court, devils. And yet,

[6] See Harry Levin, 'Notes toward a Definition of City Comedy', in Barbara Lewalski (ed.), *Renaissance Genres* (Cambridge, Mass., 1986), 143.

[7] Knights, *Drama and Society*, 258.

[8] Whigham, *Ambition and Privilege*, 186.

[9] Raymond Williams, *The Country and the City* (New York, 1973), 46. Renaissance attitudes to the city could be more equivocal; see William Tydeman, 'The Image of the City in English Renaissance Drama', *E & S* 38 (1985), 29–44; and Gail Paster, *The Idea of the City in the Age of Shakespeare* (Athens, Ga., 1985), *passim*.

[10] Thomas Heywood, *An Apology for Actors* (1612), F4.

'Each elements qualities were in the'other three; |. . . And mingled thus, their issue'incestuous.'[11] One achievement of Middleton's dramaturgy is to suggest that this incestuous issue springs from indivisible premises of social organization and behaviour.

The functional interdependence of court, city, and country is expressed in these plays in terms of a Balzacian sex-money calculus.[12] What the merchant gains in money, he loses in virility; what the prodigal heir loses in estates, he gains in sex. The idea anticipates modern psychoanalysis in positing a libidinal economy in which the sphincter control of the anal erotic diverts vital energies from sex towards the accumulation of wealth.[13] Nearer our time, Mary Douglas has shown how bodily orifices can 'represent points of entry or exit to social units', and Lévi-Strauss has studied how different cultures treat the female body as the medium of economic and political exchange.[14] In Middleton's comedies, and more grimly in his tragedies, the woman acts as the sluice through which money and power circulate. As Pursenet says in *Five Gallants*:

why, this is right the sequence of the world. A lord maintains her, she maintains a knight, he maintains a whore, she maintains a captain. So in like manner the pocket keeps my boy, he keeps me, I keep her, she keeps him; it runs like quicksilver from one to another. (3.2.102–7)

In *The Widow*, the same idea is recast as a wheel of social justice in a thief's song:

How round the world goes, and everything that's in it!
The tides of gold and silver ebb and flow in a minute:
From the usurer to his sons there's a current swiftly runs;
From the sons to queans in chief, from the gallant to the thief,
From the thief unto his host, from the host to husbandmen;
From the country to the court; and so it comes to us agen. (3.1.110–15)

City comedy, according to Theodore Leinwand, sees through the conventional representations of gentleman and citizen 'to the bases of

---

[11] John Donne, 'To Sir Henry Wotton', in *The Satires, Epigrams and Verse Letters*, ed. W. Milgate (Oxford, 1967), 72.

[12] See Jameson, *Political Unconscious*, 180–1.

[13] See Sigmund Freud, 'On Transformations of Instinct as Exemplified in Anal Erotism', in James Strachey (ed.), *The Standard Edition of the Complete Psychological Works of Sigmund Freud*, 24 vols. (London, 1953–74), xvii. 125–33; and Otto Fenichel, 'The Drive to Amass Wealth', in Hanna Fenichel and David Rapaport (eds.), *The Collected Papers of Otto Fenichel*, 2 vols. (London, 1954–5), ii. 89–108.

[14] Mary Douglas, *Purity and Danger: An Analysis of Concepts of Pollution and Taboo* (London, 1966), 4; and Claude Lévi-Strauss, *The Jealous Potter*, trans. Bénédicte Chorier (Chicago, 1988), 180–2.

urban existence in sexuality and capital'.[15] The distinction of Middleton's contribution to the genre is that it offers a perspective on the
mutual implication of these bases. Not only do money and sex join
court, city, and country; court, city, and country conspire to join
money and sex. 'Porters' backs and women's bellies bear up the world,'
Shortyard tells Easy in *Michaelmas*. Easy is wiser than he knows when
his reply imitates his mentor's cynical cool: "'Tis true, i'faith; they bear
men and money, and that's the world' (2.3.320–1). The economy of
the libido is concentric to that of the market-place in Middleton's city
comedies. In his tragedies, it will be inseparable from the disposal of
political power.

COUNTRY AND CITY: *Michaelmas Term*

The Induction to *Michaelmas Term* shows Michaelmas, the inaugural
term, arriving in the city to open the law season. He sheds the white
country cloak, his 'conscience', and slips into the lawyer's black
(ll. 1–4). 'Civil', the adjective identifying the city with the law, is
linked to 'evil' and 'the devil' (ll. 3–4) by rhyme, colour, and costume.[16] The Induction signals the rake's-progress theme by another
allegorical shorthand, a dumb-show in which the other three terms rig
out a raw yokel with silk, page, and pimp (l. 29).[17]

The Captain in *Phoenix* had envied the country heir who converted
farmer's labour into mercer's profits (1.2.61–6). The semantic exchanges in the Induction's quibbles are governed by this blighting
commerce. Court fees are an 'autumnian blessing', 'hops' laced with
'harlots' emasculate men,[18] peasants' sweat delivers a 'silver harvest' for
city lawyers, writs 'fly abroad' and return 'With clients, like dried
straws, between their bills' (ll. 6–10, 14–18, 58–60). The younger terms

---

[15] Leinwand, *City Staged*, 51.

[16] Michaelmas's gloss on his change of costume recalls an allegorical figure such as Vanity
in *The Contention between Liberality and Prodigality* (1601), who presents himself by pointing at
his feathers: 'Sith this attire so plainely shewes the same, | As shewed cannot be in words
more plaine' (ll. 3–4). On the convention, see T. W. Craik, *The Tudor Interlude: Stage,
Costume, and Acting* (Leicester, 1958), 73–92; and Glynne Wickham, *Early English Stages: 1300
to 1600*, 3 vols. (London, 1959–81), iii. 100–9.

[17] For a similar instance, see Henry Medwall's *Nature*, Pt. I, ll. 462, 1024–50.

[18] 'Hopharlots' was material for coarse sheets. The pun perverts the word's association
with frugality to that with sex. See my 'Thomas Middleton's *Michaelmas Term*, Inductio
13–19', *Explicator*, 51 (1993), 209–11.

salute Michaelmas as their 'father' (l. 35), although he is capable of breeding only the money they are after: 'Where bags are fruitful'st, there the womb's most barren; | The poor has all our children, we their wealth' (ll. 22–3).

Even when country and city are thus opposed, the prodigal-son motif places the contraries of the neo-pastoral fable in a relation of complementarity. It is the desertion of the country rather than the invasion by the city which converts the ploughman's sweat into a silver bonus for lawyers and loan sharks: 'And so through wealthy variance and fat brawl, | The barn is made but steward to the hall' (ll.11–12).[19] This, of course, is a basic requirement of the prodigal-son play. But the Induction does more than foretell that country and city will live off each other. It anticipates the circuitous chase of money and sex which makes the hunter and the hunted switch roles in the play. If Quomodo the draper bluffs his way into land and respectability, Easy the country heir is anxious to acquire the stamp of a city gallant. If Quomodo swindles Easy of his inheritance, Easy robs Quomodo, at least until his estate is restored, of his wife. If city women fancy country gentlemen, impoverished country gents, such as Rearage, angle for city widows (cf. 1.1.24), and country maids, such as Salewood's cousin, are brought up to London to marry upstart money and title.

Richard Levin links the major and minor plots by tracing two triangles on the sex–money axis. Quomodo's lust for land drives his ignored wife into Easy's arms, while his daughter Susan is repelled by her lecherous suitor, a Scottish parvenu named Andrew Lethe, and turns to Rearage. In this scheme, the conflict of citizen and gentry is a consequence of their mutually exclusive commitments to sex and riches. As Quomodo puts it, 'They're busy 'bout our wives, we 'bout their lands' (1.1.107).[20]

The play, I think, resists such simple equations. Thus Easy in Levin's first triangle, by virtue of being a deserter of his country roots, matches not only Rearage in the second, but also Lethe and his punk, the Country Wench. Easy's sexual victory over Quomodo comes late. He is first drawn into the play's team of impotent sexual deviants by Shortyard. In his disguise as Blastfield, a name equally menacing for estates and fertility, Shortyard becomes Easy's 'bedfellow', and they are 'man and wife' (2.3.304, 155). Despite differences, citizens and gentlemen are all turned by their social ambitions into variants of the migrant rustic of the Induction.

The prodigals are also linked by their social and parricidal amnesia. Easy frequents London now that his father is dead (1.1.42–3), Lethe has forgotten his tooth-drawer father since arriving in London (1.1.144–6, 255), the Country Wench has been enticed away from her father by a pimp (1.2.2), Rearage gambles away his father's income in London taverns (2.1.124), and Salewood dodges his father when the latter is in town (1.1.2–7). What begins as a politic loss of memory ends in self-oblivion. Lethe wonders if he will recognize himself (1.1.171), and the spruced-up Wench is certain that her kinsmen would not know her since she scarcely knows herself (3.1.30-1). The ease with which characters slip into new social costumes declares the infirm artifice of social selves.[21] 'What base birth does not raiment make glorious?' asks Hellgill, 'And what glorious births do not rags make infamous?' (3.1.1–3).

The themes of blasted generation and self-loss are brought together when Lethe's mother and the Wench's father, unable to recognize their offspring, become their bawd and page respectively. When Lethe shifts his attention from Susan to her mother Thomasine, he employs his own mother as go-between. However, neither Mother Gruel nor the Wench's father represents the betrayed ideal of the country. Mother Gruel takes her son for a gallant, hopes to learn the fashions, and to seduce young courtiers. The father, who had wasted his youth in the 'man-devouring city' (2.2.21), finds in the gallants a mirror of his 'former follies' (3.1.271), yet mistakes his daughter for 'A mistress of a choice beauty' (3.1.54). The errors betray self-ignorance, each generation failing to recognize in the other its own reflection.

The comic nucleus of the play is the two cozening scenes (2.3, 3.4) in which Quomodo, helped by Shortyard and Falselight, traps Easy into pawning his estate. Middleton here fits the commodity-swindle documented in rogue literature within the allegorical framework of Youth mortgaging his soul to Vice.[22] To this blend, he accommodates

---

[21] See Gail Paster, 'Quomodo, Sir Giles, and Triangular Desire: Social Aspiration in Middleton and Massinger', in A. R. Braunmuller and J. C. Bullman (eds.), *Comedy from Shakespeare to Sheridan: Change and Continuity in the English and European Dramatic Tradition: Essays in Honor of Eugene M. Waith* (Newark, NJ, 1986), 169.

the prodigal theme by linking the legal 'bond' with the filial. Quomodo likens the signing of a bond to the fathering of a child since they
both entail mounting bills (3.4.135–9).

Quomodo's joke about 'bonds abroad' resembling 'boys at nurse'
(3.4.151) returns to plague him when the indenture he fathers unbinds
his wife, son, and parasite. Experience warns him 'that cozenage in the
father wheels about to folly in the son' (4.1.83–4), and, like Volpone,
he decides to outsmart destiny by a feigned death. His worst fears are
confirmed as Thomasine promptly marries Easy, and his son Sim, for
whom he had planned a lawyer's career, is dispossessed by Shortyard.
The idea of a circular justice which puts the son of the citizen sharper
in the shoes of his father's gentry victims we encounter elsewhere in
Renaissance plays. Plutarchus explains this to his goldsmith father in
Jonson's *Devil is an Ass* (3.1.28–9), and it is elaborated upon in Shirley's
Gamester (1.1, p. 201).[23] But the requital in Quomodo's case is not
simply transgenerational. Rogue and gull, ingrosser and prodigal, he
runs the entire circuit within five acts. He sinks a notch lower than Sim
in comic improvidence when he rashly signs away his possessions to
Easy, who has already replaced him in Thomasine's bed. Although
Thomasine is restored to him in the final trial, he loses his real erotic
fetish, the land he had likened to 'a fine gentlewoman i'th' waist, not
so great as pretty' (2.3.83).

Quomodo has figured in criticism as the quintessential example of
the urban climber, and his undoing has usually been viewed in a moral
light.[24] But his pre-eminence as bourgeois Machiavel is not untem-
pered by ironic affinities across class divides. The Country Wench
learns to defend 'wholesale' by the tradesman's ethics (4.2.10–15; cf.
Dutch Courtesan, 1.2.36–9). Her father and Mother Gruel, although

[22] On the debt to rogue literature, see R. C. Bald, 'The Sources of Middleton's City
Comedies', *JEGP* 33 (1934), 377–82; Margery Fisher, 'Notes on the Sources of Some
Incidents in Midleton's London Plays', *RES* 15 (1939), 284–5; and G. R. Price (ed.),
Michaelmas Term and A Trick to Catch the Old One: *A Critical Edition* (The Hague, 1976),
15–19. On a possible real-life parallel between Quomodo and a London merchant named
Howe, see Richard Levin, 'Quomodo's Name in *Michaelmas Term*', *N & Q* 218 (1973),
460–1. For an allegorical reading of the contract scenes, see Chatterji, 'Unity and Disparity',
350–1.
[23] See Levin, *Multiple Plot*, 183. The idea is also present in Robert Burton, *The Anatomy
of Melancholy*, ed. Holbrook Jackson (1932; repr. London, 1978), 'Democritus Junior to the
Reader', 67.
[24] See e.g. *Knights, Drama and Society*, 265–6; Chatterji, 'Unity and Disparity', 352; Hallett,
Middleton's Cynics, 110–23; and Laura Caroline Stevenson, *Praise and Paradox: Merchants and
Craftsmen in Elizabethan Popular Literature* (Cambridge, 1984), 104–5.

unable to recognize their children, anticipate Quomodo's later predicament as disguised beadle spying on his own family. Nor is Quomodo's end exclusively moral. It also consolidates the mutual dependence of cozenage and folly in the play's logic into a genetic bond: 'cozenage in the father wheels about to folly in the son'.

How true to life was Quomodo? Heinemann, anxious to prove that the city and the middling sort would have had no problem with him, warns against 'too literal and documentary a view' of his class fantasy. Her caveat that Quomodo was a cheat, not the 'normal' London draper, betrays a no less literal and documentary notion of audience response.[25] Leinwand more plausibly sees Quomodo as an exaggerated and parodic portrayal of the gentry's bogeyman version of the merchant.[26] Middleton, in addition, demythologizes this self-serving model by loading him with multiple actantial duties and by linking him with his antitypes.

The treatment of Quomodo is symptomatic of the play's generic irresolution. 'New Comedy is *adulescens triumphans*; prodigal son comedy is *senex triumphans*,' observes Ervin Beck. *Michaelmas* refuses victory to either, and thus it does not 'fit exclusively into a single mode'.[27] The conflicts of place, class, age, and temperament in these dramatic conventions are reproduced in unfamiliar configurations, unclinching them from their ideological moulds.

The generic paradox is reflected also in word-play. Like sectarian rhetoric in *Family of Love*, legal jargon is employed in *Michaelmas* to forge ironic linkages in the semantic subsoil. W. Nicholas Knight notes how legal terms enable the playwright to study the interdependence of marriage, family, and property, 'transferred by law but based upon the other laws of sex and economics'.[28] Law in the play is different from the divinity Phoenix praised. It is part of the authorized mechanism which regulates creatural drives into societal forms. Middleton uses its terminology as a vaulting horse to leap both ways. One could thus read into the regulatory structures themselves the institutionalized forms of desire and depredation. Law, says Quomodo, is best suited to a citizen's son, 'for our word is, "What do ye lack?" and their word is, "What do

[25] Heinemann, *Puritanism and Theatre*, 88–94.

[26] Leinwand, *City Staged*, 51–6.

[27] Ervin Beck, 'Terence Improved: The Paradigm of the Prodigal Son in English Renaissance Comedy', *RD* 6 (1973), 111, 119–20.

[28] W. Nicholas Knight, 'Sex and Law Language in Middleton's *Michaelmas Term*', in Friedenreich (ed.), '*Accompaninge the Players*', 106; see 89–108.

you give?" ' (2.3.420–2). When Quomodo concludes the act by asking the 'students at Inns of Cozenage' (2.3.441–2) to admire him, Middleton betrays the law students in the audience into uneasy complicity after having committed them to smart laughter in the Induction: 'Sat sapienti; I hope there's no fools i'th' house' (ll. 73–4).[29]

MADNESS AND MORALS: A Mad World, My Masters

A Mad World, My Masters divides swindling and seduction between two urban rakehells, Follywit and Penitent Brothel. Follywit is after the money of his grandfather, Sir Bounteous Progress, and Penitent after the wife of Harebrain. The two dupes simplify the social grouping round the divided axiology of the plot. Sir Bounteous is a country knight who gives himself lordly airs, while Harebrain is a stingy citizen who keeps his wife under lock and key. The tricksters, on the other hand, have no defined class motive. They answer to Cuthbert Cutpurse's definition of the gentleman-gallant in A Knack to Know a Knave as he who 'when all fayles, can live vpon his wit' (l. 764). They do not, like Quomodo, best class rivals. Instead, they inherit the social roles of their victims. Follywit is the heir to his grandfather's estate, and Penitent turns more genuinely 'Puritan' than Harebrain.

The familiar terms of the comic contest are soon complicated by ironic reversals. Such reversals are the essence of the world's madness, as Candido explained to the Officer in 1 Whore:

Changde sir, why true sir, is change strange, tis not fashion vnlesse it alter: Monarkes turne to beggers; beggers creepe into the nests of Princes, Maisters serve their prentises: Ladies their Seruingmen, men turne to women. . . . I, and women turne to men, you say true, ha ha, a mad world, a mad world. (4. 3. 130–7)

'Folly' and 'wit' are indistinguishable in this saturnalian madness, although in Solomon they were seen as antithetical: 'What greater foe than folly unto wit?' (Bullen, viii. 262). Follywit, a 'mad-brain o' th' first' (1.1.83) in his pranks, reaches the 'high height of madness' (4.5.13) when he takes his grandfather's whore for a virgin and marries

[29] The prefatory epistle in Ant also ends with the Plautine tag: 'Sat sapienti; and I hope there be many wise men in all the twelve Companie[s]' (Bullen, viii. 54). The Jew of Malta, the Prologue to which may have influenced Middleton's Induction, is the likely source of the boast; cf. ll. 2332–3.

her. The failure of his wit and the depravity of Penitent's will are variants of the same lunacy, and the comic delight their pranks provide ensures that the spectators are not spared the rebuke and mockery of reversal.

While the gallants pursue either sex or money, the courtesan, Frank Gullman, trades sex for money, joining the erotic and economic segments of the plot. In the keep of Sir Bounteous, she helps Penitent bed Mrs Harebrain, and, in the end, traps Follywit into marriage. The centrality of the whore's plot function is directly related to her marginal status. Like the licensed fool, she is empowered by society to milk and mock its members. She is thus a median spirit, a mean as well as a means. 'And therefore I'm constrained to use the means,' says Penitent, 'Of one that knows no mean, a courtesan' (1.1.100–1). Like the whore Sindefy in *Eastward Ho* (1605), she is a rational norm in the upside-down world, usurping the function of the disguised prince or a morality presenter. This explains the full significance of Penitent's exclamation: 'A courtesan! O admirable times! Honesty is removed to the common place!' (1.1.125–6). Her 'common place' enables her to move in and out of court, city, and country, and exploit all with equal skill. When Harebrain describes her mother as a 'woman of excellent carriage . . . in court, city, and country', Frank quips in an aside, 'Witness three bastards apiece' (1.2.31–4).

Follywit prides himself on his 'art'; so does Frank (cf. 1.1.83–4, 1.2.94, 3.3.2).[30] They lose their artistry and control the moment they try entering status and gender roles. Follywit thereafter takes Frank for a virgin 'without sophistication . . . tricks, set speeches, and artful entertainments' (4.5.56–8), and Frank, surrendering her *déclassé* immunity, shudders at the thought of marrying a thief (5.2.231).

The nature of social bondage, freedom, and art in the mad world is summed up in the image of the spider and the fly used by Frank's mother: 'Every part of the world shoots up daily into more subtlety. The very spider weaves her cauls with more art and cunning to entrap the fly' (1.1.140–2).[31] Kinship is part of the same web. Sir Bounteous says he is bound to his whore by nature, 'a poor kinswoman of mine; nature binds me to have a care of her' (3.2.73–4). Follywit binds his

---

[30] The link between a whore's cunning and playmaking is suggested in Dekker and Webster's *Northward Ho*, another Paul's play of 1605; see 1.2.101–2, 3.1.99–100.

[31] The Courtesan seems to echo ironically the moral anxiety of Greene's *Defence of Coneycatching* (1592); see Alexander B. Grosart (ed.), *The Life and Complete Works in Prose and Verse of Robert Greene*, 15 vols., Huth Library (n.p., 1881–6), xi. 51.

grandfather literally to rob him, only to be taken 'prisoner' by his punk (4.5.53). Harebrain, trying to bind his wife, is bound by the self-spun caul of jealousy: 'Even so my husband, in restraining me, | With the same ward bars his own liberty' (1.2.108–9). Spider and fly change places; none escapes the appetitive mesh which holds together court, country, and city.

While it lasts, the tricksters' ability to slip out of their class and rank enables them to exploit the social fantasies of others. Follywit has merely to visit his grandsire in the disguise of a lord, since Sir Bounteous likes to think that courtiers seek out his hospitality, as he is blessed with 'a kind of complimental gift given me above ordinary country knights', a native *grazia* 'which naturally slips' from him (2.1.51–6), and which, nevertheless, he needs constantly to advertise.

In the course of Middleton's career, the attitude to housekeeping changed from the laments for 'the long Haull tables fully furnished with good victuals'[32] to diatribes against the '*Doore-dole*'[33] which fostered idleness and impeded the 'manuall Artes'.[34] The satire on Sir Bounteous's housekeeping does not take sides in the debate, but shows how the same social jockeying lies behind the professions of city and country values. Sir Bounteous is not one of James's forty-pound knights.[35] His hospitality is still a mimicry of courtly exhibition, not an expression of social responsibility like Sir Edward Fortune's in *Jack Drum's Entertainment*. 'Liberalitie' was upheld as a mean between 'Prodigalitie' and 'Covetousnesse'.[36] Sir Bounteous is both prodigal and covetous, starving his kin to feast his lechery (cf. 4.3.90).

The first Earl of Clare said of his generous grandfather Sir William Holles (1509–91) that he 'sent all his revenues downe the privy house'. Sir William did not feast only courtiers. Between All-Hallowtide and Candlemas, 'any man was permitted freely to stay three dayes without being asked from whence he came or what he was'.[37] Sir Bounteous's

[32] I. M., *A Health to the Gentlemanly Profession of Seruing-men: or, The Seruingman's Comfort* (1598), G4ᵛ.

[33] [Thomas Scott], *The Belgicke Pismire* (1622), L2ᵛ.

[34] Fynes Moryson, *An Itinerary* (1617), 4 vols. (Glasgow, 1907), iv. 94. On the changing attitude to housekeeping, see Felicity Heal, *Hospitality in Early Modern England* (Oxford, 1990), 91–140.

[35] Sir Bounteous is wrongly described as one of James's new knights in Ayers, 'Plot, Subplot, and the Uses of Dramatic Discord', 7. Follywit distinguishes him from such knights in 1.1.58–9.

[36] I. M., *Health to the Gentlemanly Profession*, D2.

[37] Gervase Holles, *Memorials of the Holles Family 1493–1656*, ed. A. C. Wood, Camden Society, 3rd ser. 55 (1937), 41–2.

selective entertainment, being an expression of social ambition, ironically saves his revenue from going down the privy. Instead, his 'open' house allows money to flow through places and ranks. When, late in James's reign, a bill was brought in Parliament to regulate 'Excess in Apparel', it was declined on the ground that it would limit social mobility and 'damp the Spirits of Industry'. If a man of pedigree was 'so Mad and Foolish' as to beggar himself with excess, ''tis very probable that some Man of more Wisdom and Merit will enjoy that which the other hath so idly and prodigally mispent'.[38] Sir Bounteous is not beggared, and Follywit and Frank are not quite the 'Spirits of Industry'. The quotation is useful in that it shows that excess could be suffered as a lubricant of social mobility. Sir Bounteous's open house could thus serve as a passage between the axiological and narrative divisions of the play. At the same time, Middleton, by refusing to privilege the motives of his exploiters, could equate the knight's social fantasy with those of the gallant and the whore.

While Follywit dresses up as a lord, the courtesan, like Mary Faugh in *Dutch Courtesan*, eases Penitent's access to Mrs Harebrain by posing as a Familist. She is the only one Harebrain trusts with his wife, since he dreads adultery as the only mortal sin. The fake Familist is to the merchant what the fake courtier is to the knight: both deceptions appeal to the obsessions of the deceived.

The swirl of disguises reaches a heady climax when Follywit, playing an actor, robs his grandfather in the comedy appropriately named *The Slip*. Besides flaunting the theatricality of Follywit's tricks, the episode suggests the instability of social identities outside the playhouse. 'Why, art not thou the constable i' th' comedy?' asks a bewildered Sir Bounteous to the real-life constable trapped inside the play. The constable's reply brings social and dramatic artifice to a vertiginous confrontation: 'I' th' comedy? Why, I am the constable i' th' commonwealth, sir' (5.2.149–52). Playmaking in the theatre and cony-catching outside it equally exploit the indeterminacy of social selves: players and scholars, Dekker observed, live by gulling as much as vintners and punks.[39] The inset play mocks the spectators' acceptance of such selves. It makes them see that they, like the Black Knight's victims in *Game at Chess* (1.1.257–62), have been swindled with

---

[38] Arthur Wilson, *The Life and Reign of James, the First King of Great Britain*, in [W. Kennett], *A Complete History of England*, 3 vols. (1706), ii. 5U4ᵛ.

[39] See the mock-dedication to *The Guls Horne-booke* (1609), in Dekker, *Non-Dramatic Works*, ii. 197.

laughter.[40] A new twist to the series of disguises is given by the succubus appearing to Penitent in the form of Mrs Harebrain. Follywit's surrender to Frank is set off by Penitent's rejection of the succubus. But whereas Follywit's blindness is a price for submitting to the social bridle, the clear-sightedness of Penitent, who had hitherto been something of a cynical satirist, derives from a supernatural order. The shift of planes has inspired various critical explanations—mistimed moralizing, Calvinist glimpse of the human condition, gothic parody of a morality device, subversive doubling of perspectives, return of comedy's repressed.[41] Penitent's conversion, however, is entirely consistent with the mad justice of the play-world. Madnesses, according to Joseph Hall, are as various as dispositions. Follywit, going by Hall's inventory, may be said to suffer from 'the laughing madnesse of extreame mirth', while Penitent's 'adulterous motions' (1.1.94) issues in the madness 'of outragious lust'.[42] Follywit is beaten at his own game by Frank, and is laughed at by Sir Bounteous, his fellow lunatic in mirth and a prodigal in reverse.[43] It is thus appropriate that Penitent should be reformed into the piety his victim Harebrain travesties. Harebrain removes wanton pamphlets from his wife's reach and wishes her to read Robert Parsons's *Resolution* (1.2.45–9). The same tract reforms Penitent (cf. 4.1.1–29). In theatrical and structural terms, Penitent's conversion is not as big a problem as moral and psychological readings make it out to be.

In dividing the pursuit of money and sex between two tricksters, Middleton also split the contradictory images of the satirist-presenter which the disguised-prince device had brought together. The Malevolian and Falstaffian tones of the satirist are given to Penitent and

[40] The inset play is seen as an exposure of the commercial interest behind the contemporary public theatre's pretence of 'mirth' in Paul Yachnin, 'The Politics of Theatrical Mirth: *A Midsummer Night's Dream, A Mad World, My Masters*, and *Measure for Measure*', *SQ* 43 (1992), 51–66.

[41] See Michael Taylor, 'Realism and Morality in Middleton's *A Mad World, My Masters*', *L & P* 18 (1968), 172–3; Arthur F. Marotti, 'The Method in the Madness of *A Mad World, My Masters*', *Tennessee Studies in Literature*, 15 (1970), 102; Hallett, *Middleton's Cynics*, 63–92; Stephen Wigler, 'Penitent Brothel Reconsidered: The Place of the Grotesque in Middleton's *A Mad World, My Masters*', *L & P* 25 (1975), 17–26; Shapiro, *Children of the Revels*, 123–7; Robert L. Root, Jr., 'The Troublesome Reformation of Penitent Brothel: Middletonian Irony and *A Mad World, My Masters*', *CLA Journal*, 25 (1981), 82–90; David Farley-Hills, *The Comic in Renaissance Comedy* (London, 1981), 81–107; and Ayers, 'Plot, Subplot, and the Uses of Dramatic Discord', 7–10.

[42] Ios[eph] Hall, *Holy Obseruations: Lib. I* (1607), F5ᵛ; see F5–6.

[43] Leanore Leiblein, 'Thomas Middleton's Prodigal Play', *CD* 10 (1976), 55–6, notes that Sir Bounteous is a reversed prodigal-son figure.

Follywit respectively, and while the former is betrayed in moral consequence, the latter is made a comic fool. The axiological split thus coincides with the ontological one, and, since the authority of the moral presenter derives from a source outside human society, the resolution of the Penitent-end of the axis demands a transdomain intervention. If the extrinsic stimulus partially suspends the immanent social logic shaping the play, it does so in order to enlarge the blend of New Comedy and prodigal-son drama into a comic exemplum of universal madness.

COMIC TRICK AND SOCIAL FACT: *A Trick to Catch the Old One*

Trick traces the cyclical flow of wealth through a drastically simplified action. Theodorus Witgood, a Leicestershire gentleman, has his estate mortgaged to his usurer uncle in the city, Pecunius Lucre. He passes his mistress off as a rich widow, and the prospect of their marriage traps Lucre into releasing his lands. Witgood also means to marry Joyce, niece to Walkadine Hoard, another usurer and a sworn enemy of Lucre. In trying to upstage Lucre, Hoard ends up marrying Witgood's mistress, and is even blackmailed into paying off Witgood's debts. In the city, Witgood had sunk his Leicestershire estate into lechery, 'that little pit' (1.1.4). It is sex again through which wealth is pumped back to the country. The vascular function in the economy, as well as in the plot, is served by his mistress, called a Courtesan although 'She ne'er had common use, nor common thought' (5.2.118). 'Medler', the name she assumes in her incarnation as the widow, suggests this function, being a cant term for a prostitute and the vagina. Medlar the fruit was also known as 'openarse',[44] provoking puns on the widow's rumoured 'openness' and the 'open house' she kept with her former husband (cf. 2.2.59–63, 4.5.141–5).

Trick differs from *Michaelmas* and *Mad World* in allowing Witgood an unmixed triumph. This is partly because Witgood's career of riot has already run its course when the play begins. His earlier speeches imitate the tone of the reformed prodigal (cf. 1.1.1–26), but when he tries it on the Courtesan, she sharply reminds him that his estate 'thrice racked' was not worth the virginity she had 'prodigally' given him (1.1.33–5). The reformed-prodigal model, with its sexist sequence of

[44] See James T. Henke, *Renaissance Dramatic Bawdy (Exclusive of Shakespeare): An Annotated Glossary and Critical Essays*, 2 vols. [continuous pagination] (Salzburg, 1974), 65.

using, discarding, and condemning the female, does not work in Middleton's society. Witgood thus quickly turns into the trickster-artist of New Comedy, with the Courtesan as his partner.[45] He will 'beget' the trick; she will help it 'breed' (1.1.57). The only reclamation which works is a financial one, as Lucre's use of the prodigal-son idiom shows: 'I grant he has been youthful, but is he not now reclaimed?' (2.1.75–6). After they pull off their trick, Witgood and the Courtesan are both reclaimed in the banker's sense. He regains solvency, she the security and respectability of marriage. Their reformation speeches in Act 5, Scene 2, it has been pointed out, are a parody of the conversion ritual of prodigal-son plays.[46] The parody is sharpened by the timing. They kneel 'In true reclaiméd form' (5.2.154) only after they are reclaimed financially. The Courtesan even turns her pre-reformation life into social capital by persuading a dejected Hoard that a whore-turned-wife is the best insurance against cuckoldry: 'She that knows sin, knows best how to hate sin' (5.2.140).

Compared with Plautus's *Persa*, a suggested source,[47] *Trick* does not seem reliant on the trickster's ingenuity for its effect. But placed beside *Michaelmas* and *Mad World*, it does. The altered dramaturgical stress weakens the challenge to social stereotypes. It is true, as Heinemann says, that Middleton does not privilege Witgood's gentry status,[48] but that has more to do with his dissipation than with landowning. On the contrary, his flair and resourcefulness seem to confirm the intellectual and sexual presumption of the gentleman-gallant, while the usurers reflect the fears and contempt out of which the gentleman fashioned their image.[49] Witgood's creditors themselves accept their lot as trades-men since they are 'not ordained to thrive by wisdom' (4.3.39–41). Even at the citizens' game, Witgood is cleverer. Unlike Gerardine's, his romantic sentiments never punctuate his roguery. Instead he ero-ticizes the released mortgage as much as Hoard commodifies the widow's body: 'Thou soul of my estate I kiss thee, | I miss life's

---

[45] See Rowe, *Middleton and the New Comedy Tradition*, 72–92.

[46] See Shapiro, *Children of the Revels*, 64–5; Alan R. Young, *The English Prodigal Son Plays: A Theatrical Fashion of the Sixteenth and Seventeenth Centuries* (Salzburg, 1979), 271–2; and David B. Mount, 'The "[Un]reclaymed forme" of Middleton's *A Trick to Catch the Old One*', *SEL* 31 (1991), 261–2.

[47] See Signi Falk, 'Plautus' *Persa* and Middleton's *A Trick to Catch the Old One*', *MLN* 66 (1951), 19–21.

[48] Heinemann, *Puritanism and Theatre*, 96–7.

[49] On the fears and fantasies constituting the gentry's stereotype of the merchant, see Leinwand, *City Staged*, 59.

comfort when I miss thee' (4.2.87–8). Witgood's superiority to the usurers is in the ingenuity and success of his 'revenge comedy'[50] compared to theirs, not in his moral aims. The identity of their motives is mocked in the uncertainty of Lucre's wife about whether the plot she has in mind against her husband is 'a tragedy plot, or a comedy plot'. She, however, is certain that it is a revenge plot: "Tis a plot shall vex him' (2.1.349–50).

As in *Mad World*, there are two gulls in *Trick*, but the comic humours of Lucre and Hoard are not as socially differentiated as those of Harebrain and Sir Bounteous. Their paranoid hatred for each other is a more potent motive than their social ambition (2.1.197–9, 2.2.42, 3.3.100–1). This prodigal rivalry, besides distancing their conduct from simple class motivation, also ensures that the final wedding feast is not too bitter for either of them, since the torment of each is in part alleviated by that of the other.

Although less of a common prostitute than Frank Gullman, the Courtesan shares her instrumental function in the plot. She, however, is united to Witgood by motive and necessity in a way Frank never was to Sir Bounteous or Follywit: 'our states being both desperate, they're soon resolute' (1.1.63–4). It would ease Witgood's conscience to see her 'well bestowed' (1.1.113–14), and her loyalty seems to make her deserve that happiness: 'For, where I once vow, I am ever true' (4.4.143). The Courtesan makes a further claim on our moral response in reminding Hoard that she had never boasted of money or property, but 'took a plainer course' (5.2.127). Widow Medler was a projection of the gallants' and citizens' erotic and economic fetish; the woman who replaces this fiction owns 'nothing' (5.2.128). The role is disencumbered of the fantasies of possession and domination, and the nameless Courtesan is invested with a bare gender identity implied in the familiar sexual innuendo of 'nothing'. In forcing the usurers to face the emptiness of their sociosexual construct, the Courtesan promises a challenge to male prejudices which Moll Cutpurse could take further by refusing to reclaim her gendered social role.

The only interruption to the single action comes from three scenes (1.4, 3.4, 4.5) in which the usurer Dampit figures, drinking himself to death in the last two. The name, the stink of burning horns in his room (3.4.66), and his likeness to 'the devil in chains' (4.5.6) advertise his allegorical ancestry. But Dampit is not just a morality abstraction like

---

[50] The phrase is Rowe's; see *Middleton and the New Comedy Tradition*, 88.

Tangle. When Gulf waxes large on the 'just judgement shown upon usury, extortion, and trampling villainy' (4.5.150–1), the alcoholic recovers enough sharpness to show the fellow usurer his place.

The tonal leap and structural overhang of the Dampit scenes have been variously explained. Parker viewed him as a vent for Middleton's moral disgust, and Levin considered him an absorbant of the spectators' loathing of usury.[51] Recent critics have rightly stressed that Dampit forces into the open the moral issues suppressed by festive New Comedy, provoking more uncomic response than he drains off. Unlike the gentleman-sharper, Dampit reminds playgoers what sense the world makes to one who does make a career of scams. The armada in 1588 and a storm in 1599 he remembers as times when he prayed that 'Poovies' new buildings' might be pulled down (3.4.1–5). That such a man is a usurer like Lucre and Hoard, and that he lives by cunning like Witgood and the Courtesan, sour our enjoyment of their tricks rather than save them from moral scrutiny.[52]

The characterization of Dampit, despite the morality overtones, is rooted in social fact. Dampit's 'own phrase' for his occupation, 'trampler of time' (1.4.10), suggests a legal middleman, and he resembles the pettifoggers described by Thomas Wilson as those forever 'seeking meanes to sett their neighbours att variance whereby they may gayne on both sides'.[53] A pettifogger of the time was different, however, from what we would take for a lawyer. Like Tangle, he is really what was known as a 'barretor', defined by John Cowell as 'a common wrangler, that setteth men at ods, and is himselfe never quiet, but at brawle with one or other'.[54] The old Common Law offence of barretry had to be invoked to check the nuisance, and the legal records of the time teem with real-life Dampits. In the Epiphany 1604/5 Quarter Sessions Rolls of Staffordshire, we hear of one such character, incredibly named John Barrett, who stole sheep, forged documents, brokered lawsuits 'to the Impoueryshing of manye poore people', bribed the under-sheriff for

[51] Parker, 'Middleton's Experiments', 187–8; and Levin, Multiple Plot, 127–37. See also Alexander Leggatt, Citizen Comedy in the Age of Shakespeare (Toronto, 1973), 58; and Covatta, Middleton's City Comedies, 101–3.

[52] See Rowe, Middleton and the New Comedy Tradition, 84–92; Joseph Messina, 'The Moral Design of A Trick to Catch the Old One', in Friedenreich (ed.), 'Accompaninge the Players', 112–28; Ayers, 'Plot, Subplot and the Uses of Dramatic Discord', 12–18; and Rick Bowers, 'Middleton's A Trick to Catch the Old One', Explicator, 51 (1993), 211–14.

[53] Thomas Wilson, The State of England Anno Dom. 1600, ed. F. J. Fisher, in Camden Miscellany, 16 (1936), 25.

[54] Iohn Cowell, The Interpreter: or Booke Containing the Signification of Words (Cambridge, 1607), I3ᵛ.

warrants, practised usury, and 'sould cattell or goodes at the highest Rate'. He even kept 'a booke of Register' of his neighbours' tres-passes.[55] Dampit has trodden the same path as Barrett in his remarkable career. Starting off with the theft of a mastiff, he came to town with ten shillings, 'trashed and trotted for other men's causes' (1.4.60–1), and trampled his way through Westminster Hall to a fortune of ten thousand pounds (cf. 1.4.15–26).

Once we see that Dampit is no conventional usurer or lawyer, the point of his insertion in this single-action plot becomes clear. Since, as barretor, he lives by exploiting the greed, longings, and enmity of others, he shares a certain family likeness with Witgood. Dampit came up to London to fleece 'the fooliaminy and coxcombry of the country' (1.4.59–60); Witgood bests city usurers to win his way back to Lon-gacre. Their transverse careers trace the symbiotic circuit of country and city, and the closer Witgood gets to his lost roots, the more Dampit sinks into self-oblivion.[56] Witgood's pretence is fictionally tractable, Dampit's frightening lifelikeness is not. Dampit thus remains outside the web of trick and counter-trick, the only guest who does not make it to Hoard's wedding. The structure of Middleton's neatest city comedy, unlike its many imitations,[57] finds place for the most crooked timber of social fact.

WORLDLY CRAFT AND POETIC WIT: *Your Five Gallants* and *The Puritan*

Poets, we are told in a passage the reviser inserted in *Iacke of Dover*, are the truest fools, 'for *Poets* haue good wits, but cannot vse them: great store of money, but cannot keepe it' (E3). Poets, called '*Fooles of Paules*' (E3) in what might well have been a self-description for a Paul's dra-matist, were equal with scholars, who were allowed by the penniless Parliament to 'dine vpon Witte' (G3ᵛ). Shortyard in *Michaelmas* was more realistic, ''Tis worldly craft beats down a scholar's wit' (4.3.17).

---

[55] S. A. H. Burne (ed.), *The Staffordshire Quarter Sessions Rolls, v. 1603–1606, Collections for a History of Staffordshire*, ed. Staffordshire Record Society (Kendal, 1940), 212.

[56] On the Witgood–Dampit equation, see Levin, *Multiple Plot*, 132; and Scott Cutler Shershow, 'The Pit of Wit: Subplot and Unity in Middleton's *A Trick to Catch the Old One*', *SP* 88 (1991), 363–81.

[57] Barry's *Ram Alley*, Massinger's *New Way to Pay Old Debts*, and Aphra Behn's *City Heiress* derive from *Trick*; see Gibbons, *Jacobean City Comedy*, 113–16; and Leggatt, *Citizen Comedy*, 55–70.

Like Witgood, the trickster heroes of *Five Gallants* and *Puritan* are scholars who outwit worldly craft. In the former, Fitsgrave, the true gentleman, uses a scholar's disguise to expose five 'gallants' who are also his rivals for the hand of Katherine, a moneyed orphan. The 'gallants'—a pawnbroker, a pimp, a cheat, a pickpocket, and a whore-master—are really climbers and con men.[58] They are cousins of Lethe in their attempts to brazen their way up through 'impudence' (cf. 4.5.74–5), a black version of *sprezzatura*,[59] fetching privilege only for those who can grab it. Fitsgrave unmasks them by making them recite their own villainies through tell-tale devices in a masque. They are then forced to marry their punks while Fitsgrave marries Katherine.

A virtuoso display of the arts of cozening, the social scope of *Five Gallants* is limited to the swindle-joints of Stuart London. Within this shrunken space, there is an appetitive dynamics which Pursenet calls, as we saw earlier, 'the sequence of the world'. The circuit is realized in the action itself, in the farcical passage of Katherine's chain of pearls or of Fitsgrave's cloak from one rogue to another. This sequence binds and levels, turning the five into 'natural brothers' (4.7.214). In the end, the quintet decide to woo Katherine together, agreeing that whoever wins her money would help out the other four. A counterpoint to the gallants' unity is that of the whores. They first gang up on the lecherous widow Mrs Newcut, but later make common cause against the gallants when they learn of their pursuit of Katherine. The worldly sequence thus provides a clever dramaturgical logic, although its diminished social scale does not seriously unsettle the conventionality of Fitsgrave's moral rescue act.

In *Puritan*, the pranks of George Pieboard, 'a poore Gentleman, & a Scholler' (1.2.36), are derived from the fabled jests of George Peele.[60] He does not quite repeat Witgood's success with money and women. Widow Plus and her daughters are lectured by a nobleman in the last scene into giving up the scholar and his cronies. The nobleman talks big about how a widow, unable to tell 'truth from forgeries', is easily

---

[58] Heinemann, *Puritanism and Theatre*, 94, thinks that the satire attacks aristocrats and gentlemen. C. Lee Colegrove (ed.), *A Critical Edition of Thomas Middleton's Your Five Gallants* (New York, 1979), 26, and Leinwand, *City Staged*, 109–10, point out that the 'gallants' in the play are really low-life crooks. Conycatchers often claimed respectable connections; see A. L. Beier, *Masterless Men: The Vagrancy Problem in England 1560–1640* (London, 1985), 136. In *Roaring Girl*, 5.1.267, a cutpurse enters '*very gallant*'.

[59] See Leinwand, *City Staged*, 110.

[60] 'Peele' meant a 'pie-board'. On the play's debt to the jests attributed to Peele, see M. G. Christian, 'Middleton's Acquaintance with the *Merrie Conceited Jests of George Peele*', *PMLA* 50 (1935), 754–5.

won by 'An Impudent fellow' (5.4.23–7). But the moral endnote is a fake, for the nobleman has been bribed by one of the widow's suitors to play the pompous bully. He saddles the widow and her daughters with upstarts, although the only consoling thought for the women is that they have swapped the tricksters for real courtiers.

Despite the parodic twist, *Puritan* has posed problems for admirers of Middleton. Margot Heinemann even rejects the case for his author-ship on the ground that 'Puritan' in the play means the reforming party within the Church, not sectaries.[61] The equation of 'Puritans' and reformists is suggested by the names of the servingmen of Widow Plus, Nicholas St Antlings and Simon St Mary Overies. These allude to the church of St Antholin's in Watling Street, and that of St Mary Overy's, later Southwark Cathedral. The allusion is confirmed by William Crashaw's Paul's Cross sermon of 1607, which berates a recent play for giving such names to two hypocrites.[62] The names Nicholas and Simon also recall Nicholas Felton, minister at St Antholin's, and William Symonds, one of the two chaplains at St Mary Overy's.[63] Both Felton and Symonds appear to have been moderates,[64] but it does not follow that Jacobeans associated them or their congregations with modera-tion. In January 1606, Symonds requested the Bishop of London to shield him from 'the cauils and calumnations of the contentious (of whose fury I haue had too much experience:)'.[65] Sir William Dugdale described St Antholin's as 'the grand nursery' for training 'seditious preachers' in antiroyalist principles, and William Kiffin (b. 1616), leader of the Baptists in the 1640s, was won over to the 'Puritan' cause when he listened to Thomas Foxley at St Antholin's as a boy.[66] Besides, St Antholin's appears elsewhere in Middleton in unflattering contexts. Heinemann misquotes the reference in *Roaring Girl* to the loudness of St Antholin's bell (2.1.301–2),[67] but passes over in silence Quomodo's

---

[61] Heinemann, *Puritanism and Theatre*, 75 n., 284–6.

[62] See the reprint of Crashaw's sermon in Chambers, *Elizabethan Stage*, iv. 249.

[63] See Baldwin Maxwell, *Studies in the Shakespeare Apocrypha* (New York, 1956), 123–6. Mary Middleton's grandfather, John Marbeck, was tried for heresy at St Mary Overy's. See Canon Thompson, *The History and Antiquities of the Collegiate Church of St Saviour (St Marie Overie), Southwark* (London, 1904), 59–60.

[64] Felton, a moderate Calvinist, was in the 1620s close to radical Protestant divines such as Edmund Calamy the elder and John Preston. See Patrick Collinson, *The Religion of Protes-tants: The Church in English Society 1559–1625* (Oxford, 1982), 89; and Kenneth Fincham, *Prelate as Pastor: The Episcopate of James I* (Oxford, 1990), 268.

[65] Quoted in Maxwell, *Studies in the Shakespeare Apocrypha*, 125.

[66] See Edward Sugden, *A Topographical Dictionary to the Works of Shakespeare and his Fellow Dramatists* (Manchester, 1925), 21; and Isabel M. Calders, 'The St Antholin Lectures', *Church Quarterly Review*, 160 (1959), 55.

disparaging allusion, more relevant to the story of *Puritan*, to 'a widow about Saint Antlings' who married again within a month of her husband's death (*Michaelmas*, 5.1.60–2). Moreover, the only clue we have to the party allegiance of the play's 'Puritans', Pieboard's praise of Nicholas as 'worth a hundred Brownists' (3.5.355), points to the sectaries.

A more serious problem is caused by the condescension and sexism that the cleverness of the educated prankster imposes on the play. The courtesan in *Trick* checked Witgood from such arrogance. In her absence, *Puritan* seems to connive at the intellectual presumption of the privileged, and to encourage a stereotyping of gallants, citizens, and, especially, city widows and maids. Leinwand thus finds it a city comedy 'fully complicitous with conservative and unimaginative ideology'.[68] The complaint looks justified if one compares the motives behind the nameless gentleman's rescue of Pieboard from the sergeants in Act 3, Scene 4 and Moll's similar rescue of Jack Dapper in *Roaring Girl*, Act 3, Scene 3. The gentleman helps Pieboard because he is a class ally; Moll helps Dapper because the sergeants are corrupt.

The problems of *Puritan* are symptomatic of a significant change. The gentleman-trickster figure reappears in Middleton's drama after *Trick*, but he never recovers the vocation given him at Paul's. In a way different from the disguised ruler's, the masks of the trickster in the major Paul's comedies had become a metaphor for the subversive indeterminacy of theatrical selves. Such shape-shifting did not permit narrative and people, not even the trickster's own self-image, to be regarded simply as determined by social estates. Rather, the representations of social estates were themselves shown to be inventions of people and narrative.

On the other hand, the trickster-artist shared with the disguised ruler the curse of self-division. His detachment and freedom were always imperilled by the paradoxes of his privilege. He was inside and outside the fallen play-world, declassed by disguise, yet seeking to use his self-wrought fiction to beat social usurpers and recover his class inheritance. While exploiting the class fantasies of his rivals, the

---

[67] Heinemann, *Puritanism and Theatre*, 285 n. Even this mention could be a hit at 'Puritans'. Henry Machyn recorded that on 21 September 1559 'be-gane the nuw mornyng prayer at sant Antholyns in Boge-row, after Geneve fassyon,—be-gune to rynge at v in the mornyng'; see J. G. Nichols (ed.), *The Diary of Henry Machyn, Citizen and Merchant-Taylor of London, from A.D. 1550 to A.D. 1563*, Camden Society, 42 (1848), 212.

[68] Leinwand, *City Staged*, 120.

trickster was prisoner of his own. The comeuppance of Pieboard is less a concession to conservative ideology than an attempt to realize this paradox.

In the political plays Middleton wrote around this time, the trickster found uses for his wit other than catching a widow or cadging a dinner. Theatre discovered its own double in the spectacles of Stuart absolutism, and the declassed scholar could express his disgust and dispossession through the counter-violence of fiction and role-playing. Hamlet had claimed this alternative vocation for the disguised prince, Vindice would do so for the comic trickster.

3
Tyranny and Treason: Early Tragedies

Apart from Edward Archer's dubious attribution to Tourneur (re-peated by Francis Kirkman in 1661),[1] there is no external evidence against Middleton's authorship of *The Revenger's Tragedy* (1606); there is overwhelming internal evidence for it.[2] The reluctance to admit the play to the Middleton canon has much to do with the stubborn grip of the authorized narrative of Middleton's development. Even critics who accept *Revenger* as Middleton's foster the three-period account of his career—early London comedies for the boys' troupes, 'Fletcherian' tragicomedies for adult companies in the second decade, the great tragedies and *Game at Chess* in the final phase.[3]

If the three-period theory wobbles when we exclude *Revenger*, it collapses the moment we include it. Middleton's early comic style was shaped by Paul's, but he had tried other companies and genres. The evidence for *Revenger* being a Globe play was once considered sufficient for denying Middleton its authorship,[4] although he started his career with the adult companies of Henslowe. The lost plays, *Caesar's Fall* and *Chester Tragedy*, were tragedies; so was *Viper and her Brood*. David George made Middleton's 'Fletcherian' phase coincide with an interest in Continental materials. However, *Phoenix* and *1 Whore* had dealt with such materials, not to mention the classical themes of *Lucrece* and *Caesar's Fall*.

Timon of Athens and *A Yorkshire Tragedy*, two more early tragedies,[5] were written for the King's Men. In 1605, Middleton collaborated

---

[1] See R. A. Foakes (ed.), *The Revenger's Tragedy*, Revels Plays (London, 1966), p. xlviii.
[2] See Lake, *Canon*, 136–62; Jackson, *Studies in Attribution*, 33–40; and Holdsworth, 'Revenger's Tragedy as a Middleton Play', in id. (ed.) *Three Jacobean Revenge Tragedies*, 79–105.
[3] The three-period thesis dominates Barker, *Middleton*; Samuel Schoenbaum, *Middleton's Tragedies: A Critical Study* (New York, 1955); and Frost, *School of Shakespeare*, 23–76.
[4] See Inga-Stina Ekeblad, 'A Note on *The Revenger's Tragedy*', *N & Q* 200 (1955), 98–9.
[5] See Lake, *Canon*, 163–74; Jackson, *Studies in Attribution*, 43–51, 54–66; and Stanley Wells and Gary Taylor, *William Shakespeare: A Textual Companion* (Oxford, 1987), 140–1, 501.

with Shakespeare on *Timon*, a play which may be read as an oblique text on the relationship of munificence and authority. By 1605, the theme should have been worrying James's subjects, as their king had all but emptied the treasury to illustrate his divine claims on the world. Palace bills jumped from £47,000 in the last year of Elizabeth's reign to £93,000 in James's first. Between 1603 and 1605, payments for causes and rewards rose more than three times, and those for fees and annuities almost doubled.[6] 'His Maiesty *hath had more compassion of other mens necessities, than of his owne Coffers,*' Walter Ralegh later remarked, hard on the heels of his statement that 'Kings liue in the world and not aboue it.'[7]

The largesse of the kingdom-dealing Timon expresses his desire for a transcendence of social traffic, turning others' gifts into usury and his own into bribes. His denial of the finite and contractual nature of wealth assumes that his 'free' gifts would impose an obligation of like 'freedom' in others. By freeing people, he hopes to bind them (cf. 1.1.105–6).

In a scene contributed by Middleton, a creditor's servant likens Timon's prodigal course to that of the sun, a royal emblem (3.4.14– 15). Money exposes the incoherence in Timon's royal fantasy. It gives absolutist authority its aura of transcendence, but is revealed to be a token of bargain and exchange, a means of buying awe and subjection. It is not surprising that *Pale Fire*, Nabokov's novel about a madman who thinks he is a king, should have borrowed its title from *Timon*.

Middleton's share in *Timon* shows how easily he could make the fiscal concerns of his comedies fit into a tragic play.[8] The same may be said of *Yorkshire* (1605), in which he turns a news-pamphlet on a sensational crime into a high-strung one-act play. Middleton moves away from the stress on a dysfunctional marriage in George Wilkins's play on the subject, suitably titled *The Miseries of Enforced Marriage* (1606).[9] The text concentrates instead on the denaturing grip of the devil on a prodigal who has lost his self-mastery and, therefore, his comic licence. His recourse is violence, a desecration of natural law

[6] See G. P. V. Akrigg, *Jacobean Pageant or The Court of King James I* (London, 1962), 85–8.

[7] Walter Ralegh, *The History of the World*, abridged and ed. C. A. Patrides (Philadelphia, 1971), 58–9.

[8] Middleton's major contributions are in 1.2, 3.1–6, and 4.3.460–537.

[9] On sources and analogues, see A. C. Cawley and Barry Gaines (eds.), *A Yorkshire Tragedy*, Revels Plays (Manchester, 1986), 6–13.

which he associates with the powerful. At the moment of breaking his wife's neck, he remembers the Earl of Leicester's rumoured uxoricide, 'a pollitician did it' (5.14). The 'vnnaturall tragedies' (10.24) the devil breeds in *Yorkshire* are a lower-order reflection of what will be seen as political tyranny in *Revenger*.

TYRANNY, THEATRE, AND TREASON: *The Revenger's Tragedy*

Vindice's first speech is well known. As the Duke, the Duchess, Lussurioso, and Spurio pass over the stage in a torchlit procession, Vindice, skull of his beloved in hand, introduces the 'Four excellent characters' to the audience: 'royal lecher . . . grey-hair'd adultery', 'his duchess, that will do with devil', 'his son, as impious steep'd as he', 'his bastard, true-begot in evil'. Vindice then directs his venom at the unnaturalness of the Duke's lust. He is a 'dry duke, | A parch'd and juiceless luxur', old, yet driven to 'riot it like a son and heir' (1.1.1–11).

Vindice's opening speech can be read as a reflection on tyranny. The Duke is a ruler who lacks self-rule, untrue to the dignity of his age and office. He breaks natural law in family and State, fathering bastards and raping his subjects. All these were the classic symptoms of what the Renaissance understood as tyranny. The ruler was unfit to command others if he failed to command his own passions, as Alexander is made to say at the end of Lyly's *Campaspe* (5.4.150–1). Middleton himself had characterized true kings in *Solomon* as 'Both rulers of themselves and their land' (Bullen, viii. 185). From the princes of Phrygia and Pontus in Sidney's *Arcadia* to Macbeth,[10] all literary tyrants lack self-mastery and infringe natural law in family and State. In a tyranny, wrote Pierre de La Primaudaye, the prince 'accounteth all his will as a just law . . . doth al things for his owne private profit, revenge or pleasure'. He cared little for the 'the honor of chaste women', and turned the commonwealth into 'a stewes'.[11]

Middleton, typically, examines tyranny and treason as manifested in sex and kinship. The figures of patriarchal discourse made this displacement easy. The Treason Act of 1351 included the murder of the husband by a wife with petit treason. As Matthew Hale later explained,

---

[10] See William A. Armstrong, 'The Elizabethan Conception of the Tyrant', *RES* 22 (1946), 161–81.

[11] Peter de La Primaudaye, *The French Academie*, trans. T. B[owes] (1586), 2R3, 2Q3.

'If the husband kills the wife it is murder, not petit treason, because there is subjection due from the wife to the husband, but not $\bar{e}$ converso'.[12] The man who got into the pulpit of a Wiltshire church on the anniversary of the Gunpowder Plot in 1613, and instructed 'Man' to love his wife and, 'if she will not do as thou wilt have her, take a staff and break her hands and legs', was perhaps not entirely drunk; he certainly had a sense of occasion.[13] In Revenger, the 'treason' which Lussurioso commits on his father's 'lawful bed' (4.1.23) is, at the same time, filial disobedience. 'Is't possible,' asks the Duke, 'a son should be disobedient as far as the sword?' (2.3.66–7). Emperor Trajan had given one of his generals a drawn sword to use against him if he turned tyrant. Milton recalled that the coins stamped at James's coronation showed, in an obvious allusion to the story, a naked sword with the inscription, Si mereor in me.[14] Such professions were, however, inconsistent with the monarch's paternalist notion of kingship. James had been asking the same question as Middleton's Duke in his 1598 attack on theories of political resistance, The Trew Law of Free Monarchies:

Or can any pretence of wickednes or rigor on his [father's/king's] part be a iust excuse for his children to put hand into him? . . . Yea, suppose the father were furiously following his sonnes with a drawen sword, is it lawfull for them to turne and strike againe, or make any resistance but by flight?

Rebels and tyrannicides, the king had concluded, followed the unnatural example of 'vipers',[15] the species named in the lost play which some think was an alternative title for Revenger.

Middleton's interest and method were fed by the ambiguity in the play's sources. The historical source is the life of Alessandro de' Medici, the Duke of Florence assassinated by his nephew Lorenzino in 1537. Lorenzino's motive, according to many historians, was to rid Florence of tyranny. But in Marguerite of Navarre's version in the Heptaméron, translated in William Painter's Palace of Pleasure (1566–7), Lorenzino avenges the Duke's attempt to employ him to seduce his sister. Marguerite of Navarre, says Bawcutt, mentions the political motive so

[12] Matthew Hale, Historia Placitorum Coronae: The History of the Pleas of the Crown, 2 vols. (1778), i. 381, as quoted in Susan Staves, Players' Sceptre: Fictions of Authority in the Restoration (Lincoln, Neb., 1979), 112.

[13] See David Underdown, Revel, Riot, and Rebellion: Popular Politics and Culture in England 1603–1660 (Oxford, 1985), 70–1.

[14] See John Milton, The Tenure of Kings and Magistrates (1649), in Political Writings, ed. Martin Dzelzainis (Cambridge, 1991), 12, 25.

[15] McIlwain (ed.), Political Works, 65.

briefly as to make it seem incidental.[16] Bawcutt overlooks the centrality in the *Heptaméron* of the relation of sexual desire to political authority.[17] Even the brief mention, in Painter's rendering, of Lorenzino's political purpose is precisely of the sort likely to interest Middleton. Tyranny is depicted by Painter as an outrage on both male and female honour, and Lorenzino faces the same conflict of loyalties experienced by rebels and regicides:

> Wherefore hee concluded, that better it were for hym to die, than to commit a mischief so great vnto his sister, whiche was one of the honestest women in all Italie. And therewithall considered how he might deliuer his countrie from such a tyrant, which by force would blemishe and spot the whole race of his auncient stock and familie.

Lorenzino's personal motive is inseparable from political resistance to the ruler, 'by whose death he thought to set at libertie the common wealth'.[18]

The rape of Lady Antonio in the play by Junior Brother, the Duchess's youngest son, and her subsequent suicide allude to another classical instance of tyranny. Salingar links this episode to the story of Lucrece, which Middleton had handled earlier, and to the expulsion of the Tarquins.[19] That Junior's crime is a figural iteration of the tyrant's original trespass is suggested by the similarity between Antonio's account of the rape and Spurio's conjectural reconstruction of how the Duke had sired him. Spurio thinks he was 'begot | After some gluttonous dinner . . . when deep healths went round, | And ladies' cheeks were painted red with wine' (1.2.180–3). Lady Antonio was likewise raped on a 'revelling night' at court, 'When music was heard loudest, courtiers busiest, | And ladies great with laughter' (1.4.26, 38–9). Spurio promises himself just revenge (1.2.191); a nobleman comforts Antonio by prophesying vengeance (1.4.73). Vindice later incites Piero and other friends of Antonio 'to stab home their discontents' (5.2.4), and after the revenge is accomplished he reminds Antonio that 'The rape of your good lady has been quited | With death on death' (5.3.90–1). Vindice's personal cause and recourse are shown to be inalienable from the ills of State and from the revenge-fantasies of the aggrieved.

[16] N. W. Bawcutt, '*The Revenger's Tragedy* and the Medici Family', *N & Q* 202 (1957), 192–3.

[17] See John D. Bernard, 'Sexual Oppression and Social Justice in Marguerite de Navarre's *Heptaméron*', *JMRS* 19 (1989), 251–81.

[18] William Painter, *The Palace of Pleasure*, ed. Joseph Jacobs, 3 vols. (London, 1890), ii. 76, 78.

[19] L. G. Salingar, '*The Revenger's Tragedy*: Some Possible Sources', *MLR* 60 (1965), 6–7.

Shortly before *Revenger*, the King's Men had provoked James by putting on a play on the Gowrie conspiracy (1604).[20] In 1603–4, they played *Sejanus his Fall*, an attack on tyranny which led to the summoning of Jonson before the Privy Council on charges of treason and popery. The authorities might have detected allusions to the Essex rebellion in the original script. It is more probable, as Philip Ayers argues, that the play was read as criticism of Ralegh's trial in 1603.[21] Its attack on the divine pretence of Stuart absolutism, which survives Jonson's self-censorship for publication, was reopened when the Queen's Revels performed *The Tragedy of Philotas* in January 1605, bringing a Privy Council summons for its author Samuel Daniel. Although accused of referring to the Essex rebellion,[22] *Philotas* was also an attack on tyranny, with the pointed implication that the Jacobean divine right theory led to it:

> He that aboue the state of man will straine
> His stile, and will not be that which we are,
> Not only vs contemnes but doth disdaine
> The gods themselues with whom he would compare. (ll. 2055–8)

By June 1604, the French ambassador Beaumont had noticed that the players were gunning for a king 'universally hated by the whole people'.[23] Margot Heinemann speaks of the increase of plays on the 'crisis of authority' just about this time. These plays, like *Philotas*, dramatize the conflict of conscience and obedience, a question raised again by the Gunpowder Plot, seen by many contemporaries as a climax to the treason of Essex and Ralegh.[24] Fawkes's defence, 'saying he was moved thereunto onely for Religion and Conscience sake, denying the King to be his lawful Sovereign or the Anointed of God, in regard he was a Heretick',[25] reopened the debate on Calvinist as well

---

[20] See Chambers, *Elizabethan Stage*, i. 327–8.

[21] Philip J. Ayers, 'Jonson, Northampton, and the "Treason" in *Sejanus*', *MP* 80 (1983), 356–63.

[22] See Laurence Michel's Introduction in his edition (New Haven, Conn., 1949), 36–66.

[23] Frederich von Raumer, *History of the 16th and 17th Centuries Illustrated by Original Documents* (London, 1835), ii. 206–7, as quoted in Margaret Hotine, '*Richard III* and *Macbeth*: Studies in Tudor Tyranny?', *N & Q* 236 (1991), 485.

[24] Margot Heinemann, 'Rebel Lords, Popular Playwrights, and Political Culture: Notes on the Jacobean Patronage of the Earl of Southampton', *YES* 21 (1991), 76.

[25] J. H., *A True and Perfect Relation of that Most Horrid and Hellish Conspiracy of the Gunpowder Treason* (1662), B2ᵛ.

as Jesuit theories of political resistance, which had never been entirely dormant since the days of Buchanan, Knox, and Goodman.

Hippolito's metaphor of 'gunpowder i' th' court' promising a 'Good, happy, swift' wildfire-revenge (2.2.171), makes it probable that the writing of *Revenger* followed the Gunpowder Plot. This impression is strengthened by its debt to *Volpone* (played late 1605 or early 1606),[26] and by the fact that all the decisive actions in the play—Lussurioso's midnight attack on the royal couple, the murder of the Duke, the revenge masque—are described as forms of treason (cf. 2.3.10, 66–7, 3.5.156–7, 196, 4.1.23, 63, 5.1.181, 5.3.15, 48–50, 56), and it ends with a prayer that the blood of the dead 'may wash away all treason' (5.3.128).

Contemporaries immediately grasped the theatrical possibilities of the Gunpowder Plot. Coke described it as 'beyond all examples, whether in fact or fiction, even of the tragick poets, who did beat their wits to represent the most fearful and horrible murders'.[27] Another account, attributed to James, praised God for making 'such a conclusion of this tragedy to the traitors, but tragi-comedy to the king, and all his true subjects'.[28] In his 1605 speech to Parliament, the king remarked on the apparent motivelessness of the plotters:

Secondly, how wonderfull it is when you shall thinke vpon the small, or rather no ground, whereupon the practisers were entised to inuent this Tragedie. For if these Conspirators had onely bene bankrupt persons, or discontented vpon occasion of any disgraces done vnto them; this might haue seemed to haue bene but a worke of reuenge.[29]

The plotters, in other words, did not have the motives of Vindice, whose father died of 'discontent' after suffering 'disgrace' at court (cf. 1.1.125–7). The conventions of the revenge play could thus be used by the monarch to present their apparent selflessness as motiveless malice. And this motivelessness, in turn, could make treason itself into a version of tyranny. Thus James's history of the Plot likened the aims of the conspirators to that of the

[26] See Salingar, '*Revenger's Tragedy*: Some Possible Sources', 11–12; and id., '*The Revenger's Tragedy* and the Morality Tradition', *Scrutiny*, 6 (1938), 415.

[27] [James I *et al.*], *The Gunpowder Treason. Trials of the Conspirators . . . Also, History of the Gunpowder Plot, Written by King James*, repr. in *Tracts (Chiefly Rare and Curious Reprints), Relating to Northamptonshire* (Northampton, 1870), 9.

[28] Ibid. 38.

[29] McIlwain (ed.), *Political Works*, 283.

'Roman tyrants, who wished all the bodies, in Rome, to have but one neck'.[30]

When Vindice describes vengeance as 'tenant to Tragedy' (1.1.40) in his opening speech, he summons to his cause the preconceptions underlying Coke and James's account of the Gunpowder Plot. Middleton did not write a play about the Plot in the sense that Jonson might be shown to have written one in *Catiline his Conspiracy* (1611).[31] The event probably helped bring to a flashpoint his intuitions about the contradiction in absolutist ideology exposed by the equation of tyranny and treason as forms of deviancy. Such a contradiction is evident in the way treason is turned to tyranny through the mediating trope of the theatre in Coke and James's accounts of the Gunpowder Plot.

The contradiction also symptomatizes a long-standing ambiguity in the definitions of the civic purpose of tragedy. Nashe claimed that plays showed 'the ill successe of treason', and Sidney praised tragedy since it 'maketh Kinges feare to be Tyrants, and Tyrants to manifest their tyrannicall humours'.[32] These two opposed answers to the stage-baiters' linking of plays with regicides and tyrants open up an ambiguous space between them which *Revenger* exploits. Absolutism precedes tyranny, and tyranny breeds the seditious anarchy absolutism is designed to stamp out. On the stage, the paradox is focused in the vengeance produced by misrule. Belsey neatly sums up this ambiguity of revenge: 'An act of injustice on behalf of justice, it deconstructs the antithesis which fixes the meanings of good and evil, right and wrong.'[33] Vindice's career of 'innocent' villainy (1.3.170) is a poetic study of this paradox of agency in the ideology of absolutism.

Rebels against monarchs in baroque plays, complained Walter Benjamin, show no trace of 'revolutionary conviction'. 'Baroque drama knows no other historical activity than the corrupt energy of

[30] [James I *et al.*], *Gunpowder Treason*, 38.

[31] See B. N. De Luna, *Jonson's Romish Plot: A Study of* Catiline *and its Historical Context* (Oxford, 1967).

[32] Thomas Nashe, *Pierce Penilesse*, in Ronald B. McKerrow (ed.), *The Works of Thomas Nashe*, 5 vols. (1904–10; repr. with corrections and supplementary notes by F. P. Wilson, Oxford, 1958), i. 213; and Philip Sidney, *The Defence of Poesie*, in Albert Feuillerat (ed.), *The Prose Works of Sir Philip Sidney*, 4 vols. (Cambridge, 1912–26), iii. 23.

[33] Catherine Belsey, *The Subject of Tragedy: Identity and Difference in Renaissance Drama* (London, 1985), 115.

schemers.'[34] Vindice is a baroque hero in this sense, and his 'corrupt energy' is concentrated in the 'quaintness' of his malice (3.5.108-9). This quaintness is in itself an image of the licence of tyranny turned into that of treason. The tragedy of the revenger, as the charge of tyranny brought against the Gunpowder plotters shows, is that he can only play by the rules set by his adversary, that is, turn tyrant to punish tyranny.

The point may be illustrated by a reference to *Hamlet*, the play's literary double. Before paying his mother the momentous visit in Act 3, Scene 4, Hamlet prays to his heart not to lose its 'nature':

> Let not ever
> The soul of Nero enter this firm bosom.
> Let me be cruel, not unnatural.
> I will speak daggers to her, but use none. (3.2.382-5)

The mention of Nero identifies the tyrannical, including matricidal, humours to which Hamlet feels he is in danger of succumbing. Foakes points out that Hamlet displaces this cruelty on to words and shows, while Vindice turns it into comic art.[35] The important thing about Vindice's choice is the symbiosis of tyranny and treason it illustrates. He masters the characteristic language of tyranny: 'policy', artistic cruelty, the phallic use of the tongue, role-playing. Above all, he abandons self-rule, submitting his anarchic passion only to the control of his theatrical genius. Unlike Hamlet, Vindice fights tyranny with the soul of Nero.

Rebecca Bushnell has alerted us to the nexus joining theatricality, effeminacy, and tyranny in both antityrannical and antitheatrical discourses. Playwrights shared the assumption of such discourses. Tyrants on the English Renaissance stage such as Richard III, Julius Caesar, Tiberius, Nero, and Domitian patronized the theatre, and their political presence was fundamentally histrionic.[36] Theatricality released desire, inducing in actors and tyrants an effeminate surrender to pleasure. Lucilius in Garnier's *Antonius*, translated by the Countess of

---

[34] Walter Benjamin, *The Origin of German Tragic Drama*, trans. John Osborne (London, 1977), 88.

[35] R. A. Foakes, 'The Art of Cruelty: Hamlet and Vindice', *SS* 26 (1973), 29-31.

[36] Rebecca Bushnell, *Tragedies of Tyrants: Political Thought and Theater in the English Renaissance* (Ithaca, NY, 1990), 5-9, 29-36, 56-63, 116-53; and Jonathan Goldberg, *James I and the Politics of Literature: Jonson, Shakespeare, Donne and their Contemporaries* (Baltimore, 1983), 164-209.

Pembroke (1592), called pleasure a 'poison' which worked 'greatest outrage' in kings, banishing order and justice, while 'in hir seat sitts greedie Tyrannie'.[37] Surrender to incontinence was feminine, and the unnaturalness of tyranny, like that of play-acting, was imaged as gender-hybridization. Patroclus in *Troilus and Cressida* appeals to the two set images of misrule in saying that 'A woman impudent and mannish grown | Is not more loathed than an effeminate man | In time of action' (3.3.210–12). John Knox marshalled pagan and biblical authorities to prove that public office was unsuitable for not only women, 'but also . . . men subiect to the counsel or empire of their wyues'.[38] The Duke and the Duchess in *Revenger* represent these two varieties of hybrid which tyranny engendered.

Tyranny is theatricalized and effeminized in *Revenger*. Junior 'has play'd a rape on lord Antonio's wife' (1.1.110), although her suicide, brags Antonio, turns 'Violent rape' into 'a glorious act' (1.4.3–4). The 'law's a woman' (1.1.115), and, although Vindice would have her chaste, she is, the Duchess says, 'grown more subtle than a woman should be' (1.2.72). At Junior's trial, Lussurioso compares 'offences | Gilt o'er with mercy' to 'fairest women | Good only for their beauties' (1.2.28–30), although this cosmetic justice later saves his neck. To play is to play the woman. When Lussurioso is pardoned against their hopes, Ambitioso and Supervacuo lie that they had pleaded for him: 'Did we dissemble? | Did we make our tears women for thee?' (3.6.83–4).

The dissolution of male rule into womanish tyranny is figured in *Revenger* as liquescence, orgasmic spills, uncontrol of purse, tongue, and sphincter—motifs familiar from the Paul's plays. Patrimonies melt in a kiss (1.1.27), estates turn into bastards (1.3.51–2), trees are felled 'to maintain head-tires' (2.1.226), 'lordships' are 'sold to maintain ladyships' (3.5.74). Death 'steals out of a lawyer's lip' (1.2.69), drink makes ladies' tongues 'as short and nimble as their heels' (1.2.184), women cast secrets in their morning urinal (1.3.83). Loosened desire roams as the wandering womb, the female disease of hysteria, or the 'mother' (cf. 1.3.79–80, 2.1.125–6, 243, 4.4.121–2). Redress demands that the revenger allow this flux to invade him. Vindice as Piato can be 'near

---

[37] R. Garnier, *Antonius*, trans. Countesse of Pembroke, in *A Discourse of Life and Death . . . Antonius, A Tragoedie* (1592), L1ᵛ.

[38] [John Knox], *The First Blast of the Trumpet against the Monstrous Regiment of Women* (Geneva, 1558), B2.

kin to this present minute' only by letting the age *swim* within him
(1.3.24–6). '*That woman is all male, whom none can enter*' (2.1.112), while
men are made 'close', to 'keep thoughts in' (1.3.80–1). Vindice has to
abandon this claustral male identity, and let himself be entered. The
feminization involved in playing Piato surfaces in the first question he
asks Lussurioso, 'When shall we lie together?' (1.3.35). But the role
displaces the actor, and Vindice is eventually betrayed by the womanish looseness of his tongue.

Unlike Hamlet, and like Quomodo and Leantio, Vindice values
desire as power. He remembers Gloriana as capable of draining a
usurer's son of his patrimony (1.1.26–7). Like Leantio again, he feels
her loss only as the raid of tyranny. He, therefore, conceives of moral
integrity as an original and inviolate possession. Virtue to him is a port
to be guarded, an ear the Indian devil cannot enter, jewel cannot
ravish, tongue cannot bewitch (cf. 2.2.104–5, 1.3.85–6, 93, 111–12).
He tries Gratiana and Castiza to assure himself of this moral core
inaccessible to money and power. The search ends in the skull, the
only irreducible certainty he can grasp and trust. But it demands a
playing out of the disturbed primal fantasy[39] of 'Drunken procreation'
and 'hour of incest' (1.3.57–61), which the rape of Gloriana has
engendered in him. Before he can execute his parricidal revenge by
nailing the Duke's tongue, he must use his own as a phallic weapon on
his sister and mother, the incestuous significance of which is revealed
in Gratiana's exclamation: 'No tongue but yours could have bewitch'd
me so' (4.4.33).[40]

Vindice's fantasies are sick, but, as William James said, even the
madman's 'visions of horror are all drawn from the material of daily
fact'.[41] The indivisibility of power in civil society and State is pointedly
revealed by the political context given in *Revenger* to the 'daily facts'
we had sampled in the city comedies. The perversion of tyranny, for
example, is fused with the unnatural breeding of usury. Honesty to
Lussurioso is an uninvested stock of money (1.3.115–17), Gratiana's

[39] 'Primal fantasy' and 'primal scene' in Freud embody the child's anxieties about sexuality
and parental intercourse. See Freud, *From the History of an Infantile Neurosis*, in Strachey (ed.),
Standard Edition, xvii. 7–122. The notions are applied to *Hamlet* in Stanley Cavell, *Disowning
Knowledge in Six Plays of Shakespeare* (Cambridge, 1987), 179–91.

[40] See J. L. Simmons, 'The Tongue and its Office in *The Revenger's Tragedy*', *PMLA* 92
(1977), 56–68; and Peter Stallybrass, 'Reading the Body: *The Revenger's Tragedy* and the
Jacobean Theater of Consumption', *RD* 18 (1987), 139–43.

[41] William James, *The Varieties of Religious Experience: A Study in Human Nature* (1902;
London, 1960), 169.

tongue turns Castiza into 'use' or 'common usury' (2.2.99, 123, 4.4.103). When Vindice plays the malcontent, he represents the Duke and Lussurioso as 'A usuring father to be boiling in hell, and his son and heir with a whore dancing over him' (4.2.88–9). Vindice's sexual rival, the 'usurer's son' who would have melted his patrimony for Gloriana, is thus also a metonymic image of Vindice's political enemy.

Primal fantasies do not haunt Vindice alone: there is Spurio. His vengeance turns a nightmare of parental lust into incest with his stepmother, willing to add murder to adultery if the Duke caught him 'hasp'd within his bed' (3.5.217). But Spurio lacks Vindice's theatrical flair. He does not play out the primal scene, he lives it. Instead of beating tyranny at its game, he becomes its unwitting tool, helping the Duchess carry out a symbolic castration of the Duke in revenge of her son's execution. In contrast, Vindice exhibits his command of the histrionic idiom of tyranny by converting their tryst into a spectacle of heavenly judgement for the dying Duke.

The same contrast of skill is evident in the final double masque. The swimming shapes of licence seek out court revels as their natural setting. The 'artificial noon' of the 'revelling night' (1.4.26–7) is a pattern of the primal scene, and Vindice's 'strange invention' (1.3.120) chooses the peak of the courtiers' festivity as the moment to strike. Ambitioso and Supervacuo plan their own revenge masque for the night. While they bungle their script and stab each other, Vindice rids himself of a nest of dukes and pins the blame on a courtier. 'A masque is treason's licence', says Supervacuo (5.1.181), but it needs Vindice's theatrical sabotage to turn tyranny's licence into treason's.

Revenger thus presents a receding perspective of repeated passions and motives,[42] with Vindice's superior skill and his awareness of the emptiness at its centre lending scale to the pattern. Anti-tyrant plays such as *Sejanus* express misrule as the repression of the upright. Barring Lady Antonio and Castiza's walled-up integrity, the world of *Revenger*, like that of Middleton's city comedies, is devoid of such uprightness. The play's interlocking tropes of sex, politics, and social evils so exhaustively studied by New Criticism[43]—face-painting, lingual

---

[42] See Philip J. Ayers, 'Parallel Action and Reductive Technique in *The Revenger's Tragedy*', *ELN* 8 (1970), 103–7.

[43] See, e.g. Peter Lisca, '*The Revenger's Tragedy*: A Study in Irony', *PQ* 38 (1959), 242–51; B. J. Layman, 'Tourneur's Artificial Noon: The Design of *The Revenger's Tragedy*', *MLQ* 34 (1973), 20–35; and Peter B. Murray, *A Study of Cyril Tourneur* (Philadelphia, 1964), 190–248.

atrophy, darkness, artificial light, legal corruption, usury—are all features of a language of radical absence which tyranny exploits, and
which Vindice learns to wield.

Tyranny, while claiming supra-human authority, can rule only by
denying that authority in practice. Julius Caesar and Sejanus ignore
supernatural portents; Lussurioso, as Duke, dismisses the blazing star
(5.3.39). Meeting them on their own grounds, Vindice scripts his
'tragic business' (3.5.99) in a celestial theatre where the heavenly
audience does not always respond to cue. His directorial promptings
to thunder and the heavens, which Dollimore takes as a parody of the
providential view of history, is also an attempt to improvise an ideal
and applauding audience.[44] By nailing the Duke's tongue, he must
'invent a silence' (3.5.195) to replace the abuse of sovereign speech, just
as he must invent a celestial chorus of roaring thunder and applauding
angels. Such 'tragic business' does not valorize suffering. The play's
resemblance to comedy, which most critics note,[45] results from its
distanced and self-conscious fashioning of the terms by which it may
be approved. Antonio describes the multiple deaths as 'A piteous
tragedy' and praises the justice of the 'law above', but Vindice cannot
but remind him of its comic nature and human origin: it was 'somewhat wittily carried' and 'well manag'd' (5.3.60, 91, 97, 100). 'For that
which would seem treason in our lives | Is laughter when we are
dead,' fears the Duke (1.2.7–8). Vindice's attempt to make tyranny and
treason risible in the Duke's lifetime, however, cannot prosper. If it
did, then treason would be shown to be the radical remedy for
absolutism, and this no new duke may allow: 'You that would murder
him would murder me' (5.3.105). In thus setting forth the reason for
Vindice's execution, Antonio demonstrates the 'vulnerability paradox'
of Tudor and Stuart absolutism, its ironic dependence on the threat of
anarchy, and, hence, on the endless reproduction of the spectacle of
sedition and punishment.[46]

The tragedy of Vindice's 'business' thus lies in the paradox of
agency involved in political and sexual mutiny against tyranny. Tyranny

[44] Jonathan Dollimore, *Radical Tragedy: Religion, Ideology and Power in the Drama of
Shakespeare and his Contemporaries* (1984; 2nd edn., Hemel Hempstead, 1989), 139–50.

[45] See, e.g. Inga-Stina Ekeblad, 'On the Authorship of *The Revenger's Tragedy*', *ES* 41
(1960), 227–33; Brooke, *Horrid Laughter*, 10–27; and Robert C. Jones, *Engagement with
Knavery: Point of View in* Richard III, The Jew of Malta, Volpone, *and* The Revenger's Tragedy
(Durham, NC, 1986), 123–48.

[46] See Curt Breight, ' "Treason Doth Never Prosper": *The Tempest* and the Discourse of
Treason', *SQ* 41 (1990), 1–28.

creates and needs the revenger. The need was well understood by contemporaries such as Godfrey Goodman, who accused the Earl of Salisbury of fabricating treason charges, 'and the more odious and hateful the treason were, his service would be the greater and the more acceptable'.[47] The revenger must play by the tyrant's rule and perish, but without his trespass, neither morality nor any other legitimating principle in politics can be validated. Against his moral instincts, Vindice has to accept the tyrant's premise of providential silence and of the futility of love and rebellion. He can resist only with wit and theatre, by capsizing the fictions and spectacles in which power is invested. Although he is destroyed in the end, the audience is reminded that his was the only remedial action of the play: 'This work was ours, which else might have been slipp'd' (5.3.120). 'Acting his *tragedies* with a *comick* face' (*Sejanus*, 4.379) till the last, Vindice out-tyrants Tiberius, with whom, wrote Arthur Wilson, some paralleled King James 'for Dissimulation'.[48]

TYRANT, MARTYR, AND ASSASSIN: *The Lady's Tragedy*

Tyranny is explicitly the subject of *The Lady's Tragedy*, or *The Second Maiden's Tragedy* (1611). The nameless Tyrant in this play, however, is a usurper, and his ousted adversary, Govianus, the legitimate prince. Since the revenger is the lawful king, his action is rewarded, not punished. The slaughter of the revenge masque, on the other hand, is displaced on to the domestic sub-plot, in which a stagy finale, scripted and counter-scripted by adversaries, goes wrong for everyone.

The changes should have made the script's passage through the censor smoother. Not only was it agreed, even by a rigid opponent of rebellion such as Jean Bodin, that force could justifiably be used against a usurper, it was also the duty of the legitimate prince to enforce the justice a subject might not.[49] The manuscript of the play, nevertheless, is one of the most guardedly censored Jacobean dramatic texts to survive. George Buc changed the Tyrant's 'Your king's poisoned' to 'I am poisoned' (5.2.167). He also clipped the Tyrant's threat to Govianus of a death 'beyond the Frenchmen's tortures' to 'beyond the

[47] Godfrey Goodman, *The Court of King James the First* (London, 1939), i. 102, as quoted in Hotine, '*Richard III* and *Macbeth*', 486.

[48] Wilson, *Life and Reign of James*, in [Kennett], *Complete History of England*, ii. 6H4^v.

[49] I. Bodin, *The Six Bookes of a Commonweale*, trans. Richard Knolles (1606), V1^v–X1^v.

extremest tortures' (5.2.140), pre-empting a sympathetic linking of
Govianus with François Ravaillac, executed for murdering Henry IV
of France in 1610. Other alterations include 'many a good man's
daughter' for 'many a good knight's daughter' (4.1.74), 'many ladies'
for 'most ladies' (4.3.100), and 'I would not trust but few' for 'I would
not trust at court' (5.2.80), in contexts which are disparaging for
knights' daughters, ladies, and the court. Buc also marked for deletion
another passage in which Govianus mocks court ladies' abhorrence of
honour, 'They'll sooner kill themselves with lust, than for it'
(3.1.221).[50]

The assassination of Henry IV made regicide and tyranny risky
topics in 1611. The Venetian ambassador reported in 1610 of James's
'dread that on account of the diversity of religion the same may happen here to
his own person'.[51] The event revived memories of the Gunpowder Plot.
The 'Intention of the Pouder-treason if it had come to Act,' declared a
1610 pamphlet, '. . . had exceeded this [the murder of Henry]'.[52] In
1616, James himself mentioned Ravaillac and Fawkes together as
'confederate of the same damned crew'.[53] One thus understands Buc's
caution about 'Frenchmen's tortures', although the mention in itself
does not indicate sympathy for the victim. A 1610 newsbook compared Ravaillac's suffering to 'the dying man tormented in the Brazen
Bull of the Tyrant Phalares', but it branded him a 'viperous homicyde',
not a martyr to tyranny.[54]

Official vigilance on plays may have been tightened following the
assassination, but the 1611 King's Men production of Catiline proves
that playwrights were not scared away from dangerous themes. This is
further borne out by the audacious, because sympathetic, allusions in
Lady to the recent imprisonment of Arbella Stuart and William Seymour, two claimants to James's throne, after their secret marriage in
1610. These appear in additional slips to folios 31 and 36 (1.1.221–40,
2.1.1–11), and might have been put in after the script passed the censor.
The afterthoughts are unlikely to have been Middleton's, the revising

[50] See Anne Lancashire (ed.), The Second Maiden's Tragedy, Revels Plays (Manchester,
1978), 275–80.
[51] CSP Ven. xi. 494.
[52] Edmund Skory, An Extract out of the Historie of the Last French King Henry the 4. of Famous
Memory (1610), D3.
[53] McIlwain (ed.), Political Works, 177.
[54] The Terrible and Deserued Death of Francis Rauilliack . . . for the Murther of the Late French
King, Henry the Fourth (1610), A4ᵛ, A2.

hand being another's, possibly Shakespeare's.[55] Nevertheless, the ease with which the apparently innocuous script yielded to such seditious topicalization shows the potential range of its political reference, a danger to which Buc seems to have been alerted.

Buc's touchiness about criticism of the privileged, however, is extraordinary by Jacobean standards. Lancashire suggests Buc's loyalty to the Carr–Northampton faction as a possible reason for his caution. The Earl of Northampton at this time was for political reasons promoting Robert Carr's affair with his grand-niece Frances, then wife of Essex. Lancashire reads the episode in which the ambitious courtier Helvetius urges his daughter, betrothed to Govianus, to yield to the Tyrant, as a comment on the conduct of Northampton. The parallel, if admitted, would be a plausible reason for Buc's care with unflattering mentions of ladies, courtiers, and their daughters.[56]

The suggestion might also explain why Middleton's text was deemed suitable for the insertions alluding to Arbella and William Seymour. After her imprisonment in 1610, Arbella, with the help of her aunt Mary Talbot, Lady Shrewsbury, lobbied Northampton and Carr, neither of whom was willing to use his influence with the king on her behalf. Earlier Northampton had joined Cecil in suggesting to the king that Arbella had no genuine need of financial favours.[57] Arbella had *Epicoene* suppressed in 1610 because of a suspected dig at her rumoured engagement to the Prince of Moldavia,[58] and playwrights could not have been unaware of her high reputation and popularity. In 1611, Emilia Lanier dedicated *Salve Deus Rex Judaeorum* to the queen, Princess Elizabeth, and Lady Arbella, describing the latter as 'Rare Phoenix', the compliment Vindice paid Castiza in *Revenger* (1.3.97).[59] There was a wave of public sympathy for her after her arrest, not least because of her unwavering Protestantism. A pawn in earlier Romish plots, and a protégé of the Catholic Mary Talbot, Arbella was being described as 'Puritan' even in June 1611 by the Venetian

---

[55] See Eric Rasmussen, 'Shakespeare's Hand in *The Second Maiden's Tragedy*', *SQ* 40 (1989), 1–26. The allusion to the affair in Webster's *Duchess of Malfi* is well known; see Sara Jayne Steen, 'The Crime of Marriage: Arbella Stuart and *The Duchess of Malfi*', *Sixteenth Century Journal*, 22 (1991), 61–76.

[56] Lancashire (ed.), *Second Maiden's Tragedy*, 278–9 .

[57] See Ian McInnes, *Arabella: The Life and Times of Lady Arabella Seymour* (London, 1968), 136, 171; and David N. Durant, *Arbella Stuart: A Rival to the Queen* (London, 1978), 184, 190–1.

[58] See *CSP Ven.* xi. 427. The allusion in *Epicoene*, 5.1.19–26, is discussed in Jonson, *Works*, v. 144–7.

[59] See E. T. Bradley, *Life of the Lady Arabella Stuart*, 2 vols. (London, 1889), ii. 273.

amabassador.[60] Her plight could thus be easily interpreted as the unfair persecution which a patriotic Protestant, even if royally descended, had to suffer under James's religious policy and favouritism. Compared to Frances's scandalous affairs, Arbella's secret wedding must have appeared the model of feminine constancy she made it out to be. In an undated letter written around October 1610, she told the king that any course other than the marriage would have made her 'an harlot' since by her betrothal vow she had already married Seymour in conscience.[61] Before the Privy Council earlier that year, 'She endeavoured to demonstrate that neither by laws Divine nor by human laws could she be prevented.'[62] Similar answers by the Lady to the Tyrant in the original script of *Lady* had, according to Lancashire, provided a contrast to the conduct of Frances. The reviser thus had little difficulty in further localizing the fiction by stressing the parallel with the most recent victim of the unprincipled politics of James's court.

The affairs involving Arbella and Frances provide contrasting examples of the interface of sex and political power, a major issue in *Lady*. Its historical and fictional sources also concern the sexual entailment of tyranny. First, there is the story of Herod, who in early modern European theatre best embodied the contemporary idea of the tyrant.[63] The Talmudic story of Herod and Mariamne is alluded to by the Tyrant himself (4.3.115–20). Mariamne, also the heroine of Elizabeth Cary's *Tragedy of Mariam* (written 1602–5) from which Middleton borrowed passages in *A Fair Quarrel* as well as in *Lady*,[64] committed suicide in this legend to escape the lust of Herod. Herod, who had the rest of her family killed, preserved Mariamne's body in honey for seven years. The other story of a heroic suicide, that of Sophronia, also concerned the lust of a tyrant, Maxentius. Foxe compared Maxentius 'to another Pharaoh or Nero', an 'utter enemy of all womanly chastity', whose defeat at the hands of Constantine ensured a just Christian millenium 'unto the time of John Wickliff', when 'the bishops of

[60] *CSP Ven.* xii. 164–5.

[61] Bradley, *Life of Arabella Stuart*, ii. 248.

[62] *CSP Ven.* xii. 19.

[63] See Benjamin, *Origin of German Tragic Drama*, 70; Maurice J. Valency, *The Tragedies of Herod and Mariamne* (New York, 1940), 35–67; and Bushnell, *Tragedies of Tyrants*, 84–8, 106–15. On the sources, see Anne Lancashire, '*The Second Maiden's Tragedy*: A Jacobean Saint's Life', *RES*, NS 25 (1974), 267–79; and ead. (ed.), *Second Maiden's Tragedy*, 23–32.

[64] See R. V. Holdsworth, 'Middleton and *The Tragedy of Mariam*', *N & Q* 231 (1986), 379–80.

Rome' revived the tyranny of their pagan political ancestors.[65] The minor sources for the main plot, the story of King John and Matilda, and that of Appius and Virginia, repeat this pattern of confrontation.

In *Philotas*, Thais teaches Antigona that victory for the politically ambitious is never complete 'Vnlesse they likewise gaine the mistresses | Of those they master' (ll. 1021–2). *Lady* starts with the Tyrant's project of completing his political usurpation with a sexual one. He stalls Govianus's banishment so that the latter may witness his marriage to the Lady. The Lady and Govianus defy the Tyrant by proclaiming the spiritual freedom of Christian Stoicism. The rest of the action develops the king–tyrant contrast. Govianus learns to command his own passions; the Tyrant becomes a slave to his. Govianus is guided by the Lady's spirit after her death; the Tyrant slakes his lust by exhuming her corpse.[66]

Bushnell points out the ironic affinities that lurk behind the schematic contrast of king and tyrant. The most revealing point Bushnell notes is that Govianus is restored through a private revenge, executed in the manner of Vindice.[67] By transferring the revenge strategy of the subject to the lawful king, Middleton gives treason and tyrannicide a problematic legitimacy. The political resistance which is vindicated is not the remedial violence of public justice, but the sabotage of the dispossessed, the treason which prospers by subverting the language of domination.

The reversal of the tropes of tyranny is most clearly figured in the metaphors of art and the theatre. Foxe says of Maxentius that he would have made a better magician than a ruler, since he was 'much addicted to the art magical'.[68] 'Art' is likewise a coveted tool of omnipotence for the Tyrant: he will 'By art force beauty on yon lady's face' (5.2.110). In taking the artist's disguise to smear the corpse's lips with poison, Govianus outschemes the tyrant in artistry. The dialogue ensures that the ironic point is not lost on the audience. 'We need that art thou art master of,' the Tyrant tells the disguised Govianus, who replies, 'My king is master both of that and me' (5.2.64–5).

---

[65] John Foxe, *The Acts and Monuments*, ed. Josiah Pratt, 8 vols. (1853–70; repr. London, 1877), i. 246–7, 249–50.

[66] See Rosalie Osmond, *Mutual Accusation: Seventeenth-Century Body and Soul Dialogues in their Literary and Theological Context* (Toronto, 1990), 171–4.

[67] Bushnell, *Tragedies of Tyrants*, 154–6.

[68] Foxe, *Acts and Monuments*, i. 247.

'Art' in *Lady* is allied to the tropes of playmaking.[69] The Tyrant's theatrical machinations are matched by the Lady's, when in Act 1, Scene 1 she appears at court in black,[70] and by Govianus, whose melodramatic pistol-shot in Act 2, Scene 1 wakes the conscience of Helvetius. Govianus's finest theatrical coup, of course, is the artful assassination of the Tyrant. The Roman tyrants were reputed to have executed convicts on the public stage, by making them play characters to be slain in tragedies.[71] Govianus inverts this mode of execution and poisons the Tyrant in his own play. The execution, however, is a furtive one. The return of legitimate kingship is thus shown to be paradoxically dependent on the illicit schemes of treason.

Theatrical metaphors also dominate the sub-plot. In this domestic story, derived from Cervantes, Govianus's brother Anselmus asks his friend Votarius to try the virtue of his wife. The wife is seduced by Votarius, and the two put on an act to convince Anselmus of their innocence. Their play is upstaged by that of Belarius, the lover of the wife's waiting woman. Belarius settles an old grudge against Votarius by poisoning the swords to be used in the lovers' charade. What follows is an inset play within an inset play (5.1), with Anselmus watching from the closet and Belarius from the gallery. The outcome imitates the carnage of the revenge masque, ending with the death of all the characters involved.

Apparently a contrast to the Tyrant–Govianus story,[72] the sub–plot brings the political action in closer touch with sexual and economic realities. The wife knows that the world of male power is a 'flesh-market' (1.2.272), and Votarius understands the likeness of cracked female honesty and the breaking of whole money (2.2.114–15). Their attitudes point to similar values dominating political and domestic life. The levelling function of sex to this end is best expressed in the maid's shrewd reminder to her mistress: 'I know no difference, virtuous madam, | But in love all have privilege alike' (4.1.84–5).

[69] See David M. Bergeron, 'Art within *The Second Maiden's Tragedy*', *MRDE* 1 (1984), 185.

[70] The Lady's appearance in black against the Tyrant's wishes may refer to James's dislike of wearing black in the English court. He probably meant to discourage public mourning for Elizabeth. See *Memoirs of Maximilian de Bethune, Duke of Sully*, trans. Charlotte Lennox, 3 vols. (1756), ii. 2B2ᵛ–3.

[71] See Heywood, *Apology for Actors*, E3ᵛ. Domitian in Massinger's *Roman Actor* (1626) kills Paris in a play.

[72] See Levin, *Multiple Plot*, 25–34

The clash of tyrant and martyr in *Lady* confirms Benjamin's insight that they are 'but two faces' of unchecked autocracy. Martyrdom in this play, like treason in *Revenger*, is an inverted image of despotic ideology. The sovereignty which realizes itself only in absolute desire and possession is encountered by an equally absolute denial and immolation of the subject self. However, the Lady's virtue is not quite the stoic absolutism of the spirit with which Benjamin matches the utopian ahistoricism of tyranny.[73] Her self-description as a treasure which Govianus must fling 'Into whales' throats than pirates should be gorged with't' (3.1.71) is not much different from Helvetius's view of her as a 'jewel', and her suicide ironically vindicates his judgement that a 'subject' cannot possess it (2.1.84–6). This ironic qualification is effected chiefly by the carnal and economic contagion of the sub-plot. The blend of the royal and domestic intrigues, which Schoenbaum thought a mistake Middleton never repeated after *Lady*,[74] is thus integral to the play's portrayal of the structures of political and sexual domination, and reappears in Middleton's later tragedies.

[73] Benjamin, *Origin of German Tragic Drama*, 69, 74.
[74] Schoenbaum, *Middleton's Tragedies*, 68.

4

Mirth and Licence: Moll at the Bankside and Moll in Cheapside

THEATRE AND THE POLITICS OF EXCESS: *The Roaring Girl*

Seven years after *1 Whore*, Middleton worked with Dekker on *Roaring Girl* (1611), another play for the Prince's Men.. His share this time was an equal, if not a major one,[1] and the plot reworks some of his earlier motifs. Sebastian Wengrave, whose wish to marry Mary Fitzallard is obstructed by his merchant father Sir Alexander, is a trickster who, like Witgood, uses one woman to trail another. The instrumental woman is again a social outcast. She is a transvestite, and a reputed thief.[2] But while the courtesans in *Trick* and *Mad World* had married the gentlemen they deceived, Moll prefers deviancy and isolation to dubious social membership.

In Moll, the moral ringmaster returns as outsider. Like that of Phoenix, her disguise enables her to slip 'from one company to another' (2.1.206). It also lets her assume Frank Gullman's role of a median agent in the romance plot.[3] Socially, Phoenix belonged to the

[1] Price gives to Dekker alone three scenes; Barker, Lake, and Jackson give him six. Hoy and Mulholland find neither author dominant. See G. R. Price, 'The Shares of Middleton and Dekker in a Collaborated Play', *Papers of the Michigan Academy of Science, Arts and Letters*, 30 (1944), 601–15; Barker, *Middleton*, 170–6; Lake, *Canon*, 53–5; Jackson, *Studies in Attribution*, 95–101; Cyrus Hoy, *Introductions, Notes, and Commentaries to Texts in* The Dramatic Works of Thomas Dekker *Edited by Fredson Bowers*, 4 vols. (Cambridge, 1980), iii. 12–13; and Mulholland (ed.), *Roaring Girl*, 8–12.

[2] Dekker mentions Moll disparagingly in *If This Be Not a Good Play*, 5.4.105–7; *Match Me in London*, 1.2.85–6; and *The Witch of Edmonton*, 5.1.159–61, and her role is negative in Nathan Field's *Amends for Ladies* (1611). Some critics thus treat her as Middleton's idea; see Eliot, *Selected Essays*, 166; W. Power, 'Double, Double', *N & Q* 204 (1959), 5; and Heinemann, *Puritanism and Theatre*, 100. But a source praising Mary Frith may have existed, as suggested by Raphael Seligmann, 'A Probable Early Borrowing from Middleton and Dekker's *The Roaring Girl*', *N & Q* 238 (1993), 229–31. The play is best seen as a close collaboration; see Norman Rabkin, 'Problems in the Study of Collaboration', *RORD* 19 (1976), 11.

[3] See Patrick Cheney, 'Moll Cutpurse as Hermaphrodite in Dekker and Middleton's *The Roaring Girl*', *Ren. & Ref.* 19 (1983), 120–34; and William R. Dynes, 'The Trickster-Figure in Jacobean City Comedy', *SEL* 33 (1993), 379–81.

centre and Frank to the margin, while Moll combines the contrary traits of prince and prostitute. A symbolic challenge to establishment norms is usually vested in such misjoinders—the wise fool, the honest whore, the gentleman tramp. A similar jolt into cognitive dissonance is threatened by the paradox of the man–woman and the honest cutpurse.

Critical response to the heroine's androgyny has also been dissonant. While some have found her resistance to patriarchy unequivocal,[4] others have marked her ambiguous gender values and restricted dissent.[5] Dollimore explains this divided response as the effect of a 'transgressive reinscription', in which the challenge of the deviant is finally contained, though not before producing knowledge of the process which excludes it.[6] The account is suggestive, if a little too centred on gender dissidence. I wish to widen that focus, and to connect it, as well as the play's introverted gaze on the theatre, with other symptoms of prodigal deviancy—outlandish clothes, bawdy songs, laughter, canting, conning, voyaging. In the play's alternation between attitudes of indulgence and self-regulation towards these images of exorbitance, one may detect the same ambiguity Dollimore analyses, subjecting Moll's structural function to contrary pulls.

The overriding paradox about *Roaring Girl* is that it merges fiction and life to the extent of publicizing a stage appearance of its heroine's original, and yet, since only the playhouse permits such a convergence, it insistently reflects on the theatre's artifice and social indeterminacy. Early in the play, when Sir Alexander describes the pictures in his 'galleries' to guests, the playwrights layer his speech to remind the

---

[4] See Heinemann, *Puritanism and Theatre*, 99–100; Shepherd, *Amazons and Warrior Women*, 77–83; Jean E. Howard, 'Crossdressing, the Theatre, and Gender Struggle in Early Modern England', *SQ* 39 (1988), 436–9; and Leah Marcus, *Puzzling Shakespeare: Local Reading and its Discontents* (Berkeley, Calif., 1988), 104.

[5] See Mary Beth Rose, *The Expense of Spirit: Love and Sexuality in English Renaissance Drama* (Ithaca, NY, 1988), 77–92, which sets the ambivalence against the *Hic Mulier/Haec Vir* pamphlet war of 1620. See also Lisa Jardine, *Still Harping on Daughters: Women and Drama in the Age of Shakespeare* (Brighton, 1983), 159–61; Leinwand, *City Staged*, 156–9; Comensoli, 'Play-making, Domestic Conduct, and the Multiple Plot', 249–66; Lorraine Helms, 'Roaring Girls and Silent Women: The Politics of Androgyny on the Jacobean Stage', *Themes in Drama*, 11 (1989), 59–73; Stephen Orgel, 'The Subtexts of *The Roaring Girl*', in Susan Zimmerman (ed.), *Erotic Politics: Desire on the Renaissance Stage* (New York, 1992), 12–26; Jean Howard, 'Sex and Social Conflict: The Erotics of *The Roaring Girl*', ibid. 170–90; and Anthony B. Dawson, 'Mistris Hic & Haec: Representations of Moll Frith', *SEL* 33 (1993), 385–404.

[6] Jonathan Dollimore, *Sexual Dissidence: Augustine to Wilde, Freud to Foucault* (Oxford, 1991), 293–99.

spectators at the Fortune of the life and art which surround them—
crammed galleries, heaving 'floor', 'Stories of men and women, mixed
together', 'a thousand heads' in 'one square'. The spectators are not
spared the warning that there are cutpurses in that crowd.[7] In the eyes
of the world, Moll herself was one. But the playwrights, quite as much
as Sir Alexander, leave that to the judgement of art and its viewers: 'By
a hanging villainous look yourselves may know him, | The face is
drawn so rarely' (1.2.14–30).

The portraits in Sir Alexander's gallery are anamorphic. They are
'like the promising titles of new books | Writ merrily'. Their 'own
eyes' read these books and 'seem to move' (1.2.24), viewing both
themselves and the comedy. The Epilogue picks up the simile, liken-
ing the play to a painting which will not please everyone (l. 28),
because the spectators will see themselves in it, and find their
prejudices, nourished on the 'nasty, obscene discourses' of the gutter
press (ll. 22–4), questioned.

Moll's transvestism holds up a mocking mirror to a blinkered world,
which includes the audience as much as the characters on stage.
Sebastian accuses his father of siding 'with the world to wrong her'
(2.2.135), and reassures Moll: 'Pish, let 'em prate abroad! Thou'rt here
where thou art known and loved' (4.1.94–5). The self-reference of that
'here' is attested by the *Consistory of London Correction Book* record of
27 January 1612 that Mary Frith was 'at a playe about 3 quarters of a
yeare since at *the* ffortune', and that she 'sat there vppon the stage . . . in
mans apparrell & playd vppon her lute & sange a songe'.[8] The Epilogue
promises that Frith herself, 'some few days hence, | Shall on this stage
give larger recompense' (ll. 35–6).[9] The action prepares spectators for
the appearance by making them reject 'the world's' view of her more
genuinely than Sir Alexander, who declares his remorse only after he
learns that the tavern wench is not marrying his son.

The most obvious register of theatrical self-reference is, of course,
cross-dressing. A man dressed as a woman diluted 'the veritie of his
owne kinde',[10] while a commoner dressed as a gentlemen upset 'the

[7] On warnings against pickpockets in plays of the time, see Leah Scragg, ' "Her C's, Her
U's, and Her T's: Why That?" A New Reply for Sir Andrew Aguecheek', *RES* , NS 42
(1991), 1–16.

[8] See Mulholland (ed.), *Roaring Girl*, 262.

[9] Paul Mulholland, 'The Date of *The Roaring Girl*', *RES*, NS 28 (1977), 21–2, suggests
that the 'recompense' might have been a jig, which drew crowds and cutpurses to the
Fortune.

[10] Phillip Stubbes, *The Anatomie of Abuses* (1583), F5^v.

order which God hath set in the states and conditions of men'.[11] Cross-dressing in the theatre could thus hint at the social construction of both gender and class.[12] The two are linked in Sebastian's defence of Moll. Her 'bold spirit', he says, 'Through her apparel somewhat shames her birth', especially since there are many 'well descended' gentlemen who are 'arrant knaves' (2.2.176–8, 167-9). By encouraging a disclosure of such connections, the theatre invited the hostility of crusaders against cross-dressing.[13] Moll's rebellious androgyny, while suggesting that social and gender norms were artifices of power, could also serve as a strange image of the theatre's potential for such revelation.

Cross-dressing is not Moll's only theatrical offence, she is also guilty of mirth. William Gager, John Rainolds's opponent in the Oxford dispute on cross-dressing in the 1590s, accused enemies of the stage of confusing mirth with lewdness: *ludicrum, petulans vocat.*[14] Stage-baiters, wrote Webster contemptuously, condemn the spring 'Because 'tis merry and renewes our bloud'.[15] The Prologue promises 'laughter' (l. 10), and it is 'mirth' which Mary Frith's advertised appearance will enhance (Epilogue, l. 37).[16] 'Mad Moll, or Merry Moll' (1.1.99) keeps the Prologue's promise in her jokes, songs, and canting. These even infect Lord Noland, who, when invited to Pimlico by the 'merry ging', says he is ready 'to sail to the World's End' with them (5.1.59–60).

Moll is 'loose in nothing but in mirth' (2.2.179), a looseness the world never trusts. Laxton, a 'gallant' whose homoerotic fancy is tickled by her, takes Moll for a whore, and is taught a celebrated lesson by her sword at Gray's Inn Fields. It is seldom noticed that what Moll

[11] William Perkins, *The Whole Treatise of Cases of Conscience* (1608), 3.4, repr. in Thomas M. Merrill (ed.), *William Perkins 1558–1602: English Puritanist. His Pioneer Works on Casuistry* (The Hague, 1966), 211.

[12] For two recent treatments, see Dollimore, *Sexual Dissidence*, 284–306; and Marjorie Garber, *Vested Interests: Cross-Dressing and Cultural Anxiety* (New York, 1992).

[13] See Jonas Barish, *The Antitheatrical Prejudice* (Berkeley, Calif., 1981), 92–3; and Jean E. Howard, 'Renaissance Antitheatricality and the Politics of Gender in *Much Ado About Nothing*', in Jean E. Howard and Marion F. O'Connor (eds.), *Shakespeare Reproduced: The Text in History and Ideology* (New York, 1987), 165-72.

[14] William Gager, *Vlysses Redvx* (Oxford, 1592), F5. Rainolds answers the charge in *Th'Overthrow of Stage-Playes, by the Way of Controversie betwixt D. Gager and D. Rainoldes* (n.p., 1599), D1ᵛ.

[15] John Webster, commendatory poem in Heywood, *Apology for Actors*, A2ᵛ.

[16] On the theatrical self-representation of the historical Mary Frith, see Dawson, 'Mistris Hic & Haec', 389–90.

thinks Laxton and 'the baser world' (3.1.107) misreads is not her deviant dress, but her deviant mirth. The world calls her names because she is 'often merry': 'Had mirth no kindred in the world but lust?' (3.1.104–5).

What Moll punishes in her encounter with Laxton is neither misogyny nor established gender norms, but the presumption that because she is merry and masterless, she is 'whorish' and easily baited by 'a golden hook' (3.1.89, 98). She is teaching Laxton and Sir Alexander really the same lesson in the two plots, for, in this respect, the gallant is no worse than the citizen. The one thinks of money as the 'aquafortis that eats into many a maidenhead' (2.1.195–6), and the other is certain that money 'May draw her that's most chaste to a man's bosom' (1.2.220). Masterless men and women were held guilty of 'the classic crime of status',[17] and Moll reproves the world for assuming that the offence was almost automatically moral.

Masterlessness, of course, was a complaint against players, whom many still wanted booked 'in the Catalogue of the seuerall kindes of Rogues and Vagabonds'.[18] Moll's speech after the skirmish with Laxton can be read as a self-distancing of players and playwrights from the masterless. At the same time, it disowns the mastery of the rich who sell themselves just as much as crooks and whores:

> she that has wit and spirit
> May scorn to live beholding to her body for meat,
> Or for apparel, like your common dame
> That makes shame get her clothes to cover shame. (3.1.133-6)

Moll Cutpurse is not one of those Middleton in *Ant* called 'common Molls' (Bullen, viii. 78). More significantly, she is no 'common dame' either. Like hers, the wit and spirit of playmakers could do without both the common and courtly forms of prostitution.

The allure and dread of the prodigious surrounding the man-woman call up images of voyages, mermaids, strange tongues. In a fable allegorizing his son's vices, Sir Alexander describes the hero as 'no prodigal' with money, but 'a traveller' who 'has more tongues in his

---

[17] Beier, *Masterless Men*, p. xxii. See also Roger B. Manning, *Village Revolts: Social Protest and Popular Disturbances in England, 1509–1640* (Oxford, 1988), 157–86.

[18] I[ohn] G[reen], *A Refutation of the Apology for Actors* (1615), E4. See M. C. Bradbrook, *The Rise of the Common Player: A Study of Actor and Society in Shakespeare's England* (London, 1962), 39–95; and G. E. Bentley, *The Profession of Player in Shakespeare's Time, 1590–1642* (Princeton, NJ, 1984), 8–11.

head than some have teeth' (1.2.118–21). Moll to Sir Alexander is a 'mermaid', the current word for a whore tempting young travellers. She herself warns Sebastian against a voyager's haste: 'never choose a wife as if you were going to Virginia' (2.2.68–9). Trapdoor, posing as a demobilized soldier, fibs about Turks, Hungarians, Moldavians, Valachians, Transylvanians, and Sclavonians (5.1.84–91). He reels off an itinerary which recalls the gargantuan title-pages of popular travel books, 'from Venice to Roma, Vecchio, Bononia, Romania, Bolonia, Modena, Piacenza, and Tuscana with all her cities, as Pistoia, Valteria, Mountepulchena, Arrezzo, with the Siennois and diverse others' (5.1.93–6). When Moll unmasks him, the tales are replaced by stranger canting and calls for the life of 'ben Rome-booze' and the open 'pad' (5.1.214, 226–7).

In 1599, the traveller Thomas Platter visited the Bankside, the red-light margin of town where Trapdoor knew he would find Moll (cf. 1.2.205). After sitting through a play at the Globe, he decided that the stay-at-home English learned about 'foreign matters' from plays.[19] Travel and the theatre gave them a taste of the exotic, such as the underworld canting in the play. Moll's command of the argot, which mixed traces of Irish, Welsh, Scottish, French, Latinisms, and gipsy dialect, is an analogue of the social mediation a heteroglot theatre might effect.[20]

Foreign travel was also an alleged antecedent of prodigality. Joseph Hall reminded travellers that the younger son in the parable turned prodigal 'because hee got his portion too soone into his hands, and wandred into a farre countrey'.[21] Travel books rehearsed the standard replies, as the one repeated by Thomas Coryat in 1611 to excuse his visit to a Venetian courtesan: 'Cognitio mali non est mala, the knowledge of evill is not evill'. On the contrary, the observation of vices makes the virtuous man 'more confirmed and settled in virtue'.[22] This exactly is Moll's justification for her familiarity with thieves. She asks Lord Noland if he would have refused to listen to an Italian pander in Venice disclose to him 'the close tricks of courtesans'. This is followed

[19] *Thomas Platter's Travels in England, 1599*, trans. Clare Williams (London, 1937), 170.

[20] See Arthur F. Kinney (ed.), *Rogues, Vagabonds, and Sturdy Beggars: A New Gallery of Tudor and Early Stuart Literature* (1973; Amherst, Mass., 1990), 40.

[21] Ioseph Hall, *Quo Vadis? A Iust Censvre of Travell as It is Commonly Undertaken by the Gentlemen of Our Nation* (1617), B6.

[22] Thomas Coryat, *Coryat's Crudities*, 2 vols. (Glasgow, 1905), i. 408.

by Coryat's logic, 'must you have | A black ill name because ill things you know?' (5.1.334–42).

The detractors of travel and those of poetry and plays shared the same mistrust of experiment and pleasure.[23] In Venice, wrote Jerome Turler, 'pleasures make a man not thinke on his returne'. He was seduced by 'Mermaids',[24] who could be papists as well as whores. Theatres, like Venetian bordellos, induced 'Whoredome and vncleanesse', driving the sensually inebriated 'daily and hourely, night and day, time and tyde, to see Playes and Enterludes'.[25] When defenders of the stage raised Coryat's argument, they were accused of self-deceit:

the sixth *deceit* is, A pretence that we will doe such and such things [euill and vngodly] for *trialls* sake . . . The like pretence is vsed for seeing of plaies, that by seeing many filthy sinnes . . . represented and acted on the stage, wee shall learne to hate those vices the more.[26]

Steven Mullaney sees Platter's account as an indication of English society's divided enthusiasm for the popular stage. Situated on the city's margin alongside brothels and gambling joints, it was 'an object of ambivalent fascination' to be enjoyed, exorcized, and cast off. Mullaney finds this pattern rehearsed in Prince Hal's brief affair with Eastcheap.[27] Moll's social apprenticeship has been in alehouses and theatres, two equally feared schools of radical levelling,[28] and, like Prince Hal, she has studied 'a strange tongue' so that 'the most immodest word' (*2 Henry IV*, 4.3.69–70) may be learnt and discarded. Sebastian foresees her reclamation in the same terms as Prince Hal did his own, as a spectacular breaking of light 'through foul mists' (2.2.166). The rest of society see her more as an Eastcheap scamp. In turning Moll's underworld skills to their advantage, they display the same anxiety to master and contain the prodigious which haunted both patronage and hostility to the theatre. One of Sir Alexander's friends calls Moll a 'poison' (1.2.148), and, to illustrate Moll's function in the

[23] See Richard Helgerson, *The Elizabethan Prodigals* (Berkeley, Calif., 1976), 16–43.

[24] *The Traveiler of Jerome Turler* (1575), as quoted in Clare Howard, *English Travellers of the Renaissance* (London, 1914), 56.

[25] G[reen], *Refutation of the Apology for Actors*, H4.

[26] Daniell Dyke, *The Mystery of Self-Deceiving, or, A Discourse and Discouery of the Deceitfulnesse of Mans Heart* (1614), O6^v.

[27] Mullaney, *Place of the Stage*, 60–87.

[28] See Peter Clark, *The English Alehouse: A Social History 1200–1830* (London, 1983), 145–76; Underdown, *Revel, Riot, and Rebellion*, 47–52; and Theodore B. Leinwand, 'Spongy Plebs, Mighty Lords, and the Dynamics of the Alehouse', *JMRS* 19 (1989), 159–84.

lovers' plot, Mary Fitzallard uses the same epithet with revealing condescension: 'No poison, sir, but serves us for some use' (4.1.148).

Princes can stop the game when they wish; the roaring girl is stuck with her pretence. Like the common player, she has to assert her probity against the endless misreadings of her dress, merriment, language, and company. The limitation sets Moll's situation apart from the one Mullaney describes in *Henry IV*, and it is turned into an assertion of social worth and independence. Moll is not cast off like Hal's companions, nor does she return to the normative. Reforming the anti-social and rescuing the innocent, she mediates the restoration of normalcy in the comic play-world. But, unlike Shakespeare's cross-dressed heroines, she remains unswerved in the course of effecting that 'happy swerving' which guides comedy to a socially licit end.[29] Her rebellious androgyny outlives its use in the lovers' scheme, and she declares her resolve to stay unmastered until honesty and truth are free of slander, and women are 'manned but never pandered' (5.2.219–20).

The text makes a special point of disclosing the theatrical and fictional nature of its curative denouement. In the romance plot, Moll plays Puck; in the sub-plot she plays Long Meg of Westminster.[30] The ploy which tidies up the sub-plot even flaunts its theatrical precedent. The shopkeepers, their wives, and the gallants sail to Brentford, where lechers are unmasked and women saved on the brink of dishonour. The device is a repetition of the one Dekker and Webster had used in *Westward Ho* (1604), which featured an equally momentous expedition to Brentford.[31] As the wives embark on the journey, Openwork asks, 'Come, what's the comedy?' '*Westward Ho*,' replies Mrs Gallipot (4.2.137). And when the gallants are exposed, Gallipot collapses into the role of a dazed playgoer: 'I pray, who plays | *A Knack to Know an Honest Man* in this company?' (4.2.283–4). Serious mischief is forgiven as 'merriment' (4.2.333), thanks to the arbitration of theatrical pretence.

At the time the play was written, aldermen and preachers had stepped up attacks on the stage.[32] One way of hitting back was to write,

---

[29] Stephen Greenblatt, *Shakespearean Negotiations: The Circulation of Social Energy in Renaissance England* (Oxford, 1988), 67–70.

[30] Cf. 5.1.3–5. See Shepherd, *Amazons and Warrior Women*, 70–83, on the play's use of the story of Long Meg.

[31] See M. T. Jones-Davies, *Un peintre de la vie Londonienne, Thomas Dekker* (circa 1572–1632), 2 vols. (Paris, 1958), i. 131.

[32] See Elbert N. S. Thompson, *The Controversy between the Puritans and the Stage* (New York, 1903), 134–45.

as Heywood did in 1612, an apology for actors. A second way, as the one taken in *Histriomastix* (*c*.1589; printed 1610), was to shift the charges on to strolling players. A third option was to attack the hypocrisy of the theatre's enemies, as Jonson did in *Bartholomew Fair* (1614). *Roaring Girl* is a different response, and in many ways a unique one. Moll and her Bankside crew are associated with every slander brought against players—theft, prostitution, sodomy, vagrancy, levity, shape-shifting, cross-dressing. In the end, mirth is decriminalized, and the charge of theatre's ungendering influence is countered with a model of spiritual freedom embodied in the virago. This is achieved not, as in Jonson's *Epicoene*, 'by banishing the feminine principle',[33] but by reinventing the 'effeminate' attributes of the theatre—festive merriment, the indeterminacy of appearance, the spell of spectacle and fiction.

We have noted the conflicting demands of involvement with and distance from the culture of excess made upon the disguised prince on the stage. The same demands defined the theatre's dilemma, and a prodigious outcast in place of the prince enabled the playwrights to address the question of its social place. That question was tied to the larger issue Leah Marcus has called 'the politics of mirth'.[34] Middleton's plea in the preface that a play was better diversion than dice and whores is curiously similar to James's defence of popular pastime.[35] The Stuart kings practised a form of repressive tolerance which sought simultaneously to countenance and contain festive misrule. The problem for city playwrights defending 'public mirth' was one of balancing social goodwill and social conscience. They needed to distance themselves from the licence of the suburbs as well as from that of the court, regarded by critics as twin curses of the royal policy on leisure. Nicolas Bownde had in 1595 asked for a ban on '*shooting, hunting, hawking, tennise, fensing, bowling,* or such like' on the Sabbath, as also on '*playing, drinking, filthy dancing, harlotting, fighting and quarreling*'.[36] This parallel assault on lordly and vulgar pastimes is evident twelve years later in John Sprint's updated list of the Sabbath's enemies, which includes

[33] Phyllis Rackin, 'Androgyny, Mimesis, and the Marriage of the Boy Heroine on the English Renaissance Stage', *PMLA* 202 (1987), 34.

[34] See Leah Marcus, *The Politics of Mirth: Jonson, Herrick, Milton, Marvell, and the Defense of Old Holiday Pastimes* (Chicago, 1986), 1–63.

[35] See Hill, *Society and Puritanism*, 188–9. On the argument as a defence of playhouses, see Barish, *Antitheatrical Prejudice*, 80–2.

[36] Nicolas Bownde, *The Doctrine of the Sabbath, Plainely Layde Forth* (1595), S2ᵛ, 2O2.

'oppressors, coseners, Epicures, and voluptuous liuers' with 'fidlers, stage-players, beare and bull-baiters, gamesters, drunkards, vsurers, papists, families of loue, theeues, vagrant rogues, swearers'.[37]

The 'harmlesse Recreation'[38] James liked to be seen promoting was a species of pastoral festivity, 'honest feasting and merrinesse', 'playes and lawfull games in Maie'.[39] Defenders of mirth flattered the king's self-image of a benign sport not unlike Lord Noland, while critics found his court a school of sloth and excess. Sabbatarians resented the staging of a court masque on a Sunday in 1608, and in the 1611 Parliament, the first bill to be passed by the Lower House concerned the observance of the Sabbath.[40] James's public behaviour with Robert Carr, made a Viscount in 1611, did little to allay the charge that the court was 'A Feast of strange Mirth'.[41] The phrase is from Dekker's If This Be Not a Good Play (2.1.215), written the same year, in which a king is shown forsaking his Sabbatarian zeal in favour of 'apish pastimes . . . base and effeminate' (2.1.76–7). It is significant that Prince Henry, patron of the company playing Roaring Girl and the hope of disaffected Protestants, decreed that his feasts 'should passe with decency and decorum, and without all rudenesse, noise or disorder'.[42]

Moll's question—'Had mirth no kindred in the world but lust?'—is a plea to release mirth from its aberrant forms among the leisured as well as the lowly. The use of the name 'Mary' for both heroines suits this purpose. Mary Fitzallard too appears once in a man's doublet, and Sebastian finds her more appetizing in 'this strange form' (4.1.56). As he kisses the boy-actor, Moll remarks, 'How strange this shows, one man to kiss another' (4.1.45). It is aggressive baiting of those who accused actors of sodomy. At another level, it is a reminder that Sebastian's tastes are not too distant from those of Laxton, who had declared Moll a pederast's delight.

The social and sexual paradox of Moll is a powerful image of the theatre's ambiguous relationship to authority installed on the fractured

[37] Iohn Sprint, Propositions, Tending to Proove the Necessarie Vse of the Christian Sabbaoth, or Lords Day (1607), E1ᵛ.

[38] The King's Maiesties Declaration to his Subjects, Concerning Lawfull Sports to be Vsed (1618), as quoted in Marcus, Politics of Mirth, 3.

[39] McIlwain (ed.), Political Works, 27.

[40] See Hill, Society and Puritanism, 156–8.

[41] See Samuel R. Gardiner, History of England from the Accession of James I to the Outbreak of the Civil War 1603–1642, 10 vols. (London, 1864–1903), ii. 111.

[42] Charles Cornwallis, A Discourse of the Most Illustrious Prince, Henry, Late Prince of Wales (1641), C2.

political terrain of public mirth. In this lower-order Britomart, Marcus has detected a nostalgia for the amazonian image of Elizabeth, a royal icon expressive of popular disappointment with the queen's male successor.[43] Bess Bridges in Heywood's *Fair Maid of the West*, Part 1, had earlier blended features of Long Meg and Elizabeth,[44] but she was in the end recalled by love to her native 'femininity'. Moll, on the contrary, chooses the social and sexual autarky which Elizabethans found disconcerting in their monarch.[45] The royal icon of heroic androgyny is now kindred of mirth at the Bankside. Her stubborn maintenance of difference guards a modality of social and political dissent which Middleton and Dekker, in their separate ways, never quite surrendered.

CARNIVAL AND CARNAL RULE: *A Chaste Maid in Cheapside*

Chaste Maid (1613) was played at the Swan by Lady Elizabeth's Men. The company, for which Middleton had earlier written *No Wit, No Help Like a Woman's* (1611), merged with the boys of the Queen's Revels in March 1613, enabling him to use a large female cast and bring back motifs from the Paul's comedies.[46]

By shuffling the old actants and indices, the play yet produces a difference in 'total effect'.[47] The gallant suitor is Touchwood Jr., the rich father is a Cheapside goldsmith named Yellowhammer, and the chaste maid with a wrong address is his daughter Moll. The Yellow-hammers' dream of marrying Moll into the titled gentry survives the revelation that the chosen groom, Sir Walter Whorehound, has been siring bastards by courtesy of a *mari complaisant* named Allwit. They are bluffed with the rumour of the lovers' death, and unwittingly consent to their daughter's wedding at what they thought was her funeral.

---

[43] Marcus, *Puzzling Shakespeare*, 104.

[44] The date is disputed. R. K. Turner's Regents Renaissance Drama edition (London, 1968), pp. xi–xiii, suggests a date before 1604 for Pt. 1.

[45] On these anxieties, see Louis A. Montrose, '*A Midsummer Night's Dream* and the Shaping Fantasies of Elizabethan Culture: Gender, Power, Form', in Margaret W. Ferguson *et al.* (eds.), *Rewriting the Renaissance: The Discourses of Sexual Difference in Early Modern Europe* (Chicago, 1986), 65–87; Marcus, *Puzzling Shakespeare*, 51–105; and Philippa Berry, *Of Chastity and Power: Elizabethan Literature and the Unmarried Queen* (London, 1989), 61–82.

[46] See Parker (ed.), *Chaste Maid*, pp. xxix–xxx.

[47] M. C. Bradbrook, *The Growth and Structure of Elizabethan Comedy* (1955; Harmondsworth, 1963), 172.

The romance is parodied by the coupling of Tim, the stupid son of the Yellowhammers, with the Welsh 'heiress' they choose for him, unaware that she is Sir Walter's mistress. A second contrast is set up between the Allwit and Kix households. Allwit the citizen is, as his name suggests, a wittol, pleased to let Sir Walter pick up the bills. Sir Oliver Kix is an impotent knight, elated when Touchwood Sr.'s expensive 'potion' (for he thinks it is that) makes his wife pregnant.[48] Allwit finds sex a waste of resources, while Sir Oliver hopes that money will achieve what his manhood cannot. In addition, Touchwood Sr. and his wife are a contrast to the Kixes and the Allwits. The Kixes accuse each other of barrenness, the Touchwoods are drawn closer by the need to curb the husband's costly potency. Allwit and Touchwood Sr. both convert their households to business partnerships. Allwit prospers by acting the willing cuckold. Touchwood Sr. secures his own future, and that of his brother (Sir Walter's fortune and marriage were conditional on the Kixes remaining childless), by cuckolding another.

The ingenious plot refuses to privilege any central figure, and disperses the mediatory functions of the intriguer and satirist among a number of unlikely candidates. Sir Walter is a key structural link, but his status in society and in the narrative is divided. In the Yellowhammer household, he plays the gallant trickster—'A brave court-spirit' expected to make city virgins 'quiver | And kiss with trembling thighs' (1.1.116–17). In the Allwit ménage, his role shrivels to a nervous mixture of gullible country knight and suspicious citizen cuckold. Sir Walter lusts and repents like Penitent Brothel, spends like Sir Bounteous, and frets like Harebrain.

While Sir Walter as adulterer displays the fussy uxoriousness of the cuckold, Allwit as cuckold acquires the cynical insouciance of the adulterer. Allwit claims he lives just as other tradesmen do, 'butchers by selling flesh, | Poulters by vending conies, or the like' (4.1.216–17). His application of the tradesman's reasoning, however, is aimed at immunizing himself from the chronic afflictions of stage merchants such as Quomodo:

> And where some merchants would in soul kiss hell
> To buy a paradise for their wives, and dye

---

[48] The episode derives from Machiavelli's *Mandragola*. See Robert I. Williams, 'Machiavelli's *Mandragola*, Touchwood Senior, and the Comedy of Middleton's *A Chaste Maid in Cheapside*', *SEL* 10 (1970), 385–96.

> Their conscience in the bloods of prodigal heirs
> To deck their night-piece, yet all this being done,
> Eaten with jealousy to the inmost bone,—
>
> .   .   .   .
>
> These torments stand I free of . . . (1. 2. 41-8)

By radicalizing mercantile logic, Allwit oversteps the prescripted role of the citizen cuckold and lays bare the duplicity of social standards. The Yellowhammers sell sex to Sir Walter as much as the Allwits, but, as Levin points out, Allwit's deal is socially indecent and the Yellowhammers' is not.[49]

As schemer, Allwit's control is tenuous. Davy Dahumma, Sir Walter's poor relation, can rattle him by revealing that his kinsman means to marry Moll. Allwit hurries to Yellowhammer posing as his distant cousin, and reveals Sir Walter's affairs in an attempt to scupper the match. The irony of the disguise recoils on himself when the goldsmith proves impeccably Allwitian and ignores the scandal. Allwit survives the disaster, but a limit is set to his ability to master-mind the moves.

Even then, Allwit is the point of reference for the characters among whom the role of the comic trickster is divided. Touchwood Sr. has some of his nonchalance, Yellowhammer and Davy a bit of his reptilian cool, and Sir Walter, in the Yellowhammer household at least, a little of his brazenness. These affinities across status lines, as well as the flawed efficacy of all the tricksters (even Touchwood Jr.'s first two attempts at elopement miscarry) confirm Joanne Altieri's point that no form of hierarchy, of age or rank or money or wit, is allowed to assert itself at the end of the saturnalia.[50]

The sex–money calculus is again central to the several plots. 'Some only can get riches and no children,' laments Touchwood Sr. 'We only can get children and no riches!' (2.1.11–12). But fertility is no longer an attribute of the country as it was in *Michaelmas*. The proportion of virility to riches is no index of rank or place, and potency makes Touchwood Sr.'s marriage as much a business partnership as that of Allwit and Yellowhammer. Besides solving some of Cheapside's problems, his phenomenal seed had seven country girls pregnant in the wake of his last rural rides. One of them enters with his bastard to interrupt his praise of wedlock, and we learn from her that he has also

---

[49] Levin, *Multiple Plot*, 200.
[50] Joanne Altieri, 'Against Moralizing Jacobean Comedy: Middleton's *Chaste Maid*', *Criticism*, 30 (1988), 171–87.

ruined the marriage of one poor Ellen in Derbyshire (2.1.24–6). Marriage for him is exemplary only when a wife can cut her appetite according to her purse. The Prospero of Cheapside is one with Allwit in using sex as personal capital.

Touchwood Sr. and Allwit adopt contrasting strategies of controlling the female body as a valve for getting and spending. Here again, one transaction has social and comic sanction, while the other breaks social and generic rules. Readers and producers remark on the play's strange blend of delight and disgust.[51] Middleton's point seems to be that the two are functions of hegemonic approval and censure. The logic of power, and of the comic conventions it underwrites, can turn one thing into the other just as Tim's Latin syllogisms can prove a fool rational and a whore honest (cf. 4.1.1–18, 5.4.95–104).

Tim's bride, of course, knows all about club-law, and says that marriage will make her 'honest' sooner than his logic (5.4.105–6). Power remains insuperably phallic, and Middleton has now a keener sense of how its expressions are slotted by the validational norms of society and of comedy. Sir Oliver's 'brevity' (2.1.147–8) is risible since it turns his wife's 'greater cut' (2.1.135) to Touchwood Sr.'s ministration and holds back 'goodly lands and livings' (2.1.150–1). Touchwood Sr.'s 'fatal finger' (2.1.59), on the other hand, releases lands, livings, brides, and heirs, and is accepted by even his victims as 'manly dealings' (2.1.101). Allwit's freedom from cares costs him his gender rights. As one of his servants says, he is not their 'master' but their 'mistress's husband', since his horns place him 'but one pip above a serving man' (1.2.60–6). Touchwood Jr. 'break[s] through' the 'stop' which checks his 'hopeful fortunes' (4.4.56–7) by beating Sir Walter in swordplay, the phallic import of which is made clear by placing it immediately after Tim's pledge to guard his sister, just hauled back from her attempted elopement, with Harry the Fifth's sword (4.4.45–6). Social and comic privilege depends on the skill men display in controlling the 'frays' and 'bracks' (1.1.36) of the female body, on the husband's ability to solder up 'all cracks' (1.1.37),[52] and the father's to guard his daughter as well as his plates (cf. 4.2.1–2). In this, the play

---

[51] See e.g. Samuel Schoenbaum, 'A Chaste Maid in Cheapside and Middleton's City Comedy', in Shakespeare and Others (Washington, DC, 1985), 213; and David Richman, 'Directing Middleton's Comedy', in Friedenreich (ed.), 'Accompaninge the Players', 81–2.

[52] On Middleton's use of such words for the vagina, see Holdsworth, 'Measure for Measure, Middleton, and "Brakes of Ice" ', 65–6.

shows the smart as morally equal with the stupid, hinting at the hegemonic basis of valorization in city comedy.

Gail Paster's study of the metonymic chain connecting female tears, speech, food, drink, menses, and urine in *Chaste Maid* concludes that the play focuses on containment of female appetite, fertility, and leakage, and on promotion of male potency. Male 'water' represents power; female, uncontrol.[53] I think the stress is not so much on the difference between male and female leakage as on the dissimulation of society, and of comedy, which allows hegemonic interests to choose between forms of male domination, to fashion their cultural images, and to selectively flaunt or repress the phallic truth about them.

The Lenten–Easter setting of the action gives carnality and comic resurrection an ironic temporal context. Lenten injunctions against the sale of meat were tightened in 1613 following the bad harvest of 1612, which left cattle without winter feed.[54] The Privy Council appointed its own spies to stop butchers from selling meat even to the sick and the pregnant, and their dishonesty and bullying were a source of annoyance. In *The Insatiate Countess*, written between 1607 and 1613, a jealous husband accuses his wife's suspected lover of sneaking into his house 'like a promoter to spy flesh in lent' (4.1.61–2).[55]

The promoters scene in *Chaste Maid*, more biting than the searchers episode in Greene's *A Looking Glass for London and England* (1594), Act 5, Scene 4, satirizes iniquities revealed by Lenten bans. The promoters, whom Allwit calls 'rich men's dogs' (2.2.55), turn a blind eye when Master Beggarland's servant smuggles out meat, since the merchant had 'purchas'd the whole Lent together' by bribing them on Ash Wednesday (2.2.125–6). They are finally saddled with Touchwood Sr.'s bastard when the Country Wench tricks them into confiscating the basket, hiding the baby under a loin of mutton. Entering the scene as 'ravenous creditors' (2.2.59), they end up looking as silly as the two knights, holding someone else's baby and paying someone else's bills.

The promoters episode topicalizes the play's vision of power as carnal rule. Lent might be assumed to have depressed those who could afford appetites more than those who could not. John Taylor's *Jack A*

[53] See Gail Paster, 'Leaky Vessels: The Incontinent Women of City Comedy', *RD* 18 (1987), 59–60.
[54] See Parker (ed.), *Chaste Maid*, pp. xxx–xxxi, 138–40.
[55] On the date, see Giorgio Melchiori (ed.), *The Insatiate Countess*, Revels Plays (Manchester, 1984), 16–17.

Lent (1630) alleges that 'through the royal court, the inns of courts, the city and country, all the better sort wear mourning black as long as *Lent* is in town'.[56] Middleton's play, however, shows 'religious wholesome laws' (2.1.112) as instrumental in defining the very privilege they were meant to suspend.[57] For the Beggarlands, the carnival never stops; for country wenches, survival the year round depends on the 'politic' (2.2.146) remedies of wit.

The Lenten–Easter season provides a wider allusive framework. The three leading themes of the Lenten liturgy, baptism, penance, and the passion, may be seen to correspond to the Allwit-christening, the penitence of Sir Walter, and the mock-deaths of the lovers, while the final resurrection and wedding coincide with the Easter celebrations. The spiritual significance of all three are desecrated.[58] The sire acts the godfather to avoid a scandal at the christening—one of Middleton's masterly ensemble scenes.[59] The gossips, all Puritans opposed to Lenten superstition, wolf phallic sweetmeats, get drunk, and queue up to kiss Tim. Sacramental water issues in slobbering kisses, spilt wine, and wetting under the stools before the women stagger off to the Pissing Conduit.[60] Lancelot Andrewes's 1619 Ash Wednesday sermon prayed 'that He which *turneth* the *flint stone* into a *springing well*, would vouchsafe us (even as dry as *flints*) *gratiam lachrymarum*', tears appropriate to the season of repentance.[61] In *Chaste Maid*, it is Touchwood Sr.'s semen which waters the barrenness of Kix, a name meaning dry stalk.[62] The repentance of Sir Walter ('water horehound' is a plant growing in ditches and moist soil[63]) seems to promise a genuine

---

[56] *Works of John Taylor, the Water Poet*, ed. Charles Hindley (London, 1876), *Jack A Lent*, 18.

[57] Cf. 'And this indeed is another end and fruit of Fasting, to make us more able and more willing to relieve those in necessity.' — *The Holy Fast of Lent Defended against All its Prophaners* (1677), G1. Weatherwise's zodiacal banquet in *No Wit* has his starving tenants stand in for fasting days, 'Or the six weeks in Lent' (2.1.96–8).

[58] See Rowe, *Middleton and the New Comedy Tradition*, 134–46.

[59] The scene is in the tradition of 'caquets' discussed by Mikhail Bakhtin in *Rabelais and his World*, trans. Hélène Iswolsky (Cambridge, Mass., 1968), 105–6. Bullen, v. 56 n., and Parker (ed.), *Chaste Maid*, p. xxxviii, suggest possible sources.

[60] On the flesh and water imagery, see Ruby Chatterji, 'Theme, Imagery, and Unity in *A Chaste Maid in Cheapside*', *RD* 8 (1965), 120–5; and Rowe, *Middleton and the New Comedy Tradition*, 130–52.

[61] Lancelot Andrewes, *Sermons*, ed. G. M. Story (Oxford, 1967), 137.

[62] 'Kix' or 'kex' was also a name for the cicuta, a medicinal plant used for swellings of the breasts and genitals. See E. J. Devereux, 'The Naming of Sir Oliver Kix', *N & Q* 232 (1987), 297–8.

[63] See G. B. Shand, 'The Naming of Sir Walter Whorehound', *N & Q* 227 (1982), 136–7.

spiritual rebirth. When the sergeants come to arrest him for killing Touchwood Jr. and Allwit gives him the parting kick, Sir Walter exclaims, 'O death! Do I hear this with part | Of former life in me?' (5.1.128–9). The recoil from his past sins looks like the spiritual 'turning' Andrewes explained in his great Ash Wednesday sermon.[64] But Sir Walter's contrition coincides with his disinheritance, and his confession is also that of a gamester's bankruptcy (cf. 5.1.148–9). The only character who turns to a spiritual order of values ends up in the knight's ward, while the Allwits flounce off to the Strand to take up new lodgings and the Yellowhammers are saved from marrying their daughter to a bankrupt. A very different drama of death and resurrection is played by Moll and Touchwood Jr. While it mimes the miraculous deliverance of Eastertide plays such as *The Winter's Tale*,[65] their scheme profits at the same time from the birth of a bastard in the Kix household. Middleton later wrote his own version of the battle of Carnival and Lent in the Plumporridge–Fasting Day match in *The Masque of Heroes* (1619).[66] *Chaste Maid* does not side with either Plumporridge or Fasting Day. It explores instead the social and secular realities of appetite and prohibition.

The secular stress is evident in the allusions to butchers and fishmongers, the combatants in the 'uncivil civil commotions' of Taylor's *Jack A Lent*.[67] Lenten injunctions since Edward VI's reign had served the interests of the fish trade.[68] The flesh and fish images of *Chaste Maid* suggest an indifferent carnal economics governing the supporters and enemies of Lent. Allwit sells his wife as butchers sell flesh and poulters conies (4.1.216–17); Sir Walter brings his 'ewe-mutton to find | A ram at London' (1.1.135–6); Touchwood Sr. keeps a few gulls 'in pickle' to take chewed country 'mutton' off his plate (2.1.81–2); Tim kisses his bride-to-be to taste the delights of 'Welsh mutton' (4.1.146); the promoters 'lard their whores with lamb-stones' (2.2.64); the Country Wench dumps her 'half yard of flesh' (2.1.84) under 'A good fat loin of mutton' (2.2.149). On the other hand, when Moll tries escaping by

---

[64] Andrewes, *Sermons*, 122–3.

[65] See R. Chris Hassel, Jr., *Renaissance Drama and the English Church Year* (Lincoln, Neb., 1979), 140–55.

[66] See ibid. 107–9.

[67] Taylor, *Jack A Lent*, 9. See also Nashe, *Lenten Stuffe* (1594), in McKerrow (ed.), *Works*, iii. 183–4. The economic causes of the conflict are discussed in Michael D. Bristol, *Carnival and Theater: Plebeian Culture and the Structure of Authority in Renaissance England* (New York, 1985), 72–7.

[68] See S. C. Carpenter, *The Church in England 597–1688* (London, 1954), 259.

water, her mother goes 'a-fishing for her' on a smelt boat (4.4.16), and brings back what Tim describes as a 'mermaid', 'She's half my sister now, as far as flesh goes, | The rest may be sold to fishwives' (4.4.26–8). The image of the mermaid, one of the period's many names for a prostitute, turns the chaste maid into Cheapside's oxymoronic buy of the season, composed of the equally vendible halves of flesh and fish.

The social reality behind Lenten austerity is sharply localized by a risky allusion. The Privy Council's order tightening Lent prohibitions was issued on 5 February 1613.[69] On the previous day, John Chamberlain informed Alice Carleton of the birth of the Countess of Salisbury's daughter and of the lavish expenses on her childbed, 'for the hanging of her chamber, being white satin, embroidered with gold (or silver) and perle is valued at fowreteen thousand pounds'.[70] Middleton was quick to seize the satiric opportunity provided by the coincidence. Allwit says that 'A lady lies not in', like his wife, thanks to Sir Walter's absurd expenses on

> her embossings,
> Embroid'rings, spanglings, and I know not what,
> As if she lay with all the gaudy-shops
> In Gresham's Burse about her . . . (1. 2. 31-4)

'See, gossip, and she lies not in like a countess,' marvels an envious guest at the christening (3.2.89). Allwit calls the baby a 'little countess' (2.2.25), and, before moving to the Strand, he reckons he has furniture enough to 'lodge a countess' (5.1.162).

History has repeatedly borne out Petrarch's maxim that people are driven to despair 'more from a lack of foodstuffs than from a deficiency in moral qualities',[71] and the Salisbury allusion confirms that in Cheapside too, the colon is the register of social privilege and privation. As Allwit asks the promoters, 'What cares colon here for Lent?' (2.2.79). For Mrs Touchwood, all year is Lent; for Mrs Allwit, all year is carnival. Donne explained the spiritual paradox of Lent and Easter as the presence of the redemptive feast in the penitential fast.[72] As far as

---

[69] *CSP Dom. James I 1611–1618*, 169; and Parker (ed.) *Chaste Maid*, 139.

[70] Norbert Egbert McClure (ed.), *The Letters of John Chamberlain*, 2 vols. (Philadelphia, 1939), i. 415–16.

[71] Francesco Petrarca, 'How a Ruler ought to Govern his State', trans. Benjamin G. Kohl, in Benjamin G. Kohl *et al.* (eds.), *The Earthly Republic: Italian Humanists on Government and Society* (Manchester, 1978), 56.

[72] Evelyn M. Simpson and George R. Potter (eds.), *The Sermons of John Donne*, 10 vols. (Berkeley, Calif., 1953–62), vii. 73.

its enforced observance in Jacobean London is concerned, the cheer of
Lent is experienced only in the power confirmed by privileged indulgence, self-denial being a token of dispossession, suffered 'for the profit
of purse, back, and belly' (*Heroes*, l. 141).

Sexual negotiations map out the division of power between gentry and
citizenry in *Chaste Maid*. The division highlights collusion rather than
conflict. As sex and money blur distinctions, court, city, and country
begin to seem ruses of rhetorical codes, held in place by linguistic
policing. Yellowhammer is annoyed at words his gadding wife has
fetched from Westminster, and expressions such as 'Honour' and
'faithful servant', which Sir Walter lavishes on his daughter, 'sound too
high for the daughters of the freedom' (1.1.26–7, 122–3). Sir Walter
has no need for such eloquence with his Welsh mistress, and finds it
'unnatural' that he should lie with her so often and leave her 'without
English' (1.1.98–9). Yellowhammer's 'plain, sufficient, subsidy words'
(1.1.125) are not, however, prescribed for his son, who sends letters in
hideous Latin from Cambridge to be conveniently mistranslated by his
mother and the porter. His mother's lawyer cousin cannot help with
the letter since the Inns of Court 'are all for French'. Nor can her
puritanical parson, who 'calls Latin "papistry" ' (1.1.89–91). The fit
match for the Latin-speaking Tim, nevertheless, is the Welsh-speaking
whore. In the brief encounter of the anointed and the outlawed of the
language kingdom,[73] Tim takes her Welsh for the chastest Hebrew,
and she takes his Latin for smut. Each is relieved to find that the other
speaks English, and Tim is quick to taste her native country in another
tongue: 'One may discover her country by her kissing' (4.1.144). At
the end of the play, when Tim sets about proving the whore honest by
logic, he finds that ethical translation is easy once the subterfuge of
language is deciphered. Comic nemesis teaches him to read 'meretrix'
as 'merry tricks':

> I perceive then a woman may be honest
> According to the English print, when she is
> A whore in Latin; so much for marriage and logic!(5.4.108-10)

In the rare comedy he chose to write in verse, Middleton playfully
foregrounds the class codes of the stage. The device upsets the false

---

[73] Welsh was outlawed by Henry VIII in 1535; see Glanmore Williams, *Recovery Reorien-
tation and Reformation: Wales c.1415–1642* (Oxford, 1987), 259–78.

hierarchies which use rhetorical decorum to maintain divisions, just as the gossips use the social rating of their husbands' trades in their jostle for precedence at the christening (cf. 2.4).[74] There are, the devil taught the bawd in *Black Book*, 'knaves of all languages' just as there are 'harlots of all trades': 'Knowest thou not that sin may be committed either in French, Dutch, Italian or Spanish, and all after the English fashion?' (Bullen, viii. 22).

The devil knows best since, as Malevole tells Ferrardo in *Malcontent*, he is the best linguist of the age and a great traveller (1.3.28–33). Allwit inherits some of the sinister vitality of Lucifer in *Black Book*, a non-dramatic text which provided Middleton with a structural clue for reconciling moral sarcasm and buffoonery in the satiric presenter on the stage. The play has a more complex ironic texture than the satire, and its London is different from Lucifer's. Paster reminds us that there is a city in it which spreads beyond Cheapside, populated by the servants who scorn Allwit, the nameless neighbours who would hate the Yellowhammers for sending their daughter to her death (cf. 5.2.92–3), and the watermen who tell Maudlin bluntly that she is a cruel mother (cf. 4.4.20, 51–3).[75] This ambient chorus of folk judgement restricts Allwit's diabolical mediation, and makes it necessary that the mocking legacy of vices bequeathed by Lucifer (and later by Kersmas in *Heroes*) should be turned into a bitter legacy of curses left behind by a repentant Sir Walter.

The judgement of servants and watermen in *Chaste Maid* also connects graft and power in a way *Black Book* could not. Reflection on the proportion of power to improbity was encouraged in 1613 by salacious court rumours. The idea of the blasé wittol may have come from the eighth epigram in the sixth chapter of Thomas Campion's *Observations in the Art of English Poesie* (1602). The type was familiar in popular literature, and Purge in *Family* and Sophonirus in *Lady* are earlier instances in Middleton.[76] There was, however, a more topical

---

[74] On the dissolving of linguistic hierarchies on the English stage, see Mullaney, *Place of the Stage*, 76–85.

[75] See Paster, *Idea of the City*, 170–3.

[76] See E. L. Buckingham, 'Campion's *Art of English Poesie* and Middleton's *Chaste Maid in Cheapside*', *PMLA* 43 (1928), 784–92; Bald, 'Sources of Middleton's City Comedies', 375–7; Allan H. Gilbert, 'The Prosperous Wittol in Giovanni Battista Modio and Thomas Middleton', *SP* 41 (1944), 235–7; and Shanti Padhi, 'Middleton's Wittol in *A Chaste Maid* and *Guzman de Alfarache*', *N & Q* 229 (1984), 234–6. For another example from popular literature, see the ballad 'Who would not be a cuckold', in Hyder E. Rollins (ed.), *Old English Ballads 1553–1625: Chiefly From Manuscripts* (Cambridge, 1920), 196–7.

example of marriage being turned into a market venture, and public shame into private profit. In Allwit's reference to 'the foreman of a drug-shop' (1.2.35–6), the Revels Plays editor suspects an allusion to Simon Forman, the astrologer who sold love philtres. In 1613, Forman (d. 1611) might already have been figuring in the rumours surrounding the Essex–Frances divorce trial, to which Middleton later alludes extensively in *The Witch* and *Changeling*.[77] The divorce was granted under royal pressure in September 1613. Within three months, Frances, dressed as a virgin, married the king's favourite, Robert Carr. The ground of the divorce had been non-consummation, for Essex was reported impotent only with his wife. It was witchcraft which allegedly secured Essex's exclusive unmanning. At the Overbury murder trial in 1615, it was revealed that Forman was Frances's occult consultant. The allusion in *Chaste Maid* gives reason for suspecting that Forman's involvement was rumoured early in 1613. The Kix situation, with its talk of impotence, drug, divorce, and Lady Kix's court past might then be a sly hint at the Essex–Frances–Carr affair.

A clue in the scandal which leads to an analogue of the Allwit ménage has gone unnoticed. Anne, the go-between in Frances's dealings with Forman, was married to George Turner, but had a lover in Sir Arthur Manwaring. George was a *mari complaisant*, and an unusual one. When he died in 1610, he appointed Sir Arthur overseer of his will, leaving £10 'to make him a ring with this posey *Fates junguntur Amantes*'.[78] It is tempting to suppose that Middleton knew of this black posthumous joke, superior as satire to the wedding-ring 'posy' Touchwood Jr. orders from his bride's unsuspecting father (cf. 1.1.188–91).

The episode illustrates the desperate Allwitian humour needed to play the satirist in Jacobean court and city, to survive their iniquities, and even profit from them. George Turner showed his competence at translating 'meretrix' into 'merry tricks', and is, therefore, an exemplar of the Allwitian antithesis to Moll Cutpurse in the Jacobean dialectic of mirth. Contemporary authority declared merry Moll meretricious; judging by the Essex affair, it would have found Allwit gifted with the humour of a political survivor.

---

[77] Bromham, 'Date of *Witch*', 149–52, and Lancashire, '*Witch*: Stage Flop or Political Mistake?', in Friedenreich (ed.), '*Accompaninge the Players*', 164–8, argue that these scandals were topical in 1613.

[78] See A. L. Rowse, *Sex and Society in Shakespeare's Age: Simon Forman the Astrologer* (New York, 1974), 256–7.

5

The Court and the Populace:
Tragicomedy and Comitragedy

Middleton's major comedies and tragedies appeared to Eliot 'as if written by two different men'.[1] Eliot's critics tend to read Middleton's 'Fletcherian' plays as the missing link between them, making the tragicomedies the worst casualties of the three-period thesis. 'The great shift in Middleton's work is from comedy to tragicomedy and tragedy,' wrote Schoenbaum, 'from the exploitation of intrigue to the interpretation of motive.'[2] The truth is that Middleton tried the tragicomic vein as early as in *Phoenix*, that such an ingenious exploitation of intrigue as *Chaste Maid* followed his first experiment with tragicomedy, that *Timon*, *Yorkshire*, and *Revenger* were earlier tragedies which handled complex psychological situations, and that he wrote citizen comedies like *Wit at Several Weapons* (1613; with Rowley), and *Anything for a Quiet Life* (1621; with Webster) till fairly late in his career.

No Wit, No Help Like a Woman's (1611), an early play to try out the Fletcherian formula, hardly shows much concern for convincing motives.[3] The romance plot, which wards off the threat of incest by a timely disclosure of cradle-switching, is derived from della Porta's *La Sorella*,[4] and welded to an intrigue involving widow-hunting, usury, and cross-dressing. In both plots, crisis is averted by incredible turnabouts. In the first, a mother sides with the son who had declared her dead after blowing her ransom money on a girl in Antwerp. In the second, a usurer's widow lusts after the cross-dressed Kate, who uses a gallant's disguise to reclaim the estate the late usurer had extorted from

---

[1] Eliot, *Selected Essays*, 162.

[2] Samuel Schoenbaum, 'Middleton's Tragicomedies', *MP* 54 (1956), 19. See also Farr, *Middleton and the Drama of Realism*, 5–7.

[3] Mark Eccles, 'Middleton's Comedy *The Almanac, or No Wit, No Help like a Woman's*', *N & Q* 232 (1987), 296–7, identifies the play with the 'lost' *Almanac*, acted by Prince Henry's Men at the Fortune in 1611. See also David George, 'Weather-Wise's Almanac and the Date of Middleton's *No Wit No Help Like a Woman's*', *N & Q* 211 (1966), 297–301; and John Jowett, 'Middleton's *No Wit* at the Fortune', *RD* 22 (1991), 191–208.

[4] See D. J. Gordon, 'Middleton's *No Wit, No Help Like a Woman's* and Della Porta's *La Sorella*', *RES* 17 (1941), 400–14.

her husband. When the hoax is disclosed, the widow settles for Kate's brother.

A large dose of bawdy is infused into della Porta's story, and the exchange value of sex is repeatedly stressed.[5] The city-comedy material seeks collision rather than compromise with the conventions of romance, and the lesson seems to be that New Comedy and tragicomic romance both need to suppress the moral cost of its rescue-swerves.[6] Economic and poetic justice depends in the play on Kate's success in luring her brother and the rich widow into forbidden sex. A suitor is willing to give up the widow for 'a male companion' (2.1.180–3), and the hero fears he has made his sister pregnant. As the happy ending is coerced by the morally dubious application of generic formulas, a character is made to marvel: 'Here's unity forever strangely wrought!' (5.1.371).

Psychologizing approaches miss the crucial point of Middleton's departure from the Fletcherian recipe in plays such as *No Wit*. In Fletcher's tragicomedies Herbert Blau has noticed 'a structure of *unmotivatedness*', designed to gratify desire 'at almost any dramaturgical cost'. The technique, says Blau, masks the operation of civil and personal force, and deflects it into a code of honour.[7] Middleton's method of subjecting romance conventions to the behavioural mechanics of city comedy has the contrary effect of foregrounding the reality of coercion and power.

A major theme of Renaissance tragicomedies was the illustration of right rule for the self and the polity.[8] The Fletcherian version addressed this signature theme through its routine duels of tyrannical lust and resolute chastity.[9] Middleton's 'Fletcherian' plots also pit power and illicit desire against resistant virtue, and their shock disclosures and reformations seem to restore right personal and political rule. But the patriarchal fantasies of love and voluntary subjection which replace the

---

[5] See Raymond Lepage, 'A Study in Dramatic Transposition and Invention: Della Porta's *La Sorella*, Rotrou's *La Sœur*, and Middleton's *No Wit, No Help Like a Woman's*', *Comparative Literature Studies*, 24 (1987), 344.

[6] See Rowe, *Middleton and the New Comedy Tradition*, 114–30.

[7] Herbert Blau, 'The Absolved Riddle: Sovereign Pleasure and the Baroque Subject in the Tragicomedies of John Fletcher', *NLH* 17 (1986), 549–52.

[8] See James J. Yoch, 'The Renaissance Dramatization of Temperance: The Italian Revival of Tragicomedy and *The Faithful Shepherdess*', in Nancy Klein Maguire (ed.), *Renaissance Tragicomedy: Explorations in Genre and Politics* (New York, 1987), 115–38.

[9] See Robert Y. Turner, 'Responses to Tyranny in John Fletcher's Plays', *MRDE* 4 (1989), 123–41; and Philip J. Finkelpearl, *Court and Country Politics in the Plays of Beaumont and Fletcher* (Princeton, NJ, 1990), 6–7.

threatened violence turn out to be instrumental in reinforcing the privilege of force. The effect is achieved by placing tragicomic conventions inside historical and structural contexts which show their illogical fantasies to be circumscribed by the logic of power.

MISRULE AND MAGIC: *The Witch*

The King's Men played *The Witch* (1613) in the wake of the Essex-divorce scandal. Sebastian returns in the play after three years' war service to find that 'Another has possession' (1.1.6) of his contracted bride Isabella, quite as the Earl of Essex returned from abroad in 1609 to find his wife the mistress of Carr.[10] Essex's jinxed impotence with his wife is paralleled in the play by the bewitched Antonio's incapacity for sex with Isabella, whom he has married after falsely declaring Sebastian dead. A disguised Sebastian secures the charm with Hecate's help, and Isabella's virginity is preserved until she is restored to him.

The story is flanked by two other sexual intrigues. In the one derived from Machiavelli's *History of Florence*,[11] the Duchess pledges sexual favours to Almachildes if he will kill her husband, who had forced her to drink out of her father's skull. In the other, Antonio's sister Francisca is made pregnant by Aberzanes, a courtier who manages to have the bastard delivered and palmed off. The kindness of hired killers saves the delinquents in both plots for last-minute reformations.

The Duke sexualizes conquest and tyranny by marrying the beaten enemy's daughter, and then forcing her to commit symbolic parricide. Although the Duchess tries to get her own back, the play drops the political possibilities of the tyrant-revenger contest. Instead, the focus shifts to the Duchess's scheme to allure, use, and then kill Almachildes.

The shift reflects the complicity of sex, blackmail, and political misrule glimpsed in the Essex case. Francisca and the Duchess share the attributes of the real-life Countess, and the Duchess's seduction and blackmail of Almachildes anticipate the reasoning of Beatrice-Joanna. So does her willingness to confess to murder but not adultery (cf. 5.3.102–3). In a more general way, *Witch* foreshadows *Changeling* in

---

[10] See Beatrice White, *Cast of Ravens: The Strange Case of Thomas Overbury* (London, 1965), 29–30.
[11] See Bullen, v. 353–4.

attacking the sexual exercise of irresponsible privilege. 'Your best folks will be merry,' says Amoretta, the Duchess's waiting woman. They 'do what they list', yet never put their 'reputation' on the line (2.2.130–2).

Details of Frances's recourse to Simon Forman came to light in the Overbury murder trial of 1615–16. Witchcraft, however, was already topical during the divorce trial.[12] Middleton, in any case, could have drawn on other rumours. The Countess of Essex was not Forman's only high-powered client. Her cousin Frances Parnell, for example, sought his help in bewitching the Earl of Southampton.[13] Frances's case was backed by the king, and it must have appeared a pointed instance of royal duplicity. Only a year before, witch trials in Lancaster and Northampton had led to fifteen executions, and there were at least twenty more between 1603 and 1616.[14] Witches, Reginald Scot alleged in *The Discoverie of Witchcraft* (1584), were mostly 'poore women (whose cheefe fault is that they are scolds)', and they were charged with incredibly 'ridiculous or abhominable crimes'.[15] James's own *Daemonologie* (1597) was partly an answer to Scot's book, all copies of which he had destroyed on becoming English king.[16] Middleton relied on Scot for his witches' scenes, and the choice may have had its political point at a time when the Essex affair and the witch trials had made witchcraft a sensitive and marketable issue.[17]

Lamb thought the witches in the play able only to hurt the body, while those in *Macbeth* had power over the soul.[18] That the Folio text of *Macbeth* is partly an adaptation by Middleton could not have been known to him.[19] In any case, the relative infirmity of Middleton's hags serves an important dramatic function. All who resort to Hecate in the

[12] See Bromham, 'Date of *Witch*', 149–52; and Lancashire, '*Witch*: Stage Flop or Political Mistake?', in Friedenreich (ed.), '*Accomaninge the Players*', 161–81.

[13] See Rowse, *Sex and Society*, 257. See also Keith Thomas, *Religion and the Decline of Magic: Studies in Popular Beliefs in Sixteenth and Seventeenth Century England* (London, 1971), 319–20.

[14] See *The Witches of Northamptonshire* (1612), and Thomas Potts, *The Wonderfull Discoverie of Witches in the Countie of Lancaster* (1613), repr. in Barbara Rosen (ed.), *Witchcraft* (London, 1969), 344–68. See also Thomas, *Religion and the Decline of Magic*, 449–54.

[15] Reginald Scot, *The Discoverie of Witchcraft*, ed. Brinsley Nicholson (London, 1886), 26.

[16] See Anthony Harris, *Night's Black Agents: Witchcraft and Magic in Seventeenth-Century English Drama* (Manchester, 1980), 15–16.

[17] On the commercial motivation, see W. J. Lawrence, *Shakespeare's Workshop* (Oxford, 1928), 24–38. For occult sources other than Scot, see Gareth Roberts, 'A Re-examination of the Sources of the Magical Material in Middleton's *The Witch*', *N & Q* 221 (1976), 216–19.

[18] Charles Lamb, *Specimens of English Dramatic Poets who Lived about the Time of Shakespeare* (1808; London, 1854), 152.

[19] See Wells and Taylor, *Textual Companion*, 128–9.

play do so with their minds made up.[20] Hecate does not influence their choices, and her spells illustrate their prior surrender of moral control. Her clients appear like the drunkard ready 'to reel to the devil' (1.2.232–3), or like the sleepwalker driven against 'religious knowledge' (1.2.111, 114–15). Amoretta's comic oscillation in Act 2, Scene 2 between love and loathing as the magic ribbon pops in and out of her bosom is thus not much different from Antonio's violent moodswings in Act 5, Scene 1. The text's quick-change melodrama extends this play of automatism, and hardens the impression of a court enslaved to appetite.

The witches, on the other hand, are caricatures of the humans. Firestone is a clown, and Hecate's motherly complaint echoes Falso's avuncular one (cf. *Phoenix*, 2.3.68–9): 'You had rather hunt after strange women still | Than lie with your own mothers' (1.2.100–1). Sebastian finds hell and a whore 'partners . . . In one ambition' (4.2.54–5). The partnership domesticates the demonic, and governs the emphasis which Middleton, following Marston's example in *Sophonisba* (1604–6), places on the witches' lechery. This focus enables him to turn the witch scenes into a grotesque shadow of corruption in high places, comparable to the use of pornography for political satire in the modern cinema.

Anti-familial sex makes Hecate's reign the antithesis of paternalist rule. If the true prince was a 'likeness of divinity',[21] the tyrant was a likeness of the devil. The contrasts frame the context in which James's views on demonology could serve his political agenda.[22] Just as Hecate was a pattern of misrule, the Jacobean witch, having left Church and State for the devil, was an example of 'the traytor, who is an enemie to the State, and rebelleth against his lawfull Prince'.[23] When Vindice called his *alter ego* Piato a 'witch' in *Revenger* (5.3.118), he was playing off this political sense of the word against those denoting necromancer and pimp.[24]

---

[20] See Harris, *Night's Black Agents*, 83.

[21] John of Salisbury, *The Statesman's Book of John of Salisbury*, trans. John Dickinson (New York, 1927), 335.

[22] See Stuart Clark, 'King James's *Daemonologie*: Witchcraft and Kingship', in Sydney Anglo (ed.), *The Damned Art: Essays in the Literature of Witchcraft* (London, 1977), 156–81.

[23] William Perkins, *A Discourse of the Damned Art of Witchcraft* (Cambridge, 1608), Q4^v.

[24] For other interpretations, see Stephen Wigler, ' "Tis Well He Died: He Was a Witch": A Note on *The Revenger's Tragedy*, V.iii.17', *ELN* 14 (1976), 17–20; and Scott McMillin, 'Acting and Violence: *The Revenger's Tragedy* and its Departures from *Hamlet*', *SEL* 24 (1984), 286.

Witchcraft, carrying the double metaphorical charge of tyranny and treason, was sure to have been a touchy political issue when its involvement in the Essex divorce was being rumoured. James argued the admissibility of *propter maleficium versus hanc* as a ground for annulment against a sceptical Archbishop Abbot.[25] Subjects were free to read in this learned intervention an unprincipled sanction of the Countess's affair with the royal favourite. Hecate in the play 'cannot disjoin wedlock' which is 'of heaven's fastening' (1.2.172–3), but James was seen permitting sorcery to do precisely that. Insistence on the celestial ordinance and indissolubility of wedlock (cf. 4.2.8–11, 5.1.66–8) could be, under the circumstances, a way of questioning the king's claim of divine lieutenancy. The play's blend of Machiavelli and the occult is thus an instance of Middleton's socially engaged opportunism which could turn palace gossip into political fable.

HONOUR AND PRIVILEGE: *The Nice Valour* and *A Fair Quarrel*

'Possession' and 'reputation' brace the power of the 'best folks' in *Witch* (1.1.6, 2.2.130–1). Ideally, status was justified by virtue. In practice, its 'possession' and the 'reputation' for virtue relied on unequal access to force. The chivalric rationale of privilege never rid itself of the contradiction, expressed repeatedly in the competing notions of 'honour' as essence and form, legacy and acquisition, spiritual merit and physical prowess.[26]

The problem of duelling gave the conflict a spectacular form in early modern England. As V. G. Kiernan has shown, the duel was a self-imposed test by which the élite sought to prove its feudal inheritance and class rights, which otherwise rested insecurely on birth and wealth.[27] While its apology thus meant to erase the anomaly between native and acquired honour, duelling itself was becoming an anachronism. Stuart absolutism could not brook the feudal right to private warfare, nor could the Church condone the pagan ethics of trial by

[25] T. B. Howell and T. J. Howell (eds.), *A Complete Collection of State Trials*, 33 vols. (London, 1809–26), ii. 798–802.

[26] On the *topos*, see E. R. Curtius, *European Literature and the Latin Middle Ages*, trans. W. R. Trask (London, 1953), 179–80. On the theme in contemporary society, see Mervyn James, *Society, Politics and Culture: Studies in Early Modern England* (Cambridge, 1986), 308–415.

[27] See V. G. Kiernan, *The Duel in European History: Honour and the Reign of Aristocracy* (Oxford, 1986), 164.

combat. State and Church pooled resources to stamp out the menace in the early years of James's reign, when, according to Hume, there were more duels fought 'than at any other time before or since'.[28] The streets, wrote Arthur Wilson, 'swarm Night and Day with bloody Quarrels; private Duels fomented, especially betwixt the English and Scots'.[29] A few duels made news. In 1610, Sir Thomas Dutton quit his command under Sir Hatton Cheek in the Netherlands, and killed him in a duel in Calais. In 1612, two of James's favourites, Sir James Stewart and Sir George Wharton, killed each other in Islington.[30] In a single letter to Sir Dudley Carleton dated 9 September 1613, John Chamberlain reported the actual or threatened duels between Edward Sackville and Lord Bruse, Lord Norris and Sir Peregrine Willoughby, Lord Chandos and Lord Hay, the Earl of Rutland and Lord Davers, and, a few days before the end of his divorce trial, the Earl of Essex and his brother-in-law Henry Howard.[31] While the State reacted in 1614 with the 'Proclamation against Private Challenges and Combats' and with a Star Chamber censure the following year, clergymen inveighed against duelling as the sin of Cain, 'the first duellist'.[32]

In 1615–16, Middleton wrote two tragicomic scripts with sharply divergent attitudes to duelling. *The Nice Valour* alludes to a recent incident in which John Gibb left royal service after being kicked by the king. James later apologized to Gibb, just as the Duke in the play does to Shamont, the courtier whom he had switched in the face. The play defines the limits of princely authority when the Duke dooms himself 'most strictly | To Justice' (4.1.85–6).

Shamont's touchiness about 'honour', though excessive, is nobler than the creed of Lapet, the courtier who writes an anti-duelling pamphlet to prove that kicks may be suffered without indignity. The Duke later dismisses Lapet because he does not deserve the name of a gentleman. Lapet may be an attack on peers such as the Earl of Northampton, who wrote to Sir Thomas Lake in November 1613 that

[28] David Hume, *The History of England from the Invasion of Julius Caesar to the Revolution in 1688*, abridged & ed. Rodney W. Kilcup (Chicago, 1975), 220.

[29] Wilson, *Life and Reign of James*, in [Kennett], *Complete History of England*, ii. 5R1ᵛ.

[30] See ibid. ii. 5S2ᵛ; and Kiernan, *Duel in European History*, 82.

[31] McClure (ed.), *Letters of John Chamberlain*, i. 474–5.

[32] See ibid. i. 509; and John Hales, 'Of Duels', in John Chandos (ed.), *In God's Name: Examples of Preaching in England from the Act of Supremacy to the Act of Uniformity* (London, 1971), 212.

he had an anti-duelling treatise ready and would launch it as soon as the king's proclamation against duels was out.[33]

The play's attitude to duelling is ambiguous even within the Beaumont and Fletcher canon, where it has been traditionally placed.[34] The problem may owe something to revision.[35] There was an earlier incident, probably from 1607, in which Philip Herbert was reportedly showered with titles by the king for not standing up to a Scotsman named Ramsay who had switched him on the face.[36] An earlier Fletcher text might have dramatized the incident, and Middleton would have found reflections on the limits of royal authority safer when the king's exemplary behaviour with Gibb allowed the conversion of criticism into compliment.

A Fair Quarrel, again, is a play on 'honour', but it holds duelling machismo inferior to Christian fortitude. Captain Ager's native honour is slandered when his friend, the Colonel, calls him 'son of a whore' (1.1.346). Ager, following the moral course advised in the duelling manuals,[37] decides to check with his mother. Lady Ager is outraged at the insult, but later admits to the false charge to save her son from a duel. When Ager cries off, the Colonel calls him a coward, and this offers Ager a just cause. He wins the duel, and a repentant Colonel wills his sister to Ager in restitution.

The Colonel at the start stands upon rank and reputation, while Ager dismisses these 'titular shadows' and seeks to measure 'uncompounded' man by merit alone (1.1.80–3). But the Colonel's slander has Ager's sincerity trapped inside the self-contradiction of chivalry. He cannot stomach the insult since the loss of 'honor naturall', that which 'man bringeth . . . from his mother's womb',[38] means that acquired honours are lost with it. Since status is dependent on birth, 'honour' in

---

[33] *CSP Dom. James I 1611–1618*, 208.

[34] See Baldwin Maxwell, *Studies in Beaumont, Fletcher, and Massinger* (Chapel Hill, NC, 1939), 94–5, 125–6.

[35] On the possibility of revision, see E. H. C. Oliphant, *The Plays of Beaumont and Fletcher: An Attempt to Determine their Respective Shares and the Shares of Others* (New Haven, Conn., 1927), 449–50; Cyrus Hoy, 'The Shares of Fletcher and his Collaborators in the Beaumont and Fletcher Canon (V)', *SB* 13 (1960), 92–6; Lake, *Canon*, 192–7; and Jackson, *Studies in Attribution*, 139–42.

[36] See Francis Osborne, *Historical Memoirs of the Reigns of Elizabeth and King James* (1658), repr. in Walter Scott (ed.), *Secret History of the Court of James the First*, 2 vols. (Edinburgh, 1811), i. 218–21.

[37] *Vincentio Saviolo his Practise* (1595), 2C1^v, advises 'euerie one that thought his quarrell vniust, not to take it vppon him, and rather than fight against a truth, make full satisfaction to the iniuried'.

[38] Haniball Romei, *The Courtiers Academie*, trans. I[ohn] K[epers] (1598), L4–4^v.

Ager's society can never quite reward the merit of 'uncompounded' man.

Ager's regard for native honour, however scrupulous, is questioned by the stoic fortitude of Jane and Fitzallen, whose love is obstructed in the sub-plot by Jane's merchant father. The autonomy of the spirit Fitzallen displays under physical captivity Middleton echoes in *The Peacemaker* (1618), an anti-duelling pamphlet derived from *The Charge of Sir Francis Bacon Knight . . . touching Duells* (1614).[39] The pamphlet argues that a wise man is indifferent to flattery and slander, 'For reputation is but another man's opinion, and opinion is no substance for thee to consist of' (Bullen, viii. 340). The passage recalls Ager's dismissal of 'titular shadows, | Which add no substance to the men themselves' (1.1.80–1). Inner worth and reputation cannot be simultaneous determinants of honour, and Ager can be loyal to the professed values of the duelling code only by rejecting its injunctions.

The paradox forces Ager to do the right thing for the wrong reasons. His reluctance to fight seeks out, among other pretexts, the stoical wisdom of *Peacemaker*. In the duelling scene, he wonders why a man should risk his soul to avenge 'a poor hasty syllable or two' (3. 1. 82). Later, as he takes up his sword with relief on being called a coward, he is unwittingly, within the confines of chivalric values, doing the right thing, since the charge of cowardice challenges merit while that of bastardy questions birth. For less cerebral adherents of the duelling ethics, Ager's decision inverts the order of priorities: 'Impossible: coward do more than bastard? . . . Is coward a more stirring meat than bastard, my masters?' (3.1.118, 158).

To Ager's friends, war is the court 'Where all cases of manhood are determined' (3.1.7). Manhood of a different order triumphs in the Colonel's repentance, which turns his defeat into a 'happy conquest' in the Christian 'war' for the soul (4.2.48, 50). Ager, therefore, is not the exemplar of the ethical core of the duelling code, nor is he the Colonel's partner in illustrating its superficialities.[40] His honesty is

---

[39] See R. Dunlap, 'James I, Bacon, Middleton, and the Making of *The Peacemaker*', in J. W. Bennett *et al.* (eds.), *Studies in the English Renaissance Drama in Memory of Karl Julius Holzknecht* (New York, 1959), 82–94.

[40] Examples of the first view are Fredson Bowers, 'Middleton's *Fair Quarrel* and the Duelling Code', *JEGP* 36 (1937), 40–65, and Levin, *Multiple Plot*, 66–75; of the second, McElroy, *Parody and Burlesque*, 265–321, and Mooney, ' "Common Sight" and Dramatic Form', 305–23. See also Walter Cohen, 'Prerevolutionary Drama ', in Gordon McMullan and Jonathan Hope (eds.), *The Politics of Tragicomedy: Shakespeare and After* (London, 1992), 132–3.

contrasted with the shallowness of the Colonel's initial commitment to honour, but the ironic stress of events leads that honesty away from the duel's anomalous ethics and towards the radical alternative of Christian forgiveness.

The premises of political and parental authority were officially argued to be consistent in Jacobean England. *Quarrel* dramatizes their incongruity by pitting status-defining violence against familial ideals. That Lady Ager is compelled by her concern as mother to risk her reputation as woman exposes this anomaly. A similar contrastive function is served by Jane in the bourgeois setting of the sub-plot. She initially safeguards her 'honour' by having her child secretly delivered. But when the doctor tries to blackmail her into bed, she dares him to defame her (5.1.26). Although 'honour' and money determined male status in court and city, the standards of feminine virtue were the same for the Renaissance lady and her woman.[41] Motherly love and female 'honour' in the two plots could thus create a depoliticized ethical space, deflecting fatherly authority and male heroics towards the spiritual point at issue in both battlefield and market-place.

Rowley's share in the play is enhanced by the farce of the aspiring roarers, Chough and his man Trimtram. Roisterers' clowning had been a safe draw since the days of Bobadil and Shift, and a roaring scene (4.4) was added to a reissue of the play's first quarto in 1617.[42] A pimp and a whore are called upon to defend their 'honour', and Trimtram and Albo fight a farting match, which mocks the 'verbal flatulence'[43] of the play's military and medical jargon, if not the fair quarrel itself.

As the roarers and whores carnalize the quarrel, reducing it to a 'fair fall' in 'the hug and the lock between man and woman' (2.2.165–6), their bawdy becomes a black excrescence of its repressed idiom of power. Their parodic excess, as much as the leading women's plainness, refuses aristocratic notions of 'honour' in the Fletcherian main plot any social or generic privilege over similar delusions in the city and the alehouse.

---

[41] See Ruth Kelso, *Doctrine for the Lady of the Renaissance* (Urbana, Ill., 1956), 36.

[42] See G. R. Price, 'The First Edition of *A Faire Quarrell*', *Library*, 5th ser. 4 (1949), 137–41. In his Regents Renaissance Drama edition (London, 1977), Price moves the scene to an appendix. Mooney, ' "Common Sight" and Dramatic Form', 305–23, sees it as a jig planted inside the text to circumvent the 1612 ban.

[43] Levin, *Multiple Plot*, 72. On the source of the scatological duel, see my 'Medwall's *Fulgens and Lucres* as a Probable Source for Middleton and Rowley's *A Fair Quarrel*', *N & Q* 238 (1993), 214–15.

NATURE AND LAW: *The Widow, More Dissemblers besides Women,*
and *The Old Law*

During his so-called tragicomic phase, Middleton wrote for the King's
Men two plays as different as *The Widow* (1616) and *More Dissemblers
besides Women* (1619). The plot of *Widow* shuffles ingredients of a tried
recipe: comic romance in which a daring wit wins a rich widow, the
city-comedy cast of old cuckold, frustrated young wife, and widow-
hungry usurers, and the farce involving a cross-dressed runaway girl
and thieves posing as doctors. Sex and money still power the action:
'but there's two words to a bargain ever, | All the world over; and if
love be one, | I'm sure money is the other' (5.1.313–15). But the
emphasis shifts to mirth, crooks' gags, and comic errors, and psychological and moral readings make heavy weather of the token motives
and reformations.[44]

Motives and morals are subtler in *Dissemblers*. A widowed Duchess,
pledged to continence, is driven to sly shifts by sexual desire the
moment she comes out of seclusion. Her re-entry into the world is
urged by the Cardinal of Milan, who had praised her chastity in print,
and who now wishes to show her off as his 'religious triumph' (1.2.64).
His rigidity melts at the Duchess's lie that she loves his nephew
Lactantio, and he decides to promote the politically tempting match.
He annuls her vow to the dying Duke, and denies having ever ruled
out remarriage. Chastity, he now says, is 'As rare in marriage as in
single life' (3.1.271). Kenneth Muir thinks that Middleton 'leaves it
open whether the Cardinal is a deliberate, or an unconscious hypo-
crite'.[45] The point is that he is both. While the Duchess acknowledges
her frailty and risks shame, the Cardinal, leading the cast of dissemblers
besides women, deceives both himself and the Milanese lords with his
self-explanations. The portrayal of the Cardinal shows a shrewd understanding of the auto-suggestive self-righteousness needed for the political defence of moral compromise.[46]

[44] For psychological and moral readings, see Farr, *Middleton and the Drama of Realism*,
12–13, 21–2; Robert T. Levine (ed.), *A Critical Edition of Thomas Middleton's* The Widow
(Salzburg, 1975), pp. xliii–liii; and Paula S. Berggren, ' "A Prodigious Thing": The Jacobean
Heroine in Male Disguise', *PQ* 62 (1983), 390–3.

[45] Kenneth Muir, 'Two Plays Reconsidered: *More Dissemblers besides Women* and *No Wit,
No Help Like a Woman's*', in Friedenreich (ed.), *'Accompaninge the Players'*, 148.

[46] Bromham's reading of the play as a Calvinist reaction to the Synod of Dort (1619) is
far-fetched; see *Changeling and the Years of Crisis*, 149–56.

The self-understanding of moralists in *Dissemblers* and, to a lesser extent, in *Widow*, reveals the conciliatory ruses of Fletcherian plots to be the ruses of ideology. In no other tragicomedy of Middleton is this concern more explicit than in *The Old Law* (*c*.1618; with Rowley).[47] The ideals of patriarchy confront those of absolutism once again. Duke Evander of Epire passes a law condemning all men of 80 and women of 60 to death. Young courtiers cannot wait to get rid of their parents; a young wife drives her elderly husband mad by trying out suitors under his nose; a clown bribes a parish clerk to forge his wife's date of birth; dismissed menials invest in old widows. Only Cleanthes, helped by his wife Hippolita, hides his father Leonides. They are soon betrayed. As courtiers gloat over their imminent execution, the Duke discloses that the condemned are alive, and asks Cleanthes and the old men to try the unnatural spouses and offspring.

The Fletcherian conflict at the heart of the play is that between filial and political duties, or, to recall its title, between natural and human positive law.[48] The conflict is formulated in the first scene when a lawyer tells Cleanthes that he must learn the difference between 'law' and 'conscience' (1.1.102–4). Cleanthes prefers the way prescribed in anti-tyrannical literature, and chooses the laws of God and nature above those of his sovereign.

The legal aspect of the issue was magnified by the Peacham case, which saw the dismissal of Coke from the King's Bench in 1616 for upholding Common Law against the encroachment of royal prerogative.[49] According to its defendants, Common Law was 'nothing els but common reason',[50] that is, natural law embodied in ancient custom. The idea is close to Cleanthes's definition of the 'old law' as 'common laws of reason and of nature' (5.1.231).

The dispute helped topicalize the issue which had been a major concern of Middleton since *Phoenix*, namely, the conflict between patriarchal and absolutist ideals, which King James sought to unite on a common familial premise. That the premise is not working in Epire becomes clear when the state law condemns a man, whose own

---

[47] On the date and probable revision by Massinger, see Maxwell, *Studies in Beaumont, Fletcher, and Massinger*, 138–46; and Catherine M. Shaw (ed.), *The Old Law* (New York, 1982), pp. xvii–xx.

[48] On the legal and moral dilemmas in Fletcher, see Eugene M. Waith, *The Pattern of Tragicomedy in Beaumont and Fletcher* (New Haven, Conn., 1952), *passim*.

[49] See Bromham, 'Contemporary Significance of *Old Law*', 327–39.

[50] Henry Finch, *Law, or, A Discourse thereof* (1627), as quoted in J. P. Sommerville, *Politics and Ideology in England, 1603–1640* (London, 1986), 92.

'household laws' are wise enough 'to conform seven Christian kingdoms' (2.1.101–3). James wrote in the *Basilikon Doron* that a king
should rule his people 'as their naturall father', and that he was a tyrant
if he made the law serve his 'vnrulie priuate affections'.[51] At the same
time, he never allowed this breach of kingly obligation to free subjects
of their filial duty. The anomaly in this demand is problematized in *Old
Law* by having a prince command his subjects to slay their natural
parents. A parricidal Simonides could thus use Jamesian logic to lecture
Cleanthes:

> Know then, Cleanthes, there is none can be
> A good son and bad subject; for, if princes
> Be call'd the people's fathers, then the subjects
> Are all his sons, and he that flouts the prince
> Doth disobey his father . . . (5.1.195–9)

The difference between the familial and political discourses of
power, as Debora Shuger has demonstrated, was a persistent theme in
English Renaissance texts.[52] A typical example is Fulke Greville's
Mustapha, a play in which the tyrant recognizes that 'This *Father*-lan-
guage fits not Kings' (2.2.38). 'Power hath great scope,' says another
character, 'she walkes not in the wayes | Of priuate truth' (1.2.5–6).
Old Law reverses this angle of vision, representing the discrepant ways
of power and private truth as realized by the ruled, not the ruler.

The strongest dramatic treatment of both poles of the experience
was, of course, *King Lear*. The impact of Shakespeare's example may
account for one notable change in Middleton's method. Since *Phoenix*,
Middleton had responded to the familializing of politics by politicizing
the family. While the reaction of the courtiers and clowns to the
Duke's edict in *Old Law* reproduces the symmetry of power-structures
in family and State, Cleanthes and Hippolita exemplify an alternative
model of societal bonds rare in Middleton. The exposition of the
discordance of that option with the logic of absolutism, rather than the
youth-against-age theme singled out by Maxwell, justifies regarding
the play as descended from *Lear*.[53]

Old Law, however, is tragicomedy, and its tragicomic inventions are
shaped by its politics. The play's ending best illustrates the political use
it makes of its generic lineage. Disclosure of parentage, the qualms of

---

[51] McIlwain (ed.), *Political Works*, 18–19.
[52] Debora Kuller Shuger, *Habits of Thought in the English Renaissance: Religion, Politics and
the Dominant Culture* (Berkeley, Calif., 1990), 218–49.
[53] Maxwell, *Studies in Beaumont, Fletcher, and Massinger*, 140–3.

hired killers, and last-minute conversions dispel dangers in *No Wit,
Witch*, and *Quarrel*. The redemptive surprise in *Old Law* is a declaration
of the Duke's real intentions, and the crisis is solved by the same
sovereign will which had occasioned it. As long as the Duke was
believed to have ordered the killings, there was no question of calling
tyranny by any other name. 'And what's that, sir,' asks one of the
condemned, 'but the sword of tyranny. . .?' (1.1.242). Seemingly an
example of the *felix culpa* paradox,[54] the solution throws Epire back on
the ruler's good faith, the only guarantee natural law is promised in
absolutism, and the fragility of which the crisis had demonstrated.

The Common Law controversy shows that the laws of reason and
nature were most endangered by the king's arrogation of emergency
powers. But absolutism was an apology of such prerogatives. Its
ideology relied on the threat of treason and anarchy, generalizing the
exceptional instance which called for the most violent and unchecked
display of force.[55] *Old Law* shows the ease with which the will raised
above the law to enforce its rule may slide into lawless tyranny,
impelling a spiral of resistance and repression. The arbitration of that
will could be taken for a remedy only if the play pretended, as it does
in the end, that the threats were unreal in the first place. Absolutist
solution, like that of tragicomic romance, argues against itself by
demanding that we see the source of the trouble as its remedy, and will
ourselves to believe that the trouble itself was a delusion.

As in *Quarrel*, the alternative is the radical one of love and familial
rule, briefly realized in 'that paradise' (5.1.698) where Evander shelters
his aged subjects. Cleanthes and Hippolita exemplify its values, and the
Duke's delegation of judicial powers in the final scene gestures towards
a co-operative, contractual model of government. But the opposed
ideals of power remain unreconciled, the arbitration of despotic wisdom
serving only to emphasize the brittle artifice of the tragicomic reprieve.

FOREIGN NATIONS AND NATIVE POPULACE:
Hengist, King of Kent

Hengist, King of Kent (1620–2), advertised in the 1661 quarto as a play
staged by the King's Men, has been read as both tragedy and tragi-

---

[54] See Carolyn Asp, *A Study of Thomas Middleton's Tragicomedies* (Salzburg, 1974), 70–5.
[55] See Benjamin, *Origin of German Tragic Drama*, 65–74.

comedy.[56] The events, derived from Fabyan and Holinshed, follow the death of Constantine, king of Britain.[57] His heir Constantius prefers the monastery from which he is dragged out and crowned by Vortiger, described in *The Mirror for Magistrates* as 'hee who subuerted the commonweale of Brittayne'.[58] Vortiger later murders him and usurps the throne. He turns to the newly arrived Saxons led by Hengist and Horsus in order to put down a popular revolt, following which Hengist is rewarded with land, and, later, the earldom of Kent. After treacherously knifing British lords at Stonehenge, Hengist forces Vortiger to acknowledge him king of Kent.

Meanwhile, Vortiger discards his virtuous queen for Roxena, Hengist's daughter and Horsus's mistress. The angry nobles lead a popular revolt against Vortiger, and crown his son, but Roxena's counter-coup has Vortiger returned and his son killed. Vortiger and Hengist are later overthrown by Constantius's brothers. Horsus and Vortiger stab each other to death, Roxena is consumed in flames, and Hengist is sentenced to death.

Foxe's *Acts and Monuments* held up the story of the Saxon invasion as an 'example to all ages and countries, what it is first to let in foreign nations into their dominion, but especially what it is for princes to join in marriage with infidels, as this Vortigern did with Hengist's daughter'.[59] In 1556, the Marian exile John Ponet used the same legend to warn his countrymen of the dangers of allowing Spanish Catholics a foothold in England.[60] These fears were once more topical in 1620–2, when James was seeking peace with Spain and a Spanish bride for his son. The Saxons in the play are compared with the Romans (cf. 2.3.1–2, 89), their difference in religion is stressed, the death of Roxena, the 'mysticall harlot' crowned by flames 'ffor a trivmphant whore' (5.2.199–201), is made to shadow the destruction of the whore of Babylon. The story of early Britain was recognized as a political fable pertinent to the time, as indicated by a play such as *The Birth of*

---

[56] See e.g. R. C. Bald (ed.), *Hengist, King of Kent*, (New York, 1938), p. xlvi; and Heinemann, *Puritanism and Theatre*, 136–7. Briggs, 'Middleton's Forgotten Tragedy', 485, notes similarities with Shakespeare's late romances.

[57] On the sources, see Bald (ed.), *Hengist*, pp. xxxvii–xlii.

[58] Lily B. Campbell (ed.), *Parts Added to* The Mirror for Magistrates *by John Higgins and Thomas Blenerhasset* (Cambridge, 1946), 422.

[59] Foxe, *Acts and Monuments*, i. 320.

[60] See A. A. Bromham, 'Thomas Middleton's *Hengist, King of Kent* and John Ponet's *Shorte Treatise of Politike Power*', *N & Q* 227 (1982), 143–5.

Merlin.[61] A recognition of relevance is in fact invited by the Prologue spoken by Ranulph Higden, the author of *Polychronicon*: 'So in story whats now told | That takes not part with days of old?' (ll. 15–16).

The clues support local readings,[62] but Middleton's pursuit of political questions goes beyond immediate history and reaches back to the issues raised in the early tragedies. The problem of tyrannical misrule, for instance, gains in complexity since one usurper is pitted against another. Of the two, Vortiger is, in name at least, the Christian. Yet, it is he who relies on scheming, while Hengist's adventurism rests on 'acts of valour' and 'redd sweate' (2.2.38, 41). Vortiger scorns the populace; Hengist realizes the importance of winning them over. Vortiger sends his fiancée to woo the king; Hengist refuses to let his daughter be made Vortiger's whore. The discordance between the Saxons' valour and their irreligion is expressed in Vortiger's disbelief: 'Neuer Came powre guided wth better starrs | Then these mens ffortitudes, yet th're misbeleeuers | Tis to my reason wondrous' (2.3.8–10).

The mentions of the Saxons' paganism and treachery are hedged with similar ambiguities. When Vortiger reminds the Saxons of their difference in religion (2.3.33–7), he is really looking for an excuse to cheat them of their dues. After violating the armistice at Stonehenge, Hengist explains the Saxons' motive with admirable clarity of political vision: 'We know ye hard Conditions of o^r peace, | Slauery or diminution wch we hate | W^th a joint loathing' (4.3.64–6). He is even made to express the play's most radical egalitarian sentiments. The Lambarde manuscript of the play has a few lines, deleted from the 1661 quarto, which complain that the poor die without shelter or food while the rich 'lye rotting | Vnder a Million spent in gold and marble' (2.3.141–2). Heinemann suspects that the lines were censored because they attacked the costly monuments, such as those of the Cecils at Hatfield, built at a time of unusual economic hardship.[63] The question Heinemann does not ask is why Hengist, the infidel, the usurper, and the Machiavel, should be chosen to voice this concern for social

---

[61] See Bald (ed.), *Hengist*, pp. xxii–xxiii; and Briggs, 'Middleton's Forgotten Tragedy', 487–90. *Birth of Merlin*, however, could be as early as 1608.

[62] See Heinemann, *Puritanism and Theatre*, 136–50; Anne Lancashire, 'The Emblematic Castle in Shakespeare and Middleton', in J. C. Gray (ed.), *Mirror up to Shakespeare: Essays in Honour of G. R. Hibbard* (Toronto, 1984), 231–5; Bromham and Bruzzi, *Changeling and the Years of Crisis*, 156–65; and Briggs, 'Middleton's Forgotten Tragedy', 479–95.

[63] Heinemann, *Puritanism and Theatre*, 143.

justice. Middleton's Saxon is clearly more than just a bogeyman representing the dreaded consequences of a Spanish takeover.

In contrasting a Christian usurper with a pagan one, Middleton is able to demystify the providential mystique of secular authority, and temper its pretences with the pagan adventurer's unblinking recognition of *realpolitik*. Hengist reflects some of the dissatisfaction and idealism which, together with its darkest dreads and fantasies, Renaissance Europe projected on to pagan cultures. We read in Knolles's rendering of Bodin, for instance, that the Turks are the only people who 'measure true nobilitie by vertue, and not by discent or the antiquitie of their stocke'.[64] The Saxons in the play exhibit a similar contempt for inherited privilege: 'The heate Comes from yᵉ bodye, not yᵉ weedes, | So mans true fame, must strike from his owne deedes' (2.3.24–5). Such praise was often intended to disparage European enemies by contrast.[65] Dramatists used this technique, as Heywood did in his flattering portrayal of Mullisheg beside his cruel Spaniards in *Fair Maid of the West*, Part 1. Middleton knew this balancing trick, since he had praised the Persians, deemed useful allies against the Turks, in his 1609 pamphlet on Sir Robert Sherley.[66] In *Hengist*, he chose to use the pagans' freedom from religious hang-ups to describe the unacknowledged reality about a political world in which cynical opportunism worked and Christian values did not. Middleton, it seems, was in sight of the same disturbing truth Moretti finds in Shakespeare, which is that the 'Christian prince', wholly Christian and wholly a prince, does not exist.[67]

The duplication of tyrants in *Hengist* disturbs the axiological congruence of action and values, and creates that generic ambiguity which makes it appear a tragedy to some and tragicomedy to others. For Vortiger, the tale ends as a moral exemplum of overweening ambition. The same standards are sought to be applied to Hengist, but he does not recognize the ethical and generic norms by which he is judged, and dies defiantly unrepentant. Middleton brings Macbeth to face Tamburlaine in the same text, and lets their incompatible ways reproduce a hidden cleavage in generic values.

---

[64] Bodin, *Six Bookes of a Commonweale*, E4ᵛ.

[65] See Samuel C. Chew, *The Crescent and the Rose: Islam and England during the Renaissance* (New York, 1937), 53.

[66] See G. B. Shand, 'Source and Intent in Middleton's *Sir Robert Sherley*', *Ren. & Ref.* 19 (1983), 257–64.

[67] Moretti, *Signs Taken for Wonders*, 68.

The task of joining 'new times loue, to old times storye' demanded by the Prologue (l. 18) is chiefly carried out by the comic sub-plot of Simon the tanner's election to the mayoralty of Queenborough. Heinemann detects here an allusion to the rivalry between the anti-Spanish peer, Philip Herbert, and the pro-Spanish Duke of Lennox over the 1621 election to the Parliamentary seat of Queenborough. Herbert, as Constable of Queenborough Castle, proposed his candidate to the town corporation on 6 November 1620, while Lennox did so three days later.[68] The suggestion is admissible in the light of the probable date of 1620–2 recently proposed for *Hengist*.[69]

There is more to the sub-plot than the anti-Spanish animus. The legend of Hengist's demand of a spot of land that could be measured by a piece of hide, which he then had sliced into thongs to encompass acres, gave Middleton the excuse to introduce a tanner.[70] That this enabled him to invoke the proverbial association of popular misrule and the Norfolk uprising in 1549 led by Kett the tanner has escaped notice. In *The Hurt of Sedition* (1549), John Cheke mocked the Norfolk rebels who sought to bring about 'A maruelous tanned common welth' by killing and gaoling gentlemen. Cheke asked the rebels if they thought it their duty 'to disobey your betters, and obey your tanners, to chaunge your obedience frõ a king to a ket . . .?'[71]

The tanner's story thus ties in with the wider theme of popular power. The action begins with the shout of 'that wide throated Beast the Multitude' (1.1.1), and the people remain audible throughout, making and unmaking kings. It is significant that the complaints against their 'mutable hearts' (2.2.18) are always heard from Vortiger, while Hengist recognizes the strategic need of popular support. To Vortiger's ears their voice 'imitates thunder' (2.2.21). When members of the mob do appear on stage, they are no more than the hard-pressed feltmonger

---

[68] Heinemann, *Puritanism and Theatre*, 144–8. See also Briggs, 'Middleton's Forgotten Tragedy', 493–5.

[69] See R. V. Holdsworth, 'The Date of *Hengist, King of Kent*', *N & Q* 236 (1991), 516–19.

[70] The legend goes back to the story, alluded to in the *Aeneid*, i. 366–7, of how Dido and the Phoenicians won a foothold in Carthage. See Virgil, *Eclogues, Georgics, Aeneid*, ed. H. Rushton Fairclough, 2 vols., Loeb Classics (1916; rev. edn., London, 1935), i. 267 n.

[71] Iohn Cheek, *The Hurt of Sedition, How Greeuous it is to a Common Welth* (1549; 4th edn., 1576), B1ᵛ–2. Kett's rebellion was rumoured to have begun during the performance of a play, a fact that might lie behind Simon's sentence that the rebel Oliver be made to watch a play. On the Norfolk uprising, see Stephen K. Land, *Kett's Rebellion* (Ipswich, 1977). Shakespeare included among Jack Cade's rabble 'Best's son, the tanner of Wingham' (*2 Henry VI*, 4.2.23–4).

and grazier who petition Constantius against the 'great enormitie in woolle' and the rise of pastures 'to twopence an acre' (1.2.101–3), and the harmless comics who cough and hum at Simon's election speech (3.3). Middleton's sympathy for them helps him debunk the more sinister game of élite politics through parodic allusions. Thus Simon also is presented as an upstart and sexual usurper. He is 'a Masterless man' (2.3.66), since he 'shott vp in one night wth Lyeing wth [his] M^{rs}' (3.3.169). His mayoral pledge to let the seven deadly sins, lechery especially, go unchecked (cf. 3.3.217–37) mocks the reign of Vortiger, besides inverting the scheme of *Triumphs of Truth*, Middleton's 1613 mayoral pageant.

Sedition troubles the tanner's government as well. The 'proud Rebell' (5.1.172) is Simon's electoral rival, a Puritan named Oliver, who is captured and sentenced to watch a play. To illustrate the efficacy of theatre as political therapy, Sidney had cited the story of the tyrant Alexander Pheraeus shedding tears at the spectacle of tyranny on the stage.[72] Oliver, in what is almost a parody of the episode, finds watching a play 'tiranny' and cries for revenge (5.1.183). The players, really rogues who 'only take ye name of Contry Comedians' (5.1.356–7), eventually rob Simon, and Oliver has the last laugh.

The episode, derived from the stealing of Cokes's purse in *Bartholomew Fair*, makes fun of the Puritans' allergy to the stage, and also shifts their charges against players to strollers, retainers, and con men. In a less obvious way, this revenger's comedy mimes the theatrical strategy of both tyranny and resistance. Simon says that 'a play may be dangerous' since he had 'knowne a greate man poysond in a play'. He is also aware that in a play, unlike in politics, 'he thats poysond, is allwayes made priuy too it' (5.1.147–8, 152). This knowledge does not make him more tolerant of players' trespasses than the Jacobean censors. He insists on his right to play the clown, but threatens to arrest all who laugh at him (5.1.298–308). In making this absurd demand Simon is neither less consistent nor more ridiculous than the defenders of absolutist culture. If by inserting the farcical sub-plot in a bleak political play Middleton risked turning *Hengist* into a 'comitragedy', that rare dramatic species the country players possessed in their repertoire (5.1.80), he certainly intended it as more than a joke on the factional wrangle over a Parliamentary seat.

---

[72] Sidney, *Defence of Poesie*, in Feuillerat (ed.), *Prose Works*, iii. 23–4.

The utopian plots of Renaissance tragicomedy have been explained as attempts to reconcile the competing demands of civil society and the State.[73] The friction and parody which connect the divided segments and modes in Middleton's tragicomedies and *Hengist* rule out the possibility of that compromise. By reproducing in the city and civil society the contests of the political world, the sub-plots in these plays demolish the myth which sought to harmonize these spheres. At the same time, Middleton implies that their structures are, as instances of political and gender domination, comparable. It is in this emphasis, rather than in any new obsession with motives and morals, that the middle plays look forward to *Women Beware* and *Changeling*.

[73] See Moretti, *Signs Taken for Wonders*, 61.

6
Strangers and Natives: *Women Beware Women*

ALTERED SOIL

In his novel *The Enigma of Arrival*, V. S. Naipaul tells us of the curious way he came to understand an obscure allusion Kent makes in *King Lear*: 'Goose, an I had you upon Sarum Plain | I'd drive ye cackling home to Camelot' (2.2.83–4; Folio text). Naipaul learnt one morning on the radio that the Romans walked geese to the markets in the capital all the way from Gaul. Camelot to Salisbury Plain is nothing near that distance: just twenty miles. Since that morning, the geese around Naipaul's Wiltshire cottage acquired a new historical life.[1]

There is more to these ancient geese. When the Gauls attacked the Capitol one night in 390 or 387 BC, the excited cackling of the sacred geese on the Capitoline Hill woke the Roman defenders. In *Women Beware Women* (1621), Livia recalls these hallowed birds while trying to stop her brother from forcing his daughter to marry a rich idiot.[2] Livia tells Fabritio that love cannot be forced, and she calls in the Capitoline geese for a simile:

> Oh soft there, brother! Though you be a justice,
> Your warrant cannot be served out of your liberty;
> You may compel out of the power of father
> Things merely harsh to a maid's flesh and blood,
> But when you come to love, there the soil alters;
> Y'are in another country, where your laws
> Are no more set by than the cacklings of geese
> In Rome's great Capitol. (1.2.131-8)

This is not an entirely appropriate image of fractional impotence: the geese were, after all, equally powerless in Gaul. The politically powerful in *Women Beware* represent a contrary situation where their writ does run outside their 'liberty'. The Duke of Florence not only

---

[1] V. S. Naipaul, *The Enigma of Arrival* (Harmondsworth, 1987), 22–3.
[2] See Mulryne's note to 1.2.137–8.

compels Bianca's 'flesh and blood', but also succeeds in using his authority to command erotic response.[3] The soil may alter for Fabritio; it never does for the Duke.

Women Beware displays Middleton's maturest understanding of the relation of power to desire, and of political culture to civil society. Its hybrid genre is not an instance of a seventeenth-century Ibsen selling out to consumer taste, or being inhibited by current discursive rules.[4] On the contrary, the change of soil within the play from court to city, from Italianate melodrama to bourgeois tragedy, from satire to revenge play, may itself be seen to register a critique of political and sexual authority.

Alteration of soil is of relevance in a more literal sense. The experience of distant cultures produced in early modern England a profound disquiet in the spheres Greenblatt has called sex, sustenance, and salvation, involving respectively the family, the State, and the Church.[5] In the strange, the period sensed the hidden violence of the familiar; in the familiar, the transparent savagery of the strange. Above all, alien structures of political and gender authority forced on the period's consciousness the historical contingency of native social formations. The story of Leantio and Bianca may be connected to this anxiety of estrangement, and other elements of the text studied in relation to the interlocked premises of sex, sustenance, and salvation that it lays bare.

ARRIVAL

Women Beware, like *Othello*, begins where New Comedy leaves off. Leantio has played the witty lover in Venice and has wrested Bianca from her parents, 'great in wealth, more now in rage' (1.1.50). Bianca too has forsaken 'friends, fortunes, and . . . country', hoping to make Leantio's native Florence the place of her 'birth' (1.1.131, 139).

Florence, however, is not a refuge from parents and princes. It submits the desires of the lovers to new modes of subjection. The city reminds Leantio of thieves from whose eyes Bianca is 'cased up'

---

[3] See Suzanne Gossett, ' "Best Men are Molded out of Faults": Marrying the Rapist in Jacobean Drama', *ELR* 14 (1984), 319–21.

[4] See Hibbard, 'Tragedies of Thomas Middleton and the Decadence of Drama', 54; Farr, *Middleton and the Drama of Realism*, 92–3; and Anthony B. Dawson, '*Women Beware Women* and the Economy of Rape', *SEL* 27 (1987), 318.

[5] See Greenblatt, *Learning to Curse*, 21.

(1.1.170). Bianca's new home reflects its economic and political relations. His mother is uneasy about the hypergamous match, and Leantio
fears that her doubts will teach Bianca 'to rebel | When she's in a good
way to obedience' (1.1.74–5). In stepping from an unwritten romance
into a bourgeois text, Leantio changes from reckless lover to hoarding
husband; and Bianca, from immured princess to imprisoned wife. The
action opens with the arrival of desire into this reality of power.

Christopher Ricks has shown that love expresses itself in the play in
words contaminated by money ('business', 'use', 'service', 'expense',
'tender').[6] The duplicity of such words is inseparable from the migra-
tion and the consequent self-betrayal of the lovers. Leantio brings from
Venice words which, like Bianca, fester in Florence. Shifted to a new
context of coercive exchange, the latent complicities of language erupt
to unsettle the self-understanding of desire, and to force their victims
into new verbal sleights. Bianca and Leantio do not rot, or expose their
repressions, or simply grow up after the rape.[7] Their self-images are
constituted, both before and after their Florentine experience, by what
they are constrained to repress.

'What make I here? These are all strangers to me' (5.2.206)—Bianca's dying question completes the pattern woven in the text by the
words 'strange' and 'stranger'. For R. B. Parker, the words signify
selfish isolation.[8] It would perhaps be more useful to relate them to the
change of cultural and generic soil. Bianca is literally a stranger in
Florence, but Leantio also suffers a split of identity in the city. His stint
as daring wooer in Venice spells danger for the stability of his uncol-
ourful bourgeois self in Florence. He disclaims change by locking up
Bianca, trying to hide away, and hide from, his Venetian experience.

Leantio's timid attempt to subject desire to duty reflects the sociosexual tensions contemporary English travel writers projected on to
their pictures of Italy. Fynes Moryson's *Itinerary*, which Middleton may
have used as a source,[9] tells English readers that Italian men locked up
their wives at home, 'as it were in prison',[10] while they were free to

---

[6] Christopher Ricks, 'Word-Play in *Women Beware Women*', *RES*, NS 12 (1961), 238–50.
See also T. McAlindon, *English Renaissance Tragedy* (London, 1986), 213–27.

[7] For instances of the three theories see, respectively, M. C. Bradbrook, *Themes and
Conventions of Elizabethan Tragedy* (Cambridge, 1935), 224; William Empson, *Some Versions
of Pastoral* (London, 1935), 55; and Leonora Leet Brodwin, *Elizabethan Love Tragedy 1587–
1625* (London, 1972), 320–36.

[8] Parker, 'Middleton's Experiments', 194.

[9] See Mulryne (ed.), *Women Beware*, pp. xlii–xliii.

[10] Moryson, *Itinerary*, i. 148.

have fun with 'strange women'.[11] Leantio is no womanizer, but he seeks in Bianca what he misses out on permitted male pleasures. What makes his behaviour 'strange' is his attempt to freeze-dry his foreign adventure, and to hoard its prize as an alternative to the temptations of native society, and as a concealed escape from its brutalities.

His opening speech in Act 3, Scene 2 is a good example of his effort to satisfy both alien pleasure and native duty. As he approaches his house for the weekend, he sniffs the air like a voyager scenting land. An instance of the association is provided by a 1599 tract on marriage:

> Thou [marriage] art the occasion, that to the pilgrime, after his long labours and wearisome iournies, his returne backe again into his owne countrey seemeth the more pleasanter vnto him. That to the sayler after many bitter stormes and boysterous tempests, the kenning of his wished land, and the sight of his much desired Hauen, is the more delightfull vnto him . . . .[12]

Leantio likewise scents 'blessings' and the 'delicious breath' of marriage in the air, although, when he speaks of 'the concealed comforts of a man, | Locked up in woman's love' being richer than 'The treasures of the deep' (3.2.3–7), he sounds more like sailing into an exotic private retreat than returning home.[13]

The private joys of Leantio's romance have turned into the 'concealed comforts' of marriage. What marriage provides him with is unlike the social haven praised in the quoted tract; it is rather a secret means of indulging proscribed urges. Marriage, he said earlier, had stopped him from fantasizing 'this man's sister, or . . . that man's wife' (1.1.29), and had enabled him to sit in church without ogling women (1.1.32–4). Now, once again, he praises wedlock as a prophylactic against illicit sex. The idea of marriage as a means of 'bridling the corrupt inclinations of the flesh within the limits of honesty'[14] was old

---

[11] Charles Hughes (ed.), *Shakespeare's Europe: Unpublished Chapters of Fynes Moryson's Itinerary* (London, 1903), 151.

[12] R. T[ofte], *Of Mariage and Wiuing* (1599), K4. Cf. Edmund Spenser, *Amoretti*, Sonnet 63.

[13] Cf. Michael Drayton, 'To the Virginian Voyage', in J. William Hebel (ed.), *The Works of Michael Drayton*, 5 vols. (Oxford, 1961), ii. 364. Leantio's phrase 'treasures of the deep' figures in Drayton and his source in Hakluyt; see J. Q. Adams, 'Michael Drayton's *To the Virginia Voyage*', *MLN* 33 (1918), 405–8. See also Beaumont and Fletcher, *The Island Princess*, 1.3.16–34.

[14] 'An Homily of the State of Matrimony', in *The Two Books of Homilies Appointed to be Read in Churches* (Oxford, 1859), 500. The quotation comes from the first half of the homily, a translation of an address by Viet Dietrich or Theodor of Nuremberg, the Latin version of which was published in Jena in 1567. On the link between matrimony and whoredom in the play, see Michael McCanles, 'The Moral Dialectic of Middleton's *Women Beware Women*', in Friedenreich (ed.), *'Accompaninge the Players'*, 213–17.

and authorized. Sir Thomas Overbury put the Pauline case for marriage in homoeopathic terms: 'Maryage our Lust as twere with fuell fire, | Doth with a medicine of the same allaye, | And not forbid, but rectifie desire'.[15] Such rectification rested on the public and social nature of matrimony. Leantio's 'Honest wedlock', on the contrary, must remain concealed in order to survive. He locks up his wife like Moryson's Italian husband, but his anxiety also seems curiously English, almost like that of Harebrain in *Mad World*.

BIZARRE *JOUISSANCE*

The problem of reconciling anarchic desire to social duty reflected in Leantio's dilemma was dramatized for the English Renaissance by its encounter with other cultures. In his *Crudities*, Coryat marvels at the respect publicly shown to courtesans in Venice. He is also intrigued by the explanation offered for such deference: 'For they think that the chastity of their wives would be sooner assaulted, and so consequently they should be capricornified . . . were it not for these places of evacuation.' Coryat is quick to see the anomaly in this coincidence of institutionalized adultery and fear of cuckoldry. Why lock up wives at all if the existence of brothels guarantees their chastity?

But I marvaile how that should be true though these Cortezans were utterly rooted out of the City. For the Gentlemen do even coope up their wives alwaies within the walles of their houses for feare of these inconveniences, as much as if there were no Cortezans at all in the City.[16]

Coryat's observations are useful for two reasons. First, the Venetian attitude to sex and marriage exaggerates that already latent in Coryat's England, proving James Boon's point that the period conceived of exotic and domestic institutions in 'inextricably intertwined' terms.[17] The justification for prostitution Coryat reports, for instance, is almost the same as the one for marriage given in the homily quoted earlier. Marriage and prostitution are both deemed safe 'places of evacuation' for socially disruptive urges.

Secondly, Coryat's narrative dramatizes the guilty fascination of discovering in other cultures the fantasies outlawed by one's own. His

---

[15] Thomas Overbury, *A Wife, Now a Widowe* (1614), B6ᵛ.

[16] Coryat, *Crudities*, i. 403.

[17] James A. Boon, *Other Tribes, Other Scribes: Symbolic Anthropology in the Comparative Study of Cultures, Histories, Religions and Texts* (Cambridge, 1982), 154.

description of the Venetian courtesan is steeped in the idiom of romance: the 'Paradise of Venus', 'the Queene and Goddesse of love', 'the quintessence of beauty', 'second Cleopatra', 'most elegant discourser'.[18] He tries dispelling her magic with reminders of Circe and the Sirens, the figures persistently invoked to demonize Italian allurements. Roger Ascham had warned travellers that 'Some Circes shall make him, of a plain Englishman, a right Italian', and Jerome Turler had lamented that many an Englishman visiting Italy 'is caught by the songs of Mermaids'.[19] Coryat likewise advises the traveller to shield his eyes and ears against the charms of the Venetian courtesans,[20] a precaution Ascham had prescribed against Italian pleasures in general. If the traveller must see and hear them, he is advised to be brief: 'for if thou dost linger with them thou wilt finde their poyson to be more pernicious then that of the scorpion, aspe, or cocatrice'.[21]

Coryat's account vacillates, to adapt Edward Said's description of post-Renaissance Western images of the Near East, 'between the contempt for what is familiar and its shivers of delight in—or fear of—novelty'.[22] During the Renaissance, what Said calls Europe's 'underground self'[23] could haunt perceptions also of the Far East, Russia, and, in spite of radical differences, the New World.[24] Italy, the gateway to the East, represented for Renaissance England some of the spell and dread of these far-off places.

Nowhere is the mental conflation of alien cultures more evident than in discussions of sex, marriage, and the status of women.[25] Moryson and Coryat's accounts of Italian courtesans are echoed in any

[18] Coryat, *Crudities*, i. 403–5.
[19] Roger Ascham, *The Scholemaster* (1570), in Revd. Dr Giles (ed.), *The Whole Works of Roger Ascham*, 4 vols. (London, 1864–5), iii. 151; *The Traveiler of Jerome Turler*, as quoted in Howard, *English Travellers of the Renaissance*, 56. See also Ann Rosalind Jones, 'Italians and Others: Venice and the Irish in *Coryat's Crudities* and *The White Devil*', *RD* 18 (1987), 101–19.
[20] Coryat, *Crudities*, i. 406.
[21] Ibid.
[22] Edward W. Said, *Orientalism* (1978; Harmondsworth, 1985), 59.
[23] Ibid. 3.
[24] These differences are studied at length in Edmundo O'Gorman, *The Invention of America: An Inquiry into the Historical Nature of the New World and the Meaning of its History* (Bloomington, Ind., 1961); and Tzvetan Todorov, *The Conquest of America: The Question of the Other*, trans. Richard Howard (New York, 1984). See also Henri Baudet, *Paradise on Earth: Some Thoughts on European Images of Non-European Man*, trans. Elizabeth Wentholt (New Haven, Conn., 1965).
[25] Consider the following passage from Thomas Heywood's 1637 tract: 'The Anthropophagi, the Medes, and some part of the Aethiopians, after they be once married, are admitted free congresse with their mothers and sisters. The Arabs make their wives common to all the kinred. The Moores, Numidians, Persians, Parthians, Garamantes, the Turkes, and some Jewes, take as many wives as they can well maintaine: and the ancient Athenians made their

number of tracts on the East, the dark enchantments of the Venetian bordello being transferred to the Eastern harem. These peep-shows into the 'bizarre *jouissances*'[26] of strange societies are the mirror image of the accounts of chained and battered wives. William Biddulph reports that Muslim fathers 'wil not suffer their owne sonnes, after they come to fourteene yeeres of age, to see their mothers'; George Sandys says that no Muslim woman is allowed a male companion above the age of 12; William Parry writes that no man, not even her brother, may see a married Muslim woman if her husband is living; and they all note that women go veiled and guarded, rarely seen outside baths and cemeteries.[27] The close watch under which wives are kept in Malta reminds Sandys of 'the maner of *Italy*'. Here too 'the iealous are better secured, by the number of allowed curtizans . . . as if chastity were onely violated by marriage'.[28] The images of permissiveness and control demand each other as enabling conditions of the sado-masochistic fantasy. Hence, the legends of Russian women who for a first gift sent a whip to their lovers,[29] and the flood of prurient reports of the willing slavery of American Indian women.[30]

The threat to local structures of authority did not come so much from the alien images in such narratives as from their uneasy suggestion that these strange societies embodied hedonist fantasies of classic European texts. Sandys believed that '*Mahomet* grounded his deuised Paradise vpon the Poets inuention of *Elisium*,' and William Bradford, governor of Plymouth, drew revealingly on the European classics to describe the misrule of his men led by an aspiring poet, Thomas Morton, at Merrymount: 'As if they had anew revived and celebrated the feasts of the Roman goddess Flora, or the beastly practices of the

wives and daughters common.'—[Heywood], *A Curtaine Lecture* (1637), G8^v. See also Chapman, *The Tragedy of Charles Duke of Byron*, 4.2.122–32.

[26] Said, *Orientalism*, 87. On European accounts of the Muslim seraglio, see Chew, *Crescent and the Rose*, 192–5.

[27] Theophilus Lavender (ed.), *The Travels of Certaine Englishmen into Africa, Asia . . . and to Sundry Other Places* (1609), L4; George Sandys, *A Relation of a Iourney Begun An. Dom: 1610* (1615; 2nd edn., 1615), G4, G5; William Parry, *A New and Large Discourse of the Trauels of Sir Anthony Sherley* (1601), repr. in E. Denison Ross (ed.), *Sir Anthony Sherley and his Persian Adventure* (London, 1933), 108, 119–20.

[28] Sandys, *Relation*, X3^v.

[29] See Robert Ralston Cawley, *The Voyagers and Elizabethan Drama* (Boston, 1938), 259–61. See also Richard Hakluyt, *Principal Navigations, Voyages, Traffiques and Discoveries of the English Nation* (1599), 12 vols. (Glasgow, 1903–5), ii. 445.

[30] See Antonello Gerbi, 'The Earliest Accounts of the New World', in Fredi Chiapelli (ed.), *First Images of America: The Impact of the New World on the Old*, 2 vols. (continuous pagination; Berkeley, Calif., 1976), 37–43.

mad Bacchanalians.'[31] Freed from cultural vigilance, repressed fantasies return like the pretty wench who was to accompany Sir Petronel Flash and his crew to the New World in *Eastward Ho*: 'Shee's one I loue dearely; and must not bee knowne till wee bee free from all that knowe vs' (3.3.69–71).

Just as attraction is betrayed in the disapproving accounts of male freedom, approval sneaks into the overtly critical reports of female subjection. Theophilus Lavender thought that travellers' stories would teach English wives to love their husbands, 'when they shal read in what slauery women liue in other Contries, and in what awe and subiection to their husbands, and what libertie and freedome they themselues enioy'.[32] Yet, in the letter from Biddulph edited by Lavender, Eastern severity is recommended for English women, especially the practice of drowning an adulterous wife, even if her husband had a hundred more.[33]

The experience of Italy, the East, and the New World, therefore, could cause the same shying away from self-discovery which, according to D. H. Lawrence, induced the Puritans to migrate to America.[34] Leantio's tragedy, it may be argued, results from his failure to face up to a comparably disturbing revelation of desire he had experienced in Venice, while Bianca's follows her initiation into the rites of power in Florence.

Middleton rehearsed some of the period's clichés on voyages and strange lands in his civic commissions and in the promotional pamphlet on Robert Sherley.[35] But it is in the story of Leantio and Bianca that he explores the increased complexity which, says Geertz, the brush with alien cultures brings to our moral lives.[36]

[31] Sandys, *Relation*, F5ᵛ–6; and William Bradford, *History of Plymouth Plantation 1620–1647*, as quoted in A. L. Rowse, *The Elizabethans and America* (London, 1959), 138–9. A less sensational account is given by Morton himself in *New English Canaan or New Canaan Containing an Abstract of New England* (Amsterdam, 1637), R2ᵛ–S1. See Wilcomb E. Washburn, 'The Clash of Morality in the American Forest', in Chiapelli (ed.), *First Images of America*, 43–4.

[32] Lavender (ed.), *Travels of Certaine Englishmen*, A2.

[33] Ibid. K2–2ᵛ.

[34] See D. H. Lawrence, *Studies in Classic American Literature* (1924; London, 1964), 1–3.

[35] See Bullen, vii. 247–9, 297–8, 340–1, 358–60, 366–7; viii. 299–318. Almost all references to voyages and strange peoples in Middleton are noted in Cawley, *Voyagers and Elizabethan Drama*; see index, 421.

[36] Geertz, *Local Knowledge*, 44.

DESIRE, POWER, AND SUBJECTIVITY

Florence urges on Leantio the realities of power stretching beyond the happy endings of New Comedy, and he seeks to save the stain and stimulus of its romance through the dubious legitimacy of a secret marriage. Sex with his wife turns into a surrogate of rare political privilege. The 'content' Leantio promised himself derived from his illegitimate possession of the conqueror's custom: 'But beauty able to content a conqueror, | Whom earth could scarce content, keeps me in compass' (1.1.26–7). The nexus of sex and political power glimpsed in this confession is one which events will force Leantio to acknowledge.

Bianca sparkles 'in beauty and destruction' (3.2.15) like the courtesans of her native Venice after being made to experience the 'content' coveted by Leantio. Reproducing Leantio's logic, she calls her new status as the Duke's mistress 'the best content | That Florence can afford' (3.2.40–1). When the Duke's messenger arrives to invite her to court, Leantio tries to drive his spoil to 'the end of the dark parlour', suggestively connected with a past crime of his father (3.1.161–5). But no recess is dark enough for the 'court sun' that now shines upon his wife (4.2.21), exposing his guilty secret to the light of public power.

If Leantio had looked upon his conquest as 'the best piece of theft' (1.1.43), then the Duke's capture of Bianca is merely a more professional conducting of 'love's businesses' (2.2.365). What for Leantio is piracy is for the Duke trade legitimized by power. That Bianca should fling back at Leantio 'a doctrine | Of [his] . . . own teaching' (3.2.87–8) after the rape is not surprising. It is a measure of the distance she has travelled since the initial seasickness her 'tender modesty' had suffered (2.2.471–3) that she can return her husband's demand of a kiss with the shop talk of the Exchange: 'Let's talk of other business . . . | What news of the pirates, any stirring?' (3.2.71–2).[37]

Leantio's thrift and timidity had always reflected the presence of money and power in Florentine reasoning. After the loss of Bianca, he has to accept its logic without the comforts of subterfuge. He is made to endure the Duke's public flaunting of Bianca, and to swallow the cuckold's sop of preferment. Hating her is Leantio's 'safest course | For

---

[37] Pirates were prominent news in 1620–1. See McClure (ed.), *Letters of John Chamberlain*, ii. 402; and *CSP Dom. 1619–23*, 301.

health of mind and body' (3.3.338–9), and he decides to accept Livia's offer of money for sex. Soon after, he returns to Bianca to show off his new clothes. As the former lovers inspect each other's pickings (cf. 4.1.41–104), they cease for the first time to be strangers to each other.

Bianca's initial optimism was neither complacence nor conviction, but a specular subjectivity forged by the fantasies Leantio had inspired in her. The desires she then said she enjoyed were 'second-order desires',[38] those that her self-understanding considered desirable. The rape makes her see that she had been a construct of Leantio's fantasies and rationalizations. Released from them, her subjectivity is now formed by the Duke's. Leantio had sought the pleasures of the forbidden in his wife; the Duke will seek the sanctioned indulgence of marriage in his whore. Bianca had played romance heroine and contented wife; she will now 'play the wise wench' (2.2.382), court beauty, and martyred Cleopatra. Bianca is a hostage of sexualized politics, and her 'deterioration', like the generic slide of the play, is really a passage from one male-forged narrative prison to another, from the bourgeois rationalization of sexual aggression plotted in New Comedy escapades to its conquest-fantasy expressed in imperial melodrama.[39]

The drift is evident in the instant political acuity which follows Bianca's loss of sexual innocence. As she curses the pimps in the new Florentine language the Duke has taught her, she echoes the political wisdom with which Antonio had sent Vindice to the gallows:

> And I'm like that great one
> Who making politic use of a base villain,
> *He likes the treason well, but hates the traitor.*
> So I hate thee, slave. (2.2.441–4)

Bianca's rape uncovers the usury of force which underwrites the stakes in comic romance. 'Romance has a vocation for cruelty but comedy can cure it,' writes John Traugott.[40] The Duke is a royal incarnation of the witty lover of Middleton's comedies, but one whose

[38] On 'second-order desires', see Charles Taylor, *Human Agency and Language: Philosophical Papers I* (Cambridge, 1985), 15–76.

[39] For a differrent route to a similar conclusion, see Ania Loomba, *Gender, Race, Renaissance Drama* (1989; Delhi, 1992), 101–3.

[40] John Traugott, 'Creating a Rational Rinaldo: A Study in the Mixture of the Genres of Comedy and Romance in *Much Ado About Nothing*', in Stephen Greenblatt (ed.), *The Forms of Power and the Power of Forms* = *Genre*, 15 (1982), 163.

special commission seems to be to rid the role of its comic and curative functions. He 'can command' (2.2.362) where others woo or deceive. He plays wooer and seducer by choice, although his success in such sport is assured by his superior force. Bianca makes a last effort to meet the Duke on his own ground by talking the language of 'love's businesses': 'Why should you seek, sir, | To take away that you can never give?' (2.2.367–8). The Duke's reply vocalizes the violence and power which ensure the epithalamic finale of comedy: 'But I give better in exchange: wealth, honour' (2.2.369).

Middleton rings a telling change here on the familiar situation, faced, for instance, by Jane and Fitzallen in *Quarrel*, where besieged virtue defends the liberty of conscience. To take an obscure though typical example, in John Mason's play *The Turk* (1606–7), when a besieged heroine asks Borgias to restore the 'honor' and 'life' he has robbed her of, he replies by offering to make her the Duchess of Florence (ll. 958–71). She spurns the offer, asserting the freedom of moral choice. Bianca is on different soil. Like the pawn on the chess-board downstairs, she cannot walk back (cf. 2.2.300–2), but must advance from one form of captivity into another.

Bianca's attempt to live the new self fashioned by the imperatives of male power shows in her sudden loathing of Leantio's mean lodgings. The misogynist pamphlets of the time had warned that within a few days of marriage a wife would start grumbling about her house and in-laws, and would be 'so loftie and proud, that euery thing stinketh in her nose'.[41] Bianca's complaints are inventoried almost entirely from these accounts. But there wives grumble because they are wives. Bianca's haughtiness, on the contrary, begins the moment she turns concubine, and is a bitter expression of her realization of political and gender subjection.[42]

Bianca thus learns to survey the world and herself in the light of the 'court-sun', even if that makes Leantio regard her as a variant of the prodigies travellers claimed to have encountered, 'A monster with all forehead, and no eyes' (4.1.93). The steadfast light Leantio's mother had attributed to the Duke's gaze (cf. 1.3.106–7) the Duke now finds in Bianca. 'Methinks there is no spirit amongst us, gallants,' he says in what sounds like a parody of Tamburlaine's odes to Zenocrate, 'But

---

[41] T[ofte], *Of Mariage and Wiuing*, D3^v.

[42] Bianca's complaints also contain smutty and cynical puns, as shown recently by R. V. Holdsworth, 'Notes on *Women Beware Women*', *N & Q* 238 (1993), 219–20.

what divinely sparkles from the eyes ⏐ Of bright Bianca' (3.3.97–9).[43]
A creation now of the Duke's desiring eyes, Bianca must see as she is
seen, that is, by the sun. She is proud to set her watch by the sun, not
'as some girls do ⏐ By ev'ry clock i' th' town' (4.1.11–12). The
reference to the sun, a royal emblem, cloaks a sharper irony. Like
Circe, Bianca is now the daughter of the sun, one of the period's many
circumlocutions for a whore.[44]

The functions of the comic lover and wit are in the play divided and
switched between Leantio and the Duke. In Venice, Leantio played
the romance hero; in Florence, he is the bourgeois husband. In Livia's
house, the Duke plays the witty trickster; back at court, he is the grand
lover with a conqueror's disdain for social rules. This movement
between social spaces dislodges actants from generic and ideological
indices. And it is in this movement between alternative social spaces
and male fantasies that the 'stranger' subjectivity of Bianca is made and
unmade. If she is frail, it is the frailty of the 'glasses' of male interest in
which, Isabella tells Angelo, women view themselves, 'Which are as
easy broke as they make forms' (*Measure for Measure*, 2.4.125–6).

PATRIARCHY AND INCEST

The political contingency of societal bonds, which English travellers
sensed in their experience of other cultures, is brought home to the
'stranger', and Bianca's nativization shows in her new use of old words
such as 'kind' and 'kindness'.[45] After the false reception at Livia's house,
her marriage appears to her a worse instance of betrayed hospitality.[46]

---

[43] Cf. *2 Tamburlaine*, ll. 2570–3.

[44] In *The Art of Living in London* (1642), Henry Peacham warns the gentleman against
'these overhot and crafty daughters of the sun, your silken and gold-laced harlots'. See Henry
Peacham, *The Complete Gentleman, The Truth of our Times* and *The Art of Living in London*, ed.
Virgil B. Heltzel (Ithaca, NY, 1962), 247; see also 162, 218.

[45] See McAlindon, *English Renaissance Tragedy*, 212–35.

[46] Hospitality could be interpreted as the obligation of the husband. Cf. 1.1.125–42; and
the following passage from a contemporary tract against wife-beating: 'A husband taketh his
wife from her friends, disacquainteth her with her kindsfolkes, debarreth her her parents
sight, and estrangeth her from whomsoever was dearest vnto her; he takes her into his own
hospitality; receives her into his protection, & himselfe becomes her sole Guardian. Where-
fore then to beat and abuse her, is the greatest iniury that can be against the law of
hospitalitie.'—W[illiam] H[eale], *An Apologie for Women* (Oxford, 1609), D3ᵛ. *The True
History of the Tragicke Loves of Hipolito and Isabella Neapolitans*, Middleton's probable source for
the sub-plot, plays on the idea: 'A wife . . . is like a guest, or the raine that becomes a trouble
in three dayes.' See Mulryne (ed.), *Women Beware*, 181.

'Kindness' and 'contentment' translate differently now that she feels she has sold herself short: 'Nay, since I am content to be so kind to you | To spare you for a silver basin and ewer' (3.1.22–3). Patriarchal ideology equates political and familial kinship, but Bianca's political nativization makes her a 'stranger' at home, perhaps in more senses than we suspect. A 'Harlot is called a stranger' in the Bible, Samuel Hieron warns the gadding wife in *The Spirituall Tillage* (1613), 'and the wife intituled the woman that *lyeth in the bosome* . . . It is for strumpets, not for wiues to be strangers.'[47]

Patriarchy derives legitimacy from the notion of natural bonds, from the identity of nature and right reason. The good life is the life according to natural law (*Idem est ergo beate vivere et secundum naturam*), and the bad is the unnatural (*omnia vitia contra naturam pugnant*).[48] The nature that rules Florence is a brutal one, and human positive law, as a result, is not applied reason, but applied power. The Duke thus promises the Cardinal not to 'keep woman . . . unlawfully' (4.1.255), and promptly arranges for the murder of Leantio, so that he might marry Bianca 'lawfully', 'Without this sin and horror' (4.1.273–4).

If *Women Beware* does not privilege patriarchal law, nor does it join the exaltation of paternalism which one finds in domestic tragedies such as *A Warning for Fair Women*.[49] The symbiotic bond holding together the spheres of sex and sustenance in Florence rules out any such binary simplism. 'As fitting is a government in love | As in a kingdom' (1.3.43–4)—the action of the play shows the ironic recoil of Leantio's simile on both tenor and vehicle. When love is mere lust, he adds, ''Tis like an insurrection in the people, | That raised in self-will wars against all reason' (1.3.45–6). The play, however, suggests that 'government' in both family and State is the political entailment of phallic 'self-will': only power makes any difference.

The legitimating principles the Church lays down for society and the State are sought to be upheld in the story by the Cardinal. He cannot rescue or subvert the fallen world, although he is ritually given the final words. When Bianca accuses him of lacking charity, and

---

[47] Samuel Hieron, *All the Sermons* (Cambridge, 1614), 2N3^v.

[48] Seneca, *De vita beata*, viii. 2, in *Moral Essays*, trans. and ed. John W. Basore, 3 vols., Loeb Classics (London, 1935), ii. 116–18; and *Ad Lucilium epistulae morales*, trans. and ed. Richard M. Gummere, 3 vols., Loeb Classics (1917–25; rev. edn., London, 1943), iii. 414.

[49] Leonard Tennenhouse, in *Power on Display: The Politics of Shakespeare's Genres* (New York, 1986), 147–86, reads Middleton's city comedies as exalting the claims of patriarchy over those of paternalism by showing that disorder in the family and civil society can be redressed only by the *parens patriae*.

obstructing the reform of sinners (cf. 4.3.47–69), what we marvel at is
her ability to twist the spirit of the directive principles while retaining
their letter. Every political system requires a set of legitimating values
concretized in ideologies. 'If ideologies decline, societies become
transparent.'[50] To the Cardinal, society is still opaque. To Bianca, it is
transparent, and she turns others' words around to let the light
through.

The study of familial and societal kinship is complemented by the
incest story in the sub-plot.[51] Isabella has none of Bianca's illusions
about playing the romance heroine or the contented wife. Like Livia,
she knows that 'Men buy their slaves, but women buy their masters'
when they marry (1.2.176). Unlike her, she believes that 'honesty and
love' can yet make marriage 'the most blest state' (1.2.177–8). She is
shocked when Hippolito declares his passion. Yet, once persuaded that
she is no more a kin to him 'Than the merest stranger is' (2.1.138), she
decides to marry the stupid Ward to camouflage her adultery. For the
native Isabella, such reasoning and reversal come easily: the moral and
generic location of her world hardly alters.

Isabella's change invites Hippolito, unaware of her newly found
excuse, to indulge in the fantasy travellers fight to repress. The most
horrifying marvels, as Renaissance voyagers guessed, are the surprises
at home to which the experience of the unfamiliar opens one's eyes.
Isabella's change appears to Hippolito more prodigious than all the
wonders he had come across in his ten years' travel (2.1.232–5). The
traveller's deviancy forces on him the traveller's hypocrisy. Secret
desires may be indulged provided native myths are not challenged. The
Duke instinctively strikes the right chord when he sets Hippolito
against Leantio, who, he says, has shamed his sister (4.1.151–2). Hippolito's reasoning is no different from that of many Florentine and
Jacobean politicians. The killing is justified since, instead of making use
of 'Art, silence, closeness, subtlety, and darkness', Leantio has chosen
to be 'An impudent daylight lecher' (4.2.7, 10). Hippolito has learnt to

---

[50] Claus Mueller, *The Politics of Communication: A Study in the Political Sociology of Language,
Socialization and Legitimacy* (London, 1973), 165.
[51] On incest in the play, see Lois E. Bueler, 'The Structural Uses of Incest in English
Renaissance Drama', *RD* 15 (1984), 135–8; and Stephen Wigler, 'Parent and Child: The
Pattern of Love in *Women Beware Women*', in Friedenreich (ed.), *'Accompaninge the Players'*,
183–201. On the political import of incest, see Thomas Bruce Boehrer, *Monarchy and Incest
in Renaissance England: Literature, Culture, Kinship, and Kingship* (Philadelphia, 1992).

love the treason and hate the traitor: the sexual hypocrisy of the colony matches the political hypocrisy of the palace.

The stories of rape and incest are linked by Livia, the only character to see clearly the relation of desire to power. She knows that the pleasures of commanding 'obedience . . . subjection, duty, and such kickshaws' (1.2.42) compensate a faithful husband's sexual self-denial. Livia is thus eligible for the median role of the comic farceur and courtesan of Middleton's early comedies. She loses her artistic control only after Leantio is killed, since "Tis harder to dissemble grief than love' (4.2.232). Love, which neither a smooth tongue nor political tact can control, betrays the cynic 'in another country'.

The gestic language of Florentine economy and power is brutalized by the Ward's careful inspection of Isabella's anatomy and by his game of cat-and-trap. Within the sub-plot, his illiterate bawdy is a contrast to the studied ambiguity of Livia's 'tongue-discourse' (2.2.152). He is 'not so base to learn to write and read' (1.2.126). His untroubled speech may be called, following Basil Bernstein, a 'restricted', as opposed to an 'elaborated', code. The user of the elaborated code perceives language as a set of alternatives for transmitting experience, while the user of the restricted code fails to see any expressive options.[52] Bernstein noticed that, although not exclusive to any class, the restricted code is used more often by the poor. In Middleton too, strategic mastery over words is an attribute of power, but different linguistic codes are very often morally equal. The Ward's language is different only in that it is not further reducible. In Bianca's new world, he is the Caliban who does not learn to curse.

PLAGUE

Some commentators have found the wedding-and-death masque weak and contrived, if not 'unperformable and rather silly',[53] while others have defended it as a grotesque consummation of the play's ironies.[54] It could be taken, I suggest, as an almost literal fulfilment of Leantio's

---

[52] See Basil Bernstein, *Class, Codes and Control*, 2 vols. (London, 1971–3), i. 118–37.

[53] Max Stafford Clark, in the programme note to the 1986 Royal Court Theatre production of Howard Barker's adaptation, as quoted in White, *Middleton and Tourneur*, 123.

[54] For close readings, see John Potter, ' "In Time of Sports": Masques and Masking in Middleton's *Women Beware Women*', *PLL* 18 (1982), 368–83; and Sarah P. Sutherland, *Masques in Jacobean Tragedy* (New York, 1983), 87–100.

curse: 'a plague will come' (4.1.104). Leantio leaves Bianca for the last time after making the prophecy, and Bianca perfumes her room to clear it of the 'corrupt air' she thinks he has left behind (4.1.105–9). But it was when he brought her to Florence that Leantio, as only his mother realized, rid another country of a plague and brought it home (cf. 3.2.91–2). The infection results in the masque's carnage, as the dying curses of the poisoned seem to imply: 'Plague of those Cupids', 'The pains and plagues of a lost soul upon him | That hinders me a moment' (5.2.140, 187–8).

Punitive notions of the plague since the Middle Ages had made the disease, to borrow Susan Sontag's phrase, 'adjectival'.[55] It was the arrow of God flying through the air,[56] the 'sudden destroyer of Mankind: the Nimble executioner of the Diuine *Iustice*'.[57] Having written plague pamphlets himself, Middleton could draw on such attitudes and memories in his audience, and make the final scene both sensational and recognizable.

Tennenhouse uses Foucault's observations on the plague to associate it with other Jacobean images of social indiscipline, such as riots and vagabondage, summoned to justify stricter imposition of hierarchical rule.[58] The image of the plague hardly serves such a strategy of containment in *Women Beware*. The masque, indeed, is an image of apocalyptic retribution for 'Lust and forgetfulness' (5.2.146), but, as Bianca realizes, one cannot escape the plagues of external power and of one's own desire by confinement to court or country. F. P. Wilson tells us the story of a woman in Shakespeare's London being struck down by the disease on her flight from the plague-infested city. On her corpse was reportedly inscribed, 'It is vain to fly from God, for He is everywhere.'[59] The futility of trying to escape contamination, physical and moral, by remaining socially immobile figures in Bianca's reflections towards the end of the play, when she marvels at her career in a

---

[55] Susan Sontag, *Illness as Metaphor* (1979; Harmondsworth, 1983), 63. For historical studies, see Paul Slack, *The Impact of Plague in Tudor and Stuart England* (Oxford, 1990); and Leeds Barroll, *Politics, Plague, and Shakespeare's Theatre: The Stuart Years* (Ithaca, NY, 1991).

[56] W. T., *A Casting Up of Accounts of Certain Errors* (1603), cited in F. P. Wilson, *The Plague in Shakespeare's London* (London, 1927), 71.

[57] Thomas Dekker, *London Looke Backe at that Yeare of Yeares 1625* (1630), in F. P. Wilson (ed.), *The Plague Pamphlets of Thomas Dekker* (Oxford, 1925), 181. On the suddenness of plague-deaths, see also *Meeting*, 133.

[58] See Tennenhouse, *Power on Display*, 162–5; and Michel Foucault, *Discipline and Punish: The Birth of the Prison*, trans. Alan Sheridan (1977; Harmondsworth, 1979), 195–200.

[59] Wilson, *Plague in Shakespeare's London*, 158.

strange land, and decides never to forbid her daughter either the court or the country (cf. 4.1.23–40). She has shed all fear of movement between places and ranks because she has learnt the lesson drawn by Foucault that it is 'vanity . . . to go questing after a desire that is beyond the reach of power'.[60]

For the audience, the masque is an image of the epidemic in the sense in which Antonin Artaud believed all meaningful theatre was like the plague. Both present 'an absolute crisis after which there is nothing left except death or drastic purification'. St Augustine thought that the pagan gods appointed theatres to infect those whom the plague spared.[61] Artaud stands the analogy of physical and moral pestilence on its head by stressing the absolute and curative nature of both: 'theatre action is as beneficial as the plague, impelling us to see ourselves as we are, making the masks fall and divulging our world's lies, aimlessness, meanness, and even two-facedness'.[62] Ducal procession, chess-play, banquet, masque—Florence had tried to fashion its self-deceiving image in such mirrors of theatrical feigning. When the cues of the masque are mistaken, Middleton's apocalyptic theatre takes over. The masks fall, if not quite for the characters, certainly for his viewers.

POLITICS, CIVIL SOCIETY, AND GENRE

Women Beware, it has been noticed often, blends the comic and the tragic, Italian courtliness and bourgeois domesticity.[63] My argument would suggest that this mixture is necessitated by Middleton's understanding of the inseparability of power and desire, and of political culture and civil society. The dispossessed Italian Duke in Edward Sharpham's *Fleer* (1606) had to move from Florence to London to spy on his daughters, who had set up a brothel there. Middleton's Duke did not need to make any such journey from Italian political play to

---

[60] Foucault, *History of Sexuality: Introduction*, 82.

[61] See St Augustine, *The City of God against the Pagans*, trans. and ed. George E. McCracken, 7 vols., Loeb Classics (London, 1957), i. 167–73.

[62] Antonin Artaud, *The Theatre and its Double*, trans. Victor Corti (London, 1970), 22.

[63] See e.g. Madeleine Doran, *Endeavors of Art: A Study of Form in Elizabethan Drama* (Madison, Wis., 1954), 136–7; Schoenbaum, *Middleton's Tragedies*, 127–30; Ornstein, *Moral Vision of Jacobean Tragedy*, 190–9; Tomlinson, *Study of Elizabethan and Jacobean Tragedy*, 158–84; Cyrus Hoy, *The Hyacinth Room: An Investigation into the Nature of Comedy, Tragedy and Tragicomedy* (London, 1964), 211–20; Krook, *Elements of Tragedy*, 146–83; Farr, *Middleton and the Drama of Realism*, 92–7; Brooke, *Horrid Laughter*, 89–110; and McAlindon, *English Renaissance Tragedy*, 209–10.

English citizen drama: he merely stepped from his palace into Livia's house.

Moretti located the political dimension of English Renaissance tragedy 'in posing the question of whether a *cultural foundation* of power is still possible, and in answering it in the negative'.[64] The tragic dimension of the politics of *Women Beware* does not consist in any simple 'negative' that might be offered to Moretti's question. Rather than affirm or deny the misalliance of cultural and political hegemony, it explores the repressed identity of their structures. The identity begins to hit the eye once the ideological scales fall off, as they threatened to do when Renaissance voyagers looked at alien cultures. Like Leantio, contemporary discourse struggled to express as well as contain the consequences of such exposure. *Women Beware* dramatizes these consequences by denuding political and cultural formations of their sacralizing myths. If the play is tragic, it is because it thereby magnifies the price of human irresponsibility. More clearly than most contemporaries, Middleton understood that power and culture, as Richard Rorty puts it, 'are equipollent indications of the social forces which make us more than animals—and which, when the bad guys take over, can turn us into something worse and more miserable than animals'.[65]

---

[64] Moretti, *Signs Taken for Wonders*, 64.
[65] Richard Rorty, *Consequences of Pragmatism: Essays: 1972–1980* (Minneapolis, 1982), 208.

7
Servants and Masters: *The Changeling*

In recent years, *The Changeling* (1622) has come to be seen as either an attack on class and gender rule,[1] or as a warning against marital and political alliance with Spain.[2] In the first approach, De Flores is a heroic iconoclast; in the second, an effigy of Spanish evils. It seems that the play may be read as politically radical only at the cost of making it socially conservative.[3]

The issues of sex and power coalesce in the sado-masochistic concerns of *Changeling*. The interests at work in sado-masochism have always been 'political in the fundamental sense of social management'.[4] Sex in *Changeling* is political in this fundamental sense. Despite Rowley's substantial share, the text displays how easily the comic Middletonian themes of sex and money can sour into the tragic politics of desire and power.[5] By sexualizing class relations, it exposes idealized loyalties of late feudalism as functions of political strength. To this purpose, the play reformulates the tropes of chivalry and courtly love, and it is more concerned with estranging their generic register on the stage than with demonized Spain.

CASTLE AND GARDEN

The action opens with Alsemero, known for his indifference to women, discovering desire in a strange country. He is overcome by his first sight of Beatrice in an Alicante temple, and prepares to leave on learning of her engagement to Alonzo. His retreat is cut off by Vermandero's unsuspecting cordiality. Marriage, Alsemero hoped,

---

[1] See Dollimore, *Radical Tragedy*, 178; and Heinemann, *Puritanism and Theatre*, 174–80.
[2] Bromham and Bruzzi, Changeling *and the Years of Crisis, passim*.
[3] A recent example of the either–or approach is Cristina Malcolmson, ' "As Tame as the Ladies": Politics and Gender in *The Changeling*', *ELR* 20 (1990), 320–39.
[4] Morse Peckham, *Victorian Revolutionaries: Speculations on Some Heroes of a Cultural Crisis* (New York, 1970), 248–9.
[5] Besides master-minding the sub-plot, Rowley is also present in the first and last scenes. See Joost Daalder's re-edited New Mermaids edition (London, 1990), pp. xiv–xvi.

would let him retrace his way back to man's lost perfection (cf. 1.1.7–12). What follows is his irreversible descent into the labyrinth of his host's castle: 'But I must on, for back I cannot go' (1.1.224). Castle, city, and temple are shown in Rowley's opening scene to be invaded by disruptive desires. From these infected enclosures, Alsemero wished to set out for the lost garden. The *hortus conclusus* was an emblem of the normative body politic in which desire accorded with power, nature with political rule.[6] When Sir Thomas Lake's wife and her daughter were found guilty of extorting false confessions of adultery from the Countess of Exeter, King James is reported to have 'compared their crimes to the first plot of the first sin in Paradise; the Lady Lake to the serpent, her daughter unto Eve, and Sir Thomas to poor Adam'.[7] The comparison implied the primacy of innocence in the king's political garden as also his providential presence. In the garden of the play, no such keeper expels corruption; his power merely stands guard over its own germinal secrets.

The most unsettling presence in the garden is that of De Flores, the 'serpent' (1.1.225). In the opening scene, he lurks in the shadows, moaning like the despised lover in courtly poetry. But his motive is pleasure, and he announces it in a most uncourtly way: 'Though I get nothing else, I'll have my will' (l. 237). It is the same unreason of the 'peevish will' (l. 107) which he knows to be the source of Beatrice's distaste for him. The insurgent will had destroyed the political covenant of the first garden. De Flores is free of the illusion of marriage being a way back to that concord. He sees his garden as a battlefield of phallic wills, and quickly realizes that the female 'will' is the breach through which he may worm into a position of vantage.

In the scene's closing episode, as De Flores gallantly picks up the glove that Beatrice lets fall, she peels off the other glove and discards the pair in a fit of rage. De Flores's fetishism sullies the courtly trope more irreparably than his touch: 'She had rather wear my pelt tann'd in a pair | Of dancing pumps, than I should thrust my fingers | Into her sockets here' (1.1.232–4). The scene recalls the glove-episode in *The Spanish Tragedy* (1.4.100–3), and reverses its consequences.[8] Unlike

---

[6] See A. Bartlett Giamatti, *The Earthly Paradise and the Renaissance Epic* (Princeton, NJ, 1966), 102–3.

[7] [William Sanderson], *Aulicus Coquinariae or A Vindication in Answer to a Pamphlet, Entituled The Court and Character of King James*, in Scott (ed.), *Secret History*, ii. 196–7.

[8] See Marion Lomax, *Stage Images and Traditions: Shakespeare to Ford* (Cambridge, 1987), 46. Cf. Ford's *Broken Heart*, 4.1.23–36.

Belimperia and Horatio, Beatrice and De Flores besmirch the symbolism of the chivalric ritual, and the ground is laid for the time when De Flores will brandish Alonzo's severed finger as a phallic trophy.

De Flores's reading of the glove-symbolism reflects the way the devitalized code of *amour courtois* had come to be applied in the Jacobean court. The episode may allude to an incident at the court involving Frances Howard and Prince Henry shortly before the latter's death in 1612.[9] It was rumoured that Frances, then Countess of Essex, had been the prince's mistress, but that she had soon switched her attentions to Carr, then Viscount Rochester. In the incident reported by Arthur Wilson, the prince snubbed her by refusing to accept the glove which she had dropped at a dance, 'saying publickly, He would not have it, it is stretcht by another, meaning the Viscount'.[10] Even if mere court gossip, the anecdote is an instance of the perverse semiotics De Flores has mastered.

The opening scene seems to imitate the structure of Vermandero's castle, 'plac'd conspicuous to outward view, | On promonts' tops; but within are secrets' (1.1.165–6). Chivalric love and honour define the outward view, while lust and deception lurk within. To see through the façade is to master its discursive optics.[11]

SERVICE

De Flores's flair for turning the rules against the rulers is most evident in the way he inverts the language and gestures of chivalry, of 'love', 'honour', 'reward', and, above all, 'service'. 'Service' could be sexual as well as social, and Christopher Ricks saw Beatrice trapped by De Flores's tactical use of the ambiguity.[12] Leo Salingar noted further quibbles. 'Service' could be privileged or low-born, chivalric or mercenary, rewarded with love, honour, or money.[13]

---

[9] Bromham and Bruzzi, Changeling *and the Years of Crisis*, 30.

[10] Wilson, *Life and Reign of James*, in [Kennett], *Complete History of England*, ii. 5S3ᵛ–4.

[11] On the castle, see Tomlinson, *Study of Elizabethan and Jacobean Tragedy*, 185–212; Thomas L. Berger, 'The Petrarchan Fortress of *The Changeling*', in G. Walton Williams (ed.), *Renaissance Papers* (Durham, NC, 1969), 37–46; and Lancashire, 'Emblematic Castle', 228–9.

[12] Christopher Ricks, 'The Moral and Poetic Structure of *The Changeling*', *EC* 10 (1960), 290–306.

[13] L. G. Salingar, '*The Changeling* and the Drama of Domestic Life', *E & S* 33 (1979), 92–3.

The semantic indecision was a symptom of the ideological incoherence of late feudal culture. In the classical phase of feudalism,
love-service or *domnei* was conceived as an analogue of the liege-hom-
age which a vassal owed his overlord. The analogy had its social point
since, as Maurice Keen observes, the lady's acceptance of love-service
was for the young climber 'the *laisser passer* into the rich, secure world
of the court of which she was mistress'.[14] Courtly love, with its concept
of 'service', was thus from the start 'a ritualized expression of anxieties
about social class and sexuality'.[15] Moreover, the 'service' of the free
vassal, as distinct from that of the servile orders, was conceived to be
prompted by his loyalty and honour, not by fear and necessity: *Basallus
servit seniori suo propter fidem suam quam professus est illi servire, ut non
inveniatur fallax.*[16] In the courtly lover, the myth promoted a peculiar
mixture of submission and proud self-regard, cultivated as a badge of
social entitlement.

By the fourteenth century, service was all but divorced from vassal-
age and tenure. The essence of the 'bastard' phase of feudalism that
followed was paid service. Feudalism hence became 'a complex network of marketable privileges', although its ideological forms survived
well beyond medieval times.[17] Bastard feudalism could employ these
vestigial forms as ideological curbs on the mobility of the ever-increas-
ing claimants of privilege. Ideas such as those of native honour and
sprezzatura were thus used, as Frank Whigham has shown, to set up
rigid ontological barriers between noble and ignoble.[18]

However, even in medieval courtly culture, the premises of inherited and cultivated honour were hard to reconcile, as is evident in
the tension between the polite norm of the early troubadours (*cortezia*)
and the Christian chivalry of northern France (*courtoisie*).[19] The fragile
truce which justified privilege was that innate grace, both of blood and
mind, must invariably express itself in visible forms. Thus in Book 6 of
The Faerie Queene we are told that 'vertues seat is deepe within the

[14] Maurice Keen, *Chivalry* (New Haven, Conn., 1984), 30.
[15] Donald R. Howard, *The Three Temptations: Medieval Man in Search of the World*
(Princeton, NJ, 1966), 97. See also Herbert Moller, 'The Social Causation of the Courtly
Love Complex', *Comparative Studies in Society and History*, 1 (1958–9), 137–63.
[16] *Expositio in regulam S. Benedicti*, as quoted in F. L. Ganshof, *Feudalism*, trans. Philip
Grierson (1952; 3rd edn., London, 1964), 29.
[17] K. B. McFarlane, ' "Bastard Feudalism" ', *Bulletin of the Institute of Historical Research*, 20
(1945), 162.
[18] Whigham, *Ambition and Privilege*, 70.
[19] See Roger Boase, *The Origin and Meaning of Courtly Love: A Critical Study of European
Scholarship* (Manchester, 1977), 49.

mynd, | And not in outward shows, but inward thoughts defynd', and that, at the same time, 'a man by nothing is so well bewrayd, | As by the manners, in which plaine is showne | Of what degree and what race he is growne' (Proem, 5.8–9; 3.1.3–5).

The compromise directed ideological strategies in the Renaissance to defend and restrict class privilege. The advantage of birth was claimed also for the gentle servingman, although he now worked for payment. Guazzo's *Civile Conversation* distinguishes 'vile and base servantes' from 'the good and suche as are gentlemen', the former 'pitching their marke at vyle gayne', the latter, 'at honour and re-nowne': 'Whereuppon it is sayd, That the gentleman loveth, and the slave feareth.'[20] The same distinction is made in *A Health to the Gentle-manly Profession of Seruing-men* (1598), a tract which deplores the devaluation of gentle service in England by an upstart élite. It sets the 'filiall feare' of the servingman above the slavish obedience of the servant, and even grants the former a native grace comparable to the courtier's, 'a decent and comely manner' in the carrying of a dish or a rapier.[21] The mystique of non-mercenary, voluntary loyalty also shapes the notion of love-service. The emphasis this time is on the well-born servant's selfless and unsensual devotion. Can one be said to truly 'serve', asked John Ford in *Honour Triumphant* (1606), 'when he more respects the liberty of his own affections than the imposition of ladies' command?'[22]

The decline of the social formations sustaining the chivalric tropes also enabled writers to exploit their anomalies. The usual strategy for such texts was to shift or play off registers within the allied *topoi* of love and honour.[23] In *Bussy d'Ambois*, Tamara uses the word 'honour' to mean unassailable and innate virtue: 'Mine honour's in mine owne hands, spite of kings.' But Monsieur turns the word round to the libertine sense of shame and prudery: 'Honour, what's that? your second maidenhead: | And what is that? a word' (Q1, 2.2.59–61).

The example from *Bussy* raises the crucial problem of the conflicting premises about women underlying polite and moral norms of

[20] Steeven Guazzo, *The Civile Conversation*, trans. George Pettie and Bartholomew Young, 2 vols. (1581–6; Tudor Translations, 2nd ser. 8, London, 1925), ii. 94.

[21] I. M., *Health to the Gentlemanly Profession of Seruing-men*, B2ᵛ.

[22] William Gifford and Alexander Dyce (eds.), *The Works of John Ford*, 3 vols. (London, 1869), iii. 347.

[23] See Hiram Haydn, *The Counter-Renaissance* (New York, 1950), 555–618. On the multiplicity of registers in the discourse of courtly love, see Paul Zumthor, *Essai de poétique médiévale* (Paris, 1972), 251–2.

'honour'. While chivalry distinguished women by status, the moral alternatives, whether Christian or libertine, reduced them to an undifferentiated gendered category. Massinger's *Renegado* (1623–4) has an English–born eunuch, Carazie, who, while briefing the Tunisian heroine on love-service as understood by court ladies in England, says that they are lobbying for a law which will allow them 'a priuate friend' to 'ease' their husbands (1.2.45–6). Carazie, however, is equally harsh on city and country women (cf. *Broken Heart*, 2.1.23–40). Ranks are irrelevant, since 'women in England | For the most part liue like *Queenes*' (1.2.27–8). The queen/quean pun collapses all social distinctions into a single moral class defined by gender.

Simultaneously, moralists tended to indict chivalric rituals as a front for misogyny and male lechery. To cite a somewhat late example, in Arthur Wilson's account of the Duke of Buckingham's womanizing, courtly phrases shrivel to reveal a core of depraved misogyny:

For the Marquis himself, as he was a Man of excellent Symetry, and proportion of Parts, so he affected Beauty, where he found it; but yet he looks upon the whole Race of Women as inferior Things, and uses them as if the Sex were one, best pleased with all. . . .[24]

For the malcontent climber, the loathing of women could disguise his awareness of the subservient status he shared with them. 'For like the woman he despises, he is bought by the highest bidder; like them his only role is service.'[25] Attacks on cosmetics, for instance, could conceal the aspiring courtier's own need for self-exhibition. Thus Bosola's criticism of women's 'face-physicke' leads on to a meditation on the insubstantiality of 'this outward forme of man' (*Duchess of Malfi*, 2.1.24, 47), not of women in particular. After all, the feminine for courtier in Italian, *cortegiana*, was never used by Castiglione, since it also meant a prostitute.[26]

The moral solidarity De Flores claims with his mistress is a powerful reminder of the shared subservience of servant and woman. Gender and class were always mixed in the complex motive for his obsession with Beatrice. Although a servingman, he had 'tumbled into th' world a gentleman' (2.1.49). Wendoll in Heywood's *Woman Killed with*

[24] Wilson, *Life and Reign of James*, in [Kennett], *Complete History of England*, ii. 5Z4ᵛ.
[25] Peter Stallybrass, 'Patriarchal Territories: The Body Enclosed', in Ferguson *et al.* (eds.), *Rewriting the Renaissance*, 134.
[26] The point is made by J. R. Woodhouse, *Baldesar Castiglione: A Reassessment of* The Courtier (Edinburgh, 1978), 55.

Kindness (1603) was 'a gentleman | Of a good house, somewhat press'd by want' (4.32–3). But he was not ugly. His motive in seducing his benefactor's wife was lust, and his worst offence was ingratitude. De Flores's ugliness, not present in the source, adds gender disinheritance to social, and makes his motive one of sexual and class revenge. Alienated in his own society, his situation is almost the reverse of Othello's. While Othello, the accepted outsider, cannot break free of the discursive framework within which his otherness is defined,[27] De Flores, the exiled insider, can exploit its contradictions. He can in turn protest like the true *chevalier* and the Puritan moralist, and yet extract his pound of flesh.

Beatrice is cast in the role of the *donna di palazzo*, loving 'with the eyes of judgement' and rewarding 'A true deserver' (2.1.13–15), but De Flores cares little for her 'intellectual eyesight' (2.1.19).[28] He knows that 'there's daily precedents of bad faces | Belov'd beyond all reason' (2.1.83–4), and that the moral pretext of privilege, like the Neoplatonic equation of beauty and virtue, is a sham. His description of ugly faces does not stop at vivid details such as witch-like chins and 'Wrinkles like troughs': it leads on to the thought of 'tears of perjury. . . | Fallen from the slimy and dishonest eye' (2.1.40–5). The 'swine-deformity' (l. 43) that high-born beauty is known to dote on is a moral deformity as well.

The key trope of domination that De Flores subverts is 'service'. Moments after lamenting his luck which has doomed him to 'servitude', he tells Beatrice with courtly equivocation, 'True service merits mercy' (2.1.48, 63). 'Servitude' and 'service'—De Flores lays siege on master tropes by forcing the semantic breach between the two words. Several contemporary plays exploit the ambiguity, and Ornstein sees parallels between *Changeling* and *The Maid's Tragedy* in this respect.[29] To take two obscurer examples, in Marston and Barksted's *Insatiate Countess*, Isabella commissions first Gniaca and then Don Sago to kill for her by playing upon the shifty notion of 'service' (cf. 4.2.20–37; 5.1.74, 131–2); and in Beaumont and Fletcher's *Cupid's Revenge* (published 1615), Bacha does the same in asking Tiamantus to murder

---

[27] See Edward Berry, 'Othello's Alienation', *SEL* 30 (1990), 315–33. Helen Gardner, 'Milton's "Satan" and the Theme of Damnation in Elizabethan Tragedy', *E & S* 1 (1948), 61, misleadingly connects the experience of exclusion with Beatrice.

[28] R. V. Holdsworth, 'Notes on *The Changeling*', *N & Q* 234 (1989), 344, compares *Lady*, 2.2.68. Beatrice's depiction of her fickleness as clearing vision is closer to Isabella's self-portrayal in *Insatiate Countess*; cf. 2.3.48–9; 3.2.39–42.

[29] Ornstein, *Moral Vision*, 179–90.

Leucippus (cf. 3.2.237–40, 3.3.19–20, 3.4.139; 4.1.211–12). But the lovers in these plays neither feel De Flores's privation nor possess his insight. Unlike them, De Flores can sabotage the discourse of power because in its ambiguities he can spy the fissured rock on which his master's castle and authority are founded.

CHALLENGE

The first of the two great encounter scenes opens with Alsemero, the 'complete gentleman' (2.2.3), arriving to keep his secret tryst with Beatrice. It is followed by another meeting, with De Flores taking the place of Alsemero. The scene develops the contrast between Beatrice's treatment of the 'complete gentleman' and the incomplete one, and between their respective responses. Alsemero proposes to her the 'One good service' (l. 21) of killing Alonzo in a duel. She restrains him, since 'Blood-guiltiness becomes a fouler visage' (l. 40). The last phrase reminds her of De Flores, the 'poison' which must now be used to 'expel another' (ll. 46–7). She hustles Alsemero out, and De Flores, who has watched the meeting, steps in.

The proverbial economy of nature whereby one poison expelled another was one to which Mary Fitzallard had referred in *Roaring Girl*. Beatrice's decision also recalls the Machiavellian maxim about liking the treason but hating the traitor to which Bianca had turned after the rape. Although the speakers in both instances were women, the cynical wisdom they mouthed was produced, as we saw in Antonio's sentence on Vindice, by male politics. They both spoke like the Duke in *1 Whore*, who had exiled a doctor after having used him, or so he had thought, for a murder: 'This principle is olde but true as fate, | Kings may love treason, but the traitor hate' (4.4.49–50). Women of 'art', who play with poison, have to exploit female subjection as well as male desire, a fact well known to Livia and Roxena, but dimly grasped by Beatrice.

The Jacobean men of art, Northampton and Suffolk, successfully used the service of one Copinger, when they planted Frances in order to be able to control the influential Carr. If we can believe Anthony Weldon, Copinger's social predicament was not unlike De Flores's. He was an impoverished gentleman, 'now, for maintenance . . . forced to lead the life of a serving man'. His service made him 'a friend to Northampton and Suffolk, though but a servant to Viscount Rochester'.[30] Copinger's self-prostitution is divided between his roles as 'friend' and 'servant', a split consequent on his social decline. If the politic artist was a woman, the acceptance of male 'service' as that from a 'friend' might trap her into difficulties not provided for in the chivalric code. We know little about Sir David Wood, the 'ill-looked, red-bearded Scot' with whom Frances was reported to have plotted Overbury's murder.[31] Other agents were used to poison Overbury, but the entire scandal shows how she was beaten by her own dependent gender status. Her sexuality was a tool in the male power-game long before she could use tools of her own devising, and the moral outrage aroused by Overbury's murder could later be deflected against her supposedly unruly female concupiscence.

Unlike Copinger, De Flores can use his 'service' to revenge his social and gender dispossession. Even before he is hired, De Flores detects signs of a promiscuous career in Beatrice's sexual wavering, for a woman who strays once 'Proves in time sutler to an army royal' (2.2.64). As the Revels editor notes, De Flores's comparison recalls *Hengist* (4.2.274–7), where the sins which are unbarred by a woman's first illicit affair are likened to the rush of an army through 'a small Breach in towne or Castle' made by one soldier.[32] In both plays, the image acquires immediacy from the presence of actual castles as symbols which guard privilege instead of virtue.

Beatrice's doublespeak about 'service' widens the breach in the castle. She uses speech as a sexual bait, calling De Flores by name, praising his face while stroking it, and offering to prepare a lotion for his bad skin. She then steers the talk round to the 'service' she needs, gives him money, and hints at further rewards. Francesco Barbaro had recommended 'that not only arms but indeed also the speech of women never be made public; for the speech of a noble woman can be no less dangerous than the nakedness of her limbs.'[33] Despite knowing that the face she 'call'd scurvy scarce an hour ago' is the same 'to a hair and pimple' (ll. 76–7), De Flores confirms Barbaro's fears by

---

[30] A[nthony] W[eldon], *The Court and Character of King James* (1651), repr. in Scott (ed.), *Secret History*, i. 377–8.

[31] W. Sanderson, *A Compleat History of the Lives and Reigns of Mary Queen of Scotland, and of her Son and Successor, James the Sixth, King of Scotland* (1656), and BM Add. MS 15476, as cited in White, *Cast of Ravens*, 58.

[32] The wild progression of loosened female lust was a misogynist commonplace. Cf. *Revenger*, 4.4.78–80; and Beaumont and Fletcher, *Love's Pilgrimage* (1615), 2.1.136–44.

[33] Francesco Barbaro, 'On Wifely Duties', trans. Benjamin Kohl, in Kohl et al. (eds.), *Earthly Republic*, 205.

finding her verbal striptease 'half an act of pleasure' (l. 86). He plays his part of the game, kneeling for 'the honour of a service' from her 'ladyship' (ll. 95–6), but rising to speak a bolder tongue once the deal is struck. Beatrice's adroit play on the language of 'service', 'manhood', 'blood and danger', and 'reward' (ll. 93, 119, 130) shows how easy it is to overturn these chivalric concepts. Her failure to read others' puns, however, derives from an imperfect awareness of how language covers ideological seams. Beatrice's remark about blood-guilt becoming a foul visage changes smoothly into 'Hardness becomes the visage of a man well' (l. 92). But when she talks of the 'experience' which 'hourly mends' a 'hard face' (ll. 88–90), her words treacherously slide into a moral register. Within moments, De Flores strikes her as 'lovely' (ll. 135–6). She casts her fears upon his 'service' (l. 140), hoping that once 'the deed's done', he can be pensioned off 'to live bravely in another country' (ll. 141–3). When he answers that they will talk of that 'hereafter' (l. 144), she catches neither the cynical quibble nor the tonal change.

Beatrice is shown as inexperienced, selfish, cruel, and sexually disturbed. The focus throughout is on the self-representations of desire and morals within a discursive economy under stress. To think of Beatrice as a spoilt child is to be influenced by her view of events; to think of her as a Lamia whose evil is progressively revealed is to sympathize with De Flores's.[34] There is a grain of truth in both versions, if only because the play explores the social conditions of their conflict.

REWARD

The space between the two encounter scenes is taken up by the swift dispatch of Alonzo. Playing the loyal 'servant' (2.2.162), De Flores

[34] For the spoilt-child view of Beatrice, see Ellis-Fermor, *Jacobean Drama*, 146–7; Schoenbaum, *Middleton's Tragedies*, 138; and Levin, *Multiple Plot*, 39–42. A few examples of the sterner view are Karl L. Holzknecht, 'The Dramatic Structure of *The Changeling*', *Renaissance Papers* (1954; repr. Ann Arbor, Mich., 1961), 80; Penelope B. R. Doob, 'A Reading of *The Changeling*', *ELR* 3 (1973), 188–9; J. L. Simmons, 'Diabolical Realism in Middleton and Rowley's *The Changeling*', *RD* 11 (1980), 140–9; Dale B. J. Randall, 'Some Observations on the Theme of Chastity in *The Changeling*', *ELR* 14 (1984), 347–66; Charles W. Crupi, 'The Transformation of De Flores in *The Changeling*', *Neophilologus*, 68 (1984), 142–9; and Martin Wiggins, *Journeymen in Murder: The Assassin in English Renaissance Drama* (Oxford, 1991), 183–92.

guides him through 'the ways and straits' (2.2.159) of the 'spacious and impregnable fort' (3.1.4). The maze leads to a 'descent ⌐ ... somewhat narrow' (3.1.5–6), and De Flores stabs Alonzo from behind as he stops to view 'the full strength of all the castle' (3.2.7). The sequence links a set of allied images—the castle, the labyrinth, the female body, the descent into hell, the crossing of the strait into *mare mortuum*.[35] The key which opens the secrets of the castle and of the female body for De Flores is the finger he cuts off the murdered Alonzo. Since the diamond ring Beatrice had sent Alonzo as a token would not 'part in death' (3.2.24), De Flores takes both ring and finger. The association of diamond with chastity and of the ringed finger with marriage are severed at a stroke.[36] The finger now serves the same purpose as Lollio's phallic whip, and Beatrice learns to obey its command just as the lunatics in the sub-plot bend to Lollio's 'pizzle'. The rebellious slaves in Massinger's *Bondman* (1623) are brought to heel by just such a show of whips,[37] and modern readers will recall the sight of the Count's boots, 'standing there so stiff and perky', which makes Jean, his servant, 'bend' in *Miss Julia*.[38] In *Changeling*, however, it is the servant who wrests the phallic key, and it is the mistress who bends. Symbolic possession, or the possession of symbols, and not any native majesty or servility, marks rulers off from the ruled.

Erving Goffman coined the terms 'presentation' and 'avoidance' rituals for the gestures which define proximity and distance in social interaction.[39] In the hiring scene, speech and social gests (kiss, touch, kneeling) had shown the extent to which Beatrice and De Flores were able to fake the presentation rituals of chivalry. In the second encounter, the phallic digit enables De Flores to cross its avoidance limits.

[35] See J. Chesley Taylor, 'Metaphors of the Moral World: Structure in *The Changeling*', *Tulane Studies in English*, 20 (1972), 41–56. Brooke, *Horrid Laughter*, 85, compares the castle to the female body. See also Frank Whigham, 'Reading Social Conflict in the Alimentary Tract: More on the Body in Renaissance Drama', *ELH* 55 (1988), 339–44.

[36] On the finger, ring, and diamond images, see Normand Berlin, 'The "Finger" Image and Relationship of Character in *The Changeling*', *English Studies in Africa*, 12 (1969), 162–6; Dorothea Kehler, 'Rings and Jewels in *The Changeling*', *ELN* 5 (1967), 15–17; and Doob, 'A Reading of *Changeling*', 202–6.

[37] On the historical sources of the story, see Philip Edwards, 'The Sources of Massinger's *The Bondman*', *RES*, NS 15 (1964), 21–6.

[38] August Strindberg, *Eight Famous Plays*, trans. Edwin Björkman and N. Erichsen (New York, 1949), 135.

[39] Erving Goffman, *Interaction Ritual: Essays on Face-to-Face Behaviour* (London, 1972), 62–76.

He drops ceremonies and addresses Beatrice as an equal from the moment he shows her Alonzo's finger. As Beatrice flinches at the sight, he shifts to a moral register: 'Why, is that more | Than killing the whole man?' (3.4.29–30). He uses the finger to remind her of the repugnant conduct of courtiers: 'A greedy hand thrust in a dish at court, | In a mistake hath had as much as this' (ll. 31–2). The greedy hand recalls the thrusting finger of the glove-episode, while the court-dish hints at Beatrice's sexual status in élite society (Bellafront refers to the gallants on stage as 'court-dishes' in *1 Whore*, 2.1.22).

De Flores maintains the tone of moral sarcasm when Beatrice gifts him the diamond: ''Twill hardly buy a capcase for one's conscience, though' (l. 44). He pockets the fee, reminding her that he has learnt to accept such dishonourable recompense from his social betters. Beatrice is anxious that appearances should be kept up: 'Why, thou mistak'st, De Flores, 'tis not given | In state of recompense' (ll. 49–50). De Flores in reply calls her 'lady' and talks of 'service' and 'performance' (ll. 50, 53–4, 57), but Beatrice does not catch the irony. As she offers him three thousand golden florins, De Flores sees his moment and, assuming the tone of the outraged *cavaliere servante*, mocks the pretence of selfless service which cloaks the trade in sex and money: 'What, salary? . . . | Do you place me in the rank of verminous fellows, | To destroy things for wages?' (ll. 63–5).

De Flores's abrupt refusal to play by the rules puts Beatrice 'in a labyrinth' (l. 71). He demands a kiss and, like the Duke in *Women Beware*, warns that he has power now to force her. Beatrice asks him to remember his place, but De Flores reminds her of her own moral amnesia: 'Push, you forget yourself! | A woman dipp'd in blood, and talk of modesty?' (ll. 125–6). Like the apologists of morally unmerited privilege, Beatrice invokes 'creation', the natural order which has set avoidance limits between her blood and his (ll. 130–1). De Flores's celebrated answer to this presumption rests on the familiar argument that if virtue justifies privilege, vice must disentitle the claims of birth. Ralegh argued that 'if honour . . . be a witnesse of vertue and well-doing', then a nobility fallen from virtue is 'like vnto painted and printed papers, which ignorant men worship in steade of *Christ*, our Ladie, and other Saints'.[40] De Flores's contempt for unearned status employs a similar skill in Protestant polemics:

---

[40] Ralegh, *History of the World*, 163.

Look but into your conscience, read me there,
'Tis a true book, you'll find me there your equal:
Push, fly not to your birth, but settle you
In what the act has made you, y'are no more now;
You must forget your parentage to me:
Y'are the deed's creature . . . (ll. 132-7)

Speaking like a Puritan, he calls her a whore at heart, though techni-
cally a virgin (l. 142).[41] The social gests of the hiring scene are now
symmetrically reversed. It is Beatrice's turn to kneel, and De Flores's
to pour contempt on her offer of money. The verbal foreplay ends
with De Flores echoing the Duke in *Women Beware* as he feels Beatrice
panting like a turtle in his arms (l. 170), a stunning measure of the
enormity of his social usurpation.

De Flores thus subverts the language of chivalry by exploiting the
anomaly between the polite and moral criteria of privilege, and that
between the ideals of feudalism and the realities of its bastard sequel.
Since coded restraint is basic to the practice of chivalry, the interplay
of its presentation and avoidance rituals is a crucial element in plays
which employ its idiom. A good example is Beatrice's juggling with its
ambiguities in *Much Ado*; a bad one is the heroine's trifling in Beaumont and Fletcher's *Scornful Lady* (1616). An intriguing instance is
Massinger's *Maid of Honour*, played at the same theatre (Phoenix) in
probably the same year as *Changeling*. The play shows Camiola spurn-
ing the love of Adorni, a gentleman servant, who has fought for her
honour against an unwelcome but influential suitor. She later sends
him to ransom Bertoldo, her lover held hostage in Siena. The 'love'
for which Adorni must undertake the service is hedged with an
avoidance clause: 'Love borne of duty, but advance noe further'
(3.3.185). She even kisses Adorni on the lips so that he might deliver
it to Bertoldo. The kiss is a sort of social hologram. Having defined the
limits of their intimacy, Camiola can pretend that it is given like the
ceremonial *osculum* which accompanied the lord's acceptance of liege-
homage,[42] and received by a desexualized, subaltern body. But the kiss
to be relayed is a lover's kiss, and Camiola is abusing a sexual incentive

[41] On the Puritan notion of whoredom as a moral condition, see Keith Thomas, 'The
Puritans and Adultery: The Act of 1650 Reconsidered', in Donald Pennington and Keith
Thomas (eds.), *Puritans and Revolutionaries: Essays in Seventeenth-Century History Presented to
Christopher Hill* (Oxford, 1978), 281.
[42] See Ganshof, *Feudalism*, 78.

from the safety of her social distance. Camiola's willingness to take advantage of the ambiguity of vestigial feudal forms suggests that Massinger's apparent approval of her was not unqualified. Massinger, however, ducks the implications the action has for Camiola's class values. He sends her to the convent when Bertoldo proves a fraud, and rewards Adorni with a share of her estate. In exposing the motivated artifice of the standards which disentitle him, De Flores does what Adorni never dares. He rewrites the rules of the avoidance game, turning 'service' into sexual mastery and 'servitude' into social revenge.

A play comparable to *Changeling* is rare until, as Robert Brustein suggested, we reach *Miss Julia*.[43] The servant in Strindberg's play, however, has no insight into the subterfuges of the rich, and secretly craves their privileges. His cowardice blurs the connection between self-righteousness and power, while Strindberg's misogyny suppresses that between class and gender subjection. De Flores, on the contrary, makes Beatrice his partner in 'death and shame' (3.4.155), sharing in sin the common degradation of servant and woman. 'Honest De Flores' (4.2.37) is the only man in Alicante who profanes the feminine ideal of honour because he has no illusions about the masculine one.

HONOUR

The bridal procession, De Flores, and Alonzo's ghost file past in succession in the opening pageant of Act 4. Social appearances and their adversary both seem superseded by a retributive moral order when the ghost freezes De Flores's smile by displaying its mutilated hand. Yet, the third order of reality makes no sustained claim on our attention in the last two acts. The main plot in Act 4 is concerned with the virginity test, which further deflates the norms of 'honour' by which De Flores's social betters live. De Flores had known Beatrice for a whore at heart when she was still a virgin; Alsemero is convinced of her chastity when she cheats through the philtre-test.

The rest of the Alicante élite come out worse.[44] Vermandero thinks only of his 'honour' when Alonzo disappears (cf. 4.2.1–2). Tomazo,

[43] Brustein, *Seasons of Discontent*, 253.
[44] See Peter Morrison, 'A Cangoun in Zombieland: Middleton's Teratological *Changeling*', in Friedenreich (ed.), '*Accompaninge the Players*', 219–41.

Alonzo's brother, hangs around like a lost revenger in search of a playwright. Jasperino dutifully passes on to Alsemero the news of Beatrice's affair with a servant, but excuses his own fling with the maid with stupefying condescension: '(for to that wench | I pretend honest love, and she deserves it)' (4.2.89–90).

The bride-substitution is another revealing instance of the rites of male power in Alicante. Beatrice's means of having the 'will' denied by her father's was to exploit that of her servant. She manipulated his lust, yet imagined that he would keep to the paradoxical discipline which conceived of the subject exclusively as a body but denied its libidinal autonomy. She repeats the pattern with Diaphanta, her proxy for the first night. When Diaphanta too shows a reluctance to 'rule her blood' (5.1.7) and overstays her hour in Alsemero's bed, Beatrice is appalled that a hired woman should serve 'her own ends' and not mind her employer's 'honour' or 'peace' (5.1.2–4). De Flores, who had vented his class-hatred in his lady's bed, knows that waiting women are termagants, 'Especially when they fall upon their masters, | And have their ladies' first fruits' (5.1.17–18). He makes sure that she does not live like him to blackmail Beatrice. He sets fire to Diaphanta's chamber and silences Beatrice's panic: 'You talk of danger when your fame's on fire?' (5.1.34). De Flores now has a stake in shows: better raze the castle than change its outward view.

In fleshing out John Reynolds's story with a variant of the 'murdered-substitute tale',[45] the dramatists were relying on sources such as Leonard Digges's translation of Cespedes, the treatment of the black servant girl Zanche in Webster's *White Devil*, and the bed-trick in Heywood's *Maidenhead Well Lost*.[46] At the same time, the test and the substitution allude to the examination of Frances's virginity in her divorce case.[47] Diaphanta's reference to 'the forewoman of a female jury' (4.1.101) reminds playgoers of the matrons appointed to examine Frances, and Beatrice's request to be allowed to 'come obscurely' (4.2.121) on her wedding night recalls the rumour that Frances came to the test 'under a Veil', and that 'another young Gentlewoman . . . was fobbed into the place'.[48] The rumour suggests that the moral ticket

---

[45] See Ernst G. Mathews, 'The Murdered Substitute Tale', *MLQ* 6 (1945), 187–95.

[46] See Bertram Lloyd, 'A Minor Source of *The Changeling*', *MLR* 19 (1924), 101–2; and Bawcutt's note to 5.1.1–25. Heinemann, *Puritanism and Theatre*, 179–80, points out Diaphanta's difference from Zanche.

[47] See Bullen, vi. 73; and Simmons, 'Diabolical Realism', 153–63.

[48] Wilson, *Life and Reign of James*, in [Kennett], *Complete History of England*, ii. 5T2ᵛ.

to social privilege was for the woman reduced to a genital norm, and it needed the genius of the playwrights to follow the ironic upshot of an ideology which demanded that female probity should declare itself in laboratory reports. If an unruptured hymen is the sole index of feminine virtue, then a servant girl who does possess it should be a better warrant of Alsemero's 'honour' than a wife of blue blood who does not. The substitution, therefore, does ironic justice to the moral claims of Vermandero's Alicante and James's London.

SHAME

Once Alsemero is undeceived, Beatrice appears to him 'all deform'd',[49] and he calls her, predictably, a 'whore' (5.3.31, 77). Beatrice's response—'What a horrid sound it hath!' (5.3.31)—has been seen as her inability to hear named what she is unafraid to do.[50] But this is not the first time she hears herself called whore. She did not protest when De Flores called her 'whore in thy affection' (3.4.142) even before she had slept with a man. Yet, when in the final scene De Flores triumphantly tells Alsemero that his wife is a whore, Beatrice screams in denial from inside the locked closet. Like the Duchess in *Witch*, she confesses to murder, but pleads innocent to adultery (cf. 5.3.62–5).

Beatrice's behaviour can be understood if one takes her encounter with Alsemero as she herself figured it—as that of a malefactor facing a tribunal (cf. 4.1.8). At the Overbury murder trial, Anne Turner was reported to have broken down when Edward Coke called her 'a whore, a bawd, a sorcerer, a witch, a papist, a felon, and a murderer'.[51] Coke's ferocity is an instance of the name-calling used to crack a defendant in a legal system where reaction to public shaming weighed as much as concrete evidence. Murder for love was less a cause of public shame for the woman than whoredom: the former might indicate a desire to be lawfully owned, the latter violated the rights of

---

[49] Cf. Heywood, *The English Traveller* (*c.*1625), 5.1, p. 90, where Wincott's wife appears like Medusa to Young Geraldine. Beatrice's contrasting discovery of beauty in De Flores defamiliarizes the motif by playing on the ambiguity of beauty as lover's gift and as virtuous condition. Cf. Andreas Capellanus, *Andreas Capellanus on Love*, trans. and ed. P. G. Walsh (London, 1982), 39: 'Love makes the hirsute barbarian as handsome as can be: it can even enrich the lowest-born with nobility of manners . . . A person in love grows to the practice of performing numerous services becomingly to all.'

[50] See e.g. Joost Daalder, 'Folly and Madness in *The Changeling*', *EC* 38 (1988), 16.

[51] Howell and Howell (eds.), *State Trials*, ii. 935.

ownership. When she married Carr, Frances made a point of being seen 'in the Habit of a Virgin'; but at the murder trial she pleaded guilty with a sobriety which 'wan pitie'.[52] Public deportment was expected to signify moral states in the legal as well as the political culture of Jacobean England, and Alsemero's disenchantment with this myth reflects contemporary response to moral slick at the top.

Since murder of a wife taken in adultery was legally condoned,[53] Alsemero's plan to lock Beatrice and De Flores in the closet and kill them in the act best combines his self-appointed roles of judge and revenger. But the play is given its final twist when De Flores wields the knife and steals the revenger's triumph-speech.[54] He carries in the bleeding Beatrice, displaying her as a trophy just as he had shown off Alonzo's finger, mocking as ever the chivalric language of his masters: 'Yes, and her honour's prize | Was my reward' (5.3.167–8). De Flores kills himself to consummate the union with the body he has devoured, making himself and his class enemy literally one. The 'broken rib of mankind' (5.3.146) is his own, and the Edenic equations change as the serpent usurps the role of Adam. Since outlawed desire can realize itself only as vengeance, De Flores now safely calls his passion 'love'. In Deloney's *The Gentle Craft* (1597), when the tyrant makes St Hugh drink St Winifred's poisoned blood, he finds in it 'a taste of sweet-nesse', and toasts the shoemakers, 'I drink to you all . . . but I cannot spare you one drop to pledge me.'[55] In the double death of *Changeling*, De Flores lifts this grand line of the martyred lover: 'it was so sweet to me | That I have drunk up all, left none behind | For any man to pledge me' (5.3.169–71). *Changeling* thus shows a remarkable consistency of actantial inversions: assassin is revenger, the serpent is Adam, and the sexual blackmailer is the tragic lover.

In her dying speech, Beatrice presents herself, recalling Lear's image for his ungrateful daughters (cf. *Lear*, Folio Text, 2.2.395–8), as her father's diseased blood (5.3.149–51). She asks Vermandero to 'Let the common sewer take it from distinction' (l. 153). The social levelling De Flores desired is thus achieved in the candour of filth. The sewer,

[52] Wilson, *Life and Reign of James*, in [Kennett], *Complete History of England* ii. 5T3; and McClure (ed.), *Letters of John Chamberlain*, ii. 5.

[53] See Thomas, 'Puritans and Adultery', 268–9.

[54] The point is noted in François André Camoin, *The Revenge Convention in Tourneur, Webster and Middleton* (Salzburg, 1972), 96.

[55] Mann (ed.), *Works*, 87. The source has escaped notice. Rowley had used Deloney in *A Shoemaker, a Gentleman* (1608). But Middleton uses drinking and pledging in contexts involving sex, poison, and death in *Mad World*, 5.2.262–4; and *Revenger*, 1.4.9–11.

where, wrote Victor Hugo, 'the spittle of Caiaphus encounters the vomit of Falstaff ',[56] takes the blood she had so presumed upon 'from distinction'.

The survivors in Alicante show themselves incapable of rage or anguish. Alsemero pompously welcomes the triumph of justice (ll. 186–7), Tomazo raves on about the problems of chasing dead killers (ll. 192–4), and sub-plot characters join Alsemero in indexing the play's turnabouts (ll. 196–215). Together they parody the redemptive rites of tragedy,[57] while Vermandero, to whom belongs the patriarchal privilege of presiding over them, stands numbed by the storming of his 'citadel' (l. 147).

Vermandero is given another revealing line. The forcing of Beatrice and De Flores into the closet to rehearse their 'scene of lust' for the 'black audience' (ll. 115–16) had made us imagine the discovery space as the tiring house of hell. De Flores emerges from it to tell Alsemero, in the metaphor of the game of barley-break, that he has coupled with his mate and that they are now left in hell (ll. 162–3). Vermandero answers: 'We are all there, it circumscribes here' (l. 164). The line echoes Marlowe's *Faustus* (cf. ll. 553–5), but the adjacent metaphor of the playhouse gives it a chilling immediacy. Castle and theatre turn to hell, and the spectators to its 'black audience'. We are betrayed into a helplessness which the routine *sententiae* of the survivors can do nothing to alleviate: 'All we can do to comfort one another, | . . . Is to no purpose' (ll. 220–3). Only the knowledge that theatre is fiction and actors die in sport, says the Epilogue, reconciles grief to pleasure (ll. 224–7).

LOWER LABYRINTH

In turning from castle to madhouse, the sub-plot pushes seduction and sexual blackmail down the social chain, repeating the playwrights' method in *Quarrel*. The keeper of the asylum, Alibius, is stingy and impotent. Two young gentlemen, Antonio and Franciscus, pose as fool and madman to gain access to his wife Isabella.[58] Alibius's servant

---

[56] Victor Hugo, *Les Misérables*, trans. Norman Denny (1976; Harmondsworth, 1982), 1065.

[57] See Pentzell, '*The Changeling*: Notes on Mannerism in Dramatic Form', 3–4.

[58] The resemblance of the lovers with Lipsalve and Gudgeon in *Family* is noted in Bawcutt's Introduction, p. xxxviii. A minor source is studied in Douglas Bruster, '*The Changeling* and Thomas Watson's *Hecatompathia*', *N & Q* 238 (1993), 222–4.

Lollio tries to blackmail Isabella into bed after finding out about her truant admirers. She first threatens to set Antonio to kill him, but later decides to make a deal.

The sub-plot is not a moral contrast to high sleaze, and Isabella is no model housewife.[59] Faking a seductive delirium, she invites Antonio to 'tread the lower labyrinth' (4.3.107), but returns infuriated when he, taking her for a freak, kicks her aside. Isabella had promised the disguised fool to speak to him when she saw the gentleman within (3.3.140–1). Antonio fails the test, and his vaunted intellect is shown equal to his fool's disguise: 'Keep your caparisons,' Isabella tells him, 'y'are aptly clad' (4.3.134). Like the virginity test and the bed-trick, Antonio's failure to tell Isabella from her clothes debunks the myth of the significative surface.

Isabella's abortive rebellion teaches her that her place is with her husband's patients, that society uses the same techniques of surveillance for unruly minds and unruly female bodies. Women and madmen are both kennelled like beasts 'under the whip' (1.2.45). Isabella is kept in her 'pinfold' lest she be 'taken in another man's corn' (3.3.8–10). Franciscus is shepherded to his 'kennel' as Isabella is to her fettered 'cage' (3.3.91, 2–3). Lollio boasts that 'a shepherd has not his dog at more obedience' (3.3.55–8) than he has the lunatics. His whip is appropriately a 'pizzle', made out of a bull's penis. When Alibius worries that his patients might scare the ladies at Beatrice's wedding (an offence which merits hanging, according to Quince in *Midsummer Night's Dream*, 1.2.70–2), Lollio assures him that they will be 'as tame as the ladies themselves' once they see the 'commanding pizzles' (4.3.61–3).

The chain of images linking animals, madmen, and women bear out Keith Thomas's point that between 1500 and 1800 animal domestication in England was the key metaphor of social management.[60] Animality was always a trope of disentitlement, but recent scholarship has shown that such tropes were reversible.[61] De Flores, with whom

[59] For exceptions to the view of Isabella as moral foil to Beatrice, see Michael Scott, *Renaissance Drama and a Modern Audience* (London, 1982), 82–5; and Maurice Charney, *Hamlet's Fictions* (New York, 1988), 46.

[60] Keith Thomas, *Man and the Natural World: Changing Attitudes in England 1500–1800* (London, 1983), 45. See also Michael MacDonald, *Mystical Bedlam: Madness, Anxiety, and Healing in Seventeenth-Century England* (Cambridge, 1981), 179.

[61] See Mary Douglas, *Implicit Meanings: Essays in Anthropology* (London, 1975), 276–314; and Natalie Zemon Davis, 'Women on Top: Symbolic Sexual Inversion and Political Disorder in Early Modern Europe', in Barbara A. Babcock (ed.), *The Reversible World: Symbolic Inversion in Art and Society* (Ithaca, NY, 1978), 147–90.

animal images are most consistently associated, is again the agent of reversal. It has been claimed that the main plot is a deviant beauty-and-the-beast fable, in which beauty is shown to be a beast as well.[62] It needs to be noted that the fable could be a socially conservative allegory of hypergamy. Christine de Pisan's *Epître d'Othea à Hector* (c.1400) had interpreted Pasiphae's love for the bull as her being 'aqueynted with a man of foul condicions'.[63] It is in a similar social sense that Beatrice had called De Flores 'foul villain'. He calls her 'fair murd'ress' in reply (3.4.140-1). By showing her beauty to be morally foul, De Flores destroys the ethical pretext of class privilege.

Isabella's disguise is a comparable attempt at figural inversion. In *1 Whore*, Bellafront the whore acts mad because she wants to be 'honest'; in *Changeling*, Isabella the wronged housewife does so to beat domestic oppression. Madness at the time, it is well known, was often a cover for radical opinions.[64] Isabella likewise tries to turn madness from an occasion of enslavement to one of liberation. Unlike De Flores, she fails. But in defeat she reveals that, in their blinkered duplicities, the men who rule her show more unreason than the caged freaks. As Vindice says in *Revenger*, "Tis we are mad in sense, they but in clothes' (3.5.82).

HYPALLAGE

Masque and antimasque, aria and recitative—many analogies have been summoned to explain the perplexing mixture of genres in *Changeling*.[65] The main plot alludes to many subgeneric precedents: revenge drama, tragedies of love, domestic tragedies, ironic inversions of Petrarchism. The sub-plot moralizes Terence, and retouches the reformed-prodigal theme. Comparisons with the mixed mode in

---

[62] See Brustein, *Seasons of Discontent*, 254; and Robert Jordan, 'Myth and Psychology in *The Changeling*', *RD* 3 (1970), 157-65.

[63] Christine de Pisan, *Epître d'Othea à Hector*, trans. Stephen Scrope, ed. Curt F. Bühler, EETS 264 (London, 1970), 57.

[64] See Hill, *World Turned Upside Down*, 223-30. For a recent study of the dramatic functions of madness, see Duncan Salkeld, *Madness and Drama in the Age of Shakespeare* (Manchester, 1993). Edgar, in the course of playing the lunatic, presented himself as a servingman, who, like De Flores, had done 'the act of darkness' with her mistress (*Lear*, Folio text, 3.4.79-84).

[65] See Wylie Sypher, *Four Stages of Renaissance Style: Transformations in Art and Literature 1400-1700* (Gloucester, Mass., 1978), 155; Bradbrook, *Themes and Conventions*, 221; and Ornstein, *Moral Vision*, 181.

Shakespeare are misleading beyond a point, since the porter, the fool, Shylock, and Falstaff are never curtained off in self-contained plots. In *Changeling*, traffic between the plots is reduced to a minimum, and within each segment narrative regularities are estranged, and actants and functions freely transposed. Assassin and revenger, persecutor and lover, master and servant trade places in the tragic plot, just as gaoler and gaoled, wit and fool, sane and mad do in the comic one.

The word 'changeling' was a synonym for hypallage, the rhetorical figure which reverses the natural relation of two terms in a sentence. It has been proposed that the title be taken in this sense, since in the play contrary qualities and values cross over and combine.[66] Within each plot, we have seen such hypallagic exchanges work their way to the surface of the narrative.

Together, the irregular plots in opposed modes do not produce that 'organic unity' the endless demonstration of which bored Greenblatt at college.[67] They collude instead in a pact of mutual occlusion. Tragedy is denied its transfigurative splendour; comedy, its validation of enduring normalcy and reason. The strategy lays open the ideological interests, especially those which need to keep political, civil, and domestic spheres separate, governing the curative formulas of moral comedy and moral tragedy. By treating generic formulas as open pretence, *Changeling* foregrounds the concentric artifice of social and literary conventions. The changeling standards of society and politics find their just image in the play's changeling form.

[66] See Ann Pasternak Slater, 'Hypallage, Barley-Break, and *The Changeling*', *RES*, NS 34 (1983), 429–40.

[67] Greenblatt, *Learning to Curse*, 168.

8

Vulgar Pasquin and Lordly Players: *A Game at Chess*

Middleton's last work for the stage, in a way different from Shakespeare's, is about playing in the related senses of the histrionic and the ludic. Chess pieces had long been metaphors for social estates; and the game, for politics and warfare. The 'eschekere' was the place where 'A man may learn to be wise and ware', wrote Thomas Hoccleve in his verse translation (1411–12) of Guido Colonna's *De regimine principium*, and Jacques de Cessoles's chess allegory, translated by Caxton (1474), viewed the game as a philosopher's invention 'to correcte and repreue the kynge'.[1] On the English stage, Chapman used the royal game as a mirror of politic sport in *Bussy d'Ambois*, Act 1, Scene 2, and *The Tragedy of Charles Duke of Byron*, Act 4, Scene 2, and Middleton improved on Chapman in *Women Beware*. But the action of *A Game at Chess* (1624) is the game itself, and its characters are both players and played. Players play live political gamesters, to the point of using the cast-off suit of one of them,[2] and yet they are all reduced to chessmen, moved by an authorial hand according to the game's fictional and ludic rules.

Middleton's play was not 'A harmlesse game raised meerely for delight', as he is alleged to have claimed in a petition from prison.[3] The inset play-game, joining the fictional to the ludic, had always been 'a mirror-image of earnest' in English drama.[4] But the game in this play

---

[1] Thomas Hoccleve, *The Regement of Princes*, in F. J. Furnivall (ed.), *Hoccleve's Works*, iii. *The Regement of Princes . . . and Fourteen of Hoccleve's Minor Poems*, EETS, extra ser. 72 (1897), 77; Jacques de Cessoles, *Game and Playe of the Chesse*, trans. William Caxton, ed. William E. A. Axon (London, 1883), 13.

[2] Chamberlain wrote to Dudley Carleton on 21 Aug. 1624 that the Black Knight's costume included a cast suit of Gondomar; see McClure (ed.), *Letters of John Chamberlain*, ii. 577. Documents relating to the play are also repr. in T. H. Howard-Hill (ed.), *A Game at Chess*, Revels Plays (Manchester, 1993), 192–212.

[3] On the disputed authenticity of the petition, see Samuel A. Tannenbaum, 'A Middleton Forgery', *PQ* 12 (1933), 33–6; Bernard M. Wagner, 'A Middleton Forgery', *PQ* 14 (1935), 287–8; and Bullough, ' "Game at Chess": How it Struck a Contemporary', 163. The quotation follows the transcript in Wagner's article, 288.

[4] Wickham, *Early English Stages*, iii. 110.

is its own alienating device, never letting playgoers forget the fantastic and ludic nature of the action. M. C. Bradbrook compared the ludic quality of the modern theatre to the medieval play-game, and singled out the ritual of the dream as a special instance of playhouse games.[5] *Game at Chess* involves a similar foregrounding of play and fantasy, the whole action being presented in the Induction as Error's dream vision.[6]

At the same time, the play alludes to the recurrent use of ludic and theatrical metaphors in the religious and political controversies which occasioned its writing. A recovery of that figurative context should enable us to see how the biggest hit in Jacobean stage history absorbed the rhetoric of propaganda to produce a subtle text on the theatre of politics and the politics of theatre.

WHITE THEATRE, BLACK THEATRE

An anonymous French pamphlet, published in London with an English translation in 1607, relates how the Jesuits that year put up at Lyons a comedy:

This Comedie was a kinde of representation, by personages, of the state of Heauen and Hell. . . . They then had a Iesuitical God . . . then was there a Iesus Christ on his right hand, enuironed with Angels holding their Trumpets on the very top of all the theater which they called Paradice. In a place somewhat lower, vpon the one side, was the Pope & his traine, yᵉ Kings Catholique & Christian, on yᵉ other side were *Turks, Prester-Iohn*, miscreants & Heretiques. Underneath was Hell, where diuers Deuilles might be descerned with Lucifer their Maister, attired according to yᵉ *Iesuites* appointment. The intent & sum of the Play, was a counterfeting of the finall iudgement . . .[7]

All went well on the first day, when the Pope and the blessed were feasted 'in the wooden Paradise'. The second day belonged to the damned, and guns and explosives were readied to simulate doomsday terrors. But before these could go off, a real thunderstorm broke out, and the 'newe created God, fled away in all haste'. The storm is seen

---

[5] M. C. Bradbrook, *English Dramatic Form: A History of its Development* (London, 1965), 14–15, 18.

[6] On the contemporary association of dream, church ritual, and plays, see Reid Barbour, 'Liturgy and Dreams in Seventeenth-Century England', *MP* 88 (1991), 227–42.

[7] *The Iesvites Comedie Acted at Lyons in France, the Seuenth and Eight Dayes of August Last Past 1607* (1607), A2ᵛ–3. A diary of the time speaks of other printed accounts; see George Roberts (ed.), *Diary of Walter Yonge, Esq. Justice of the Peace, and M.P. for Honiton*, Camden Society, 41 (1848), 15.

as divine judgement on those who dared 'to make a play-game of that wherein eternal life and death consisteth'.[8] Their punishment was no less theatrical. The Jesuits had tried to bring the spiritual world down to their wooden stage; God taught them that the universe was his playhouse. The Jesuits had planned a comedy; God turned it into a tragedy for them, and to 'laughter' for the righteous.[9]

To the English Protestant, there was an exemplary irony in the form and occasion of the judgement. The Jesuit to him had always been a diabolic actor-playwright. In Robert Burton's *Philosophaster* (1606), Aequivocus says of his Jesuit boss Polupragmaticus: *Proteus opinor non est illo mutabilior,* | *Nec vulpes mage versipellis, aut versutior.*[10] Jesuit hypocrisy and play-acting were joined at a more pragmatic level. Several tracts of the period spoke of a wardrobe at a Jesuit college which was apparently meant 'for the performance of Comedies' by younger disciples, but which supplied senior members with disguises for spying and for 'verie strange impostures'.[11] Play-acting was more than a ruse: the actor's mask defined the Jesuit's duplicitous essence. In Rome, wrote Webster, the Jesuit 'wears a Maske upon his heart; in England he shifts it, and puts it upon his face'.[12]

One thus understands the righteous glee with which English Protestants welcomed the news that on 26 October 1623 a floor in Hunsdon House, where Catholics had gathered for a Jesuit sermon, had collapsed, killing over a hundred people including the preacher, Robert Drury. The accident was publicized as retribution for apostasy and as a warning for those who still favoured alliance with Spain. This interpretation was helped by the date, which coincided with the anniversary of the Gunpowder Plot in the Roman calendar.[13] The Catholics read in the incident their own providential message. The Archdeacon of Cambrai recorded the French ambassador's view that the mishap was God's warning 'so that we might be disillusioned

---

[8] *Iesuites Comedie*, A3ᵛ–4.

[9] Ibid. A2ᵛ.

[10] Robert Burton, *Philosophaster*, trans. and ed. Paul Jordan-Smith (Stanford, Calif., 1941), 148.

[11] *Troubles in Bohemia, and Diuers Other Kingdomes* (1619), B2–2ᵛ. This text is virtually the same as *A Discouery of the Most Secret and Subtile Practises of the Iesvites* (1610).

[12] John Webster, *New and Choise Characters, of Seuerall Authors* (1615), in F. L. Lucas (ed.), *The Complete Works of John Webster*, 4 vols. (London, 1927), iv. 42.

[13] M. A. Breslow, *A Mirror of England: English Puritan Views of Foreign Nations, 1618–1640* (Cambridge, Mass., 1970), 68, lists pamphlets which report the disaster.

over the outcome before we proceed further with the marriage [between Charles and Donna Maria, Infanta of Spain]'.[14]

A most illuminating response is that of the author of *Digitus Dei*, an anonymous pamphlet included in the *Workes* (1624) of the Puritan preacher Thomas Scott, who fled from the law to Holland after annoying the king with his *Vox Populi* (1620). The author asks why the nearby Blackfriars theatre was not struck down as well, since the Jesuits' sins are apparently no worse than the players'. The playhouse escaped, he decides, 'because it professeth it selfe to be no better then it is, a Play-House'. The Jesuits' theatre lacks this saving candour. It 'playes with the Word and Sacraments in a most Anticke or Apish fashion' while pretending to be 'most serious'. It is 'Anticke' and 'Apish', theatre as well as sport, and God appropriately 'makes it a spectacle of his Iudgement'.[15]

The two episodes establish a triple theatrical hierarchy. At one end is the black theatre which lies and trifles; at the other, the white theatre of God's judgement. Between them stands the indeterminate theatre of professional players, which, although given to fiction and trivia, is not as malefic as that of spiritual dissemblers. John Gee, who narrowly escaped being killed at Hunsdon House, likens the miraculous visions faked by Jesuits to 'Theatrical and fabulous tricks', but more dull and expensive than 'the *Ghost in Hamblet*, *Don Andreas Ghost in Hieronimo* . . . the comedie of *Piramus* and *Thisbe*, where one comes in with a Lanthorne and Acts *Mooneshine*'.[16]

Playhouse metaphors had long been in use in anti-Catholic polemics. In a sermon preached at Whitehall in 1621, Isaac Bargrave, chaplain to Prince Charles, compared the church to a theatre where good men were bad actors.[17] They acted the parts scripted for them by God, while the hypocrite played many roles, being that master of '*blacke-Art*' who 'Than Satans selfe, playes better, Satans part'.[18] When Samuel Hieron described the Catholic Mass in 1613 as 'A pretty play, to see a priest | Tossing his God betweene his fist,'[19] he was following

[14] Albert J. Loomie (ed.), *Spain and the Jacobean Catholics*, 2 vols., Catholic Record Society (Records Series), 64 and 68 (n.p., 1973, 1978), ii. 160.

[15] *Digitus Dei* (n.d.), D3ᵛ–4, in *The Workes of the Most Famovs and Reverend Divine Mr. Thomas Scot. Batcheler in Diuinitie: Sometimes Preacher in Norwich* (Utrecht, 1624).

[16] Iohn Gee, *New Shreds of the Old Snare* (1624), D1ᵛ, D2ᵛ, D3ᵛ.

[17] Isaac Bargrave, *A Sermon against Selfe Policy, Preached at Whitehall in Lent, 1621* (1624), C3ᵛ.

[18] Iohn Vicars, *Babels Balm, or The Honey-Combe of Romes Religion* (1624), P3ᵛ.

[19] Hieron, *All the Sermons*, 3D6.

the example of Protestant preachers from Tyndale onward. This contempt for theatricality went together with the representation of the world as God's playhouse.[20] Foxe called schoolmen and friars 'new sort of players, to furnish the stage',[21] yet wrote didactic plays himself, and cast many episodes in his *Acts and Monuments* as tragedies and histories. The world, like the 'woodie Theatre' of Eden in *Paradise Lost* (4.141), could be the setting for both divine and diabolic artifice.

The stigma of the theatre attached itself especially to the Jesuit, who in Jacobean England had eclipsed the Machiavellian as the archetype of the evil thespian.[22] The contest between Machiavelli and Loyola at Lucifer's court in Donne's *Ignatius his Conclave* (1611) memorably dramatized this upstaging. The Machiavel changed shapes for secular ends. The Jesuit was a shade worse, 'an *Amphibion*, that conuerseth in two elements of Ciuill, and Ecclesiasticall affaires'.[23]

The tropic configurations linking play-acting with Jesuits and Machiavels hardened in the early 1620s as radical Protestant campaigners attacked James's soft line on Spain. Anxieties converged on his pursuit of a Spanish match, the toleration granted to English Catholics and Jesuits in the wake of the marriage treaty with Spain ratified in July 1623, the suppression of the Commons, and the refusal of armed support for Prince Frederick, the king's son-in-law, who had been stripped of the crown of Bohemia by the Spanish Habsburgs and Emperor Ferdinand, a trained Jesuit, in 1620. The Jesuits in England and abroad figured in these attacks as cunning gamesters plotting 'to aduance the domination of *Spaine*',[24] and the Spanish lobby at home was pictured as crafty Sinons, 'the Traytors in the Troyan horse'.[25] In Thomas Scott's *Second Part of Vox Populi* (1624), the Spanish ambassador to England, Diego Sarmiento de Acuña, after 1617 Count of Gondomar, is presented *in the likenes of Matchiauell in a Spanish Parliament*.[26] On the other hand, King James, who in 1609 portrayed himself as a player disposing his subjects 'like men at the

[20] See Barish, *Antitheatrical Prejudice*, 160–5.
[21] Foxe, *Acts and Monuments*, i. p. xxi.
[22] See Mario Praz, *The Flaming Heart: Essays on Crashaw, Machiavelli, and Other Studies in the Relations between Italian and English Literature from Chaucer to T. S. Eliot* (Garden City, NY, 1958), 90–145.
[23] Theophilus Higgons, *Mysticall Babylon, or Papal Rome* (1624), 2C1.
[24] *The Legend of the Iesuites* (1623), C3.
[25] Bargrave, *Sermon Preached before the Honorable Assembly*, E1ᵛ.
[26] [Thomas Scott], *The Second Part of Vox Populi, or Gondomar Appearing in the Likenes of Matchiauell in a Spanish Parliament* (1624).

Chesse',[27] is sometimes imagined as an amateur gamester, outsmarted by opponents: 'They say, you have lost the fayrest Game at *Maw*, that ever King had, for Want of making the best Advantage of the five Finger, and playing the other Helpes in Time.'[28] The English are easily beaten, Gondomar is made to boast in *Vox Populi*, since the Catholic clergy are 'at libertie to giue any hereticall Prince the Mate when they list'.[29]

Alternatively, the English king could be shown to be a crafty player in both senses, acting a part and disguising his hand. Scott's *Belgicke Pismire* (1622) hopes that, in appeasing Spain, the king is merely 'acting his part in the eye of the whole world', that he is 'trying his exact skill in *King-craft* vvith the greatest *State* and *Statists* in Christendome'.[30] After the prince returned from Madrid in October 1623, and especially after the marriage deal finally fell through in April 1624 and the Jesuits were ordered out of the kingdom, it became possible to compliment the monarch on his superior strategy. In a ballad published immediately following the Jesuits' expulsion, Truth tells Time that she had pretended to be asleep simply to study the Jesuits' 'Insolence and Guile'.[31] A similar explanation was given by the Duke of Buckingham to Parliament in February 1624 for the secret trip to Madrid on which he had left with the prince exactly a year before. The prince resolved to go to Spain in person, he claimed, only when 'he saw his Fathers Negotiation playnelie deluded'.[32] This re-conceived narrative is repeated in the war-party tracts. Gondomar is made to acknowledge in *The Second Part of Vox Populi* that Charles 'by comming in Person discouered our plot'.[33] The prince is recast as the knight of the white theatre, setting off on a perilous quest and overcoming the Spanish Archimago. Such would surely have been the course, had anyone cared to write it, of the heroic poem begun by Edmund Bolton entitled 'Vindex or The Blame is Spaines'. Dedicated to Buckingham, this unpublished fragment turns a mission of expediency

---

[27] McIlwain (ed.), *Political Works*, 308.

[28] *Tom Tell–Troath, or, A Free Discourse touching the Manners of the Time* (*c.*1623), repr. in *The Harleian Miscellany*, 8 vols. (1744–6), ii. 3E1[v].

[29] [Scott], *Vox Populi*, C3–3[v].

[30] [Scott], *Belgicke Pismire*, A4[v].

[31] *The Travels of Time* (1624), repr. in Rollins (ed.), *Old English Ballads*, 185.

[32] See Robert E. Ruigh, *The Parliament of 1624: Politics and Foreign Policy* (Cambridge, Mass., 1971), 163–4. See also Conrad Russell, *Parliaments and English Politics 1621–1629* (Oxford, 1979), 158–9; and Thomas Cogswell, *The Blessed Revolution: English Politics and the Coming of War* (Cambridge, 1989), 171. For a summary account of the occasion of the play see Howard-Hill (ed.), *Game at Chess*, 10–17.

[33] [Scott], *Second Part of Vox Populi*, C4[v].

into a romantic adventure, in which Charles is led by love, 'not by his father willed', to set out 'in strange disguise, | To gaine the roiyall Maide, his hazards prize'.[34] The outcome of the chivalric quest was apocalyptic. 'Babylon is fallen,' rejoices the author of *Englands Ioy* (1624),[35] and that of *Newes from Rome, Spalato's Doome* (1624) associates the fall of the apostate Archbishop of Spalatro with the final overthrow of 'a world of shadowes, a theater of disguises, a map of colours, a shop of complexion, a schoole of hypocrisie'.[36]

One of the features of such propaganda literature is its frequent fictional, if not theatrical, pretence. The scene may be set in a Spanish parliament or at a celestial conference, and historical characters may argue with imaginary ones. In *Vox Regis* (*c.*1624), Scott answers the charge of fictionalizing history:

And might I not borrow a ˙*Spanish* name or two, as well as *French*, or *Italian*, to grace this Comedie with stately Actors? Or must they onely be reserved for Kingly Tragedies? Why not *Gondomar*, aswell as *Hieronymo*, or Duke *d'Alva*?[37]

Scott adds that

Kings are content in Playes and Maskes to be admonished of diuers things . . . for Fooles and Children will often speake truth (and therefore such as speake so are counted Fooles or Children). . .[38]

Scott is claiming for his work the admonitory and heuristic functions of white theatre, a claim basic to defences of the stage.[39] Fiction and folly may address the substance precisely because they present it as shadow.

The metaphorical uses of play-game in the polemical texts we have sampled frame the figurative code of *Game at Chess*. The play has its scheming Jesuits and Machiavels, and the dissembling Knight and Duke who expose them. There is a Black House and a White, with the dissimulation proper to each. At the same time, there are black

---

[34] Philanactophil [Edmund Bolton], 'Vindex or The Blame is Spaines' (1625), in Bodleian, MS Tanner 73/2, fo. 421. James himself had eulogized the trip as the pursuit of the 'The Beauteous prize, the golden ffleece'; see James Craigie (ed.), *The Poems of James VI of Scotland*, 2 vols., Scottish Text Society (Edinburgh, 1955–8), ii. 192.

[35] [Thomas Scott], *Englands Ioy, For Suppressing the Papists, and banishing the Priests and Iesuites* (1624), C1ᵛ.

[36] *Newes from Rome, Spalato's Doome* (1624), F3.

[37] [Thomas Scott], *Vox Regis* (n.d.), B1ᵛ.

[38] Ibid. E1ᵛ–2.

[39] Cf. Massinger, *Roman Actor*, 1.3.50–142.

pretenders within the White House. More surprisingly, we are shown a forged vision within an action which is itself presented as Error's dream. In the end, virtue gains her promised victory (cf. Prologue, 7-8), but the dizzying shifts of black and white, play and earnest, cheat us of its moral comfort.

DREAM PLAY

'Machevil' had introduced Marlowe's *Jew of Malta*. His chair having been taken by Ignatius Loyola, it is now the latter's turn to open a play. He leads the Induction, appearing with Error sleeping at his feet. In the Induction to *Michaelmas Term*, Michaelmas was touching native soil in arriving from country to city. So was Lucifer in the Prologue to *Black Book*. But Ignatius's first words, parodying the *quis hic locus* formula, show him lost on English soil: 'Hah! Where? What angle of the world is this . . . ?' (l. 1). He then jolts Error out of the pleasing slumber of ignorance. The Induction thus seems to be consciously inverting the opening tableau of Dekker's *Whore of Babylon* (1607), which featured Time and his daughter Truth, the latter asleep on a rock.[40]

While Dekker's play has Truth awakened and crowned, Middleton presents an action that completes Error's interrupted dream. A lame and lost braggart being shown the dream of a blind and drowsy Error is a unique situation, even by the loose standards of Renaissance stage presenters. The choice of dreamer and spectator makes an ontic puzzle of the dream and the game. Error has no competence as visionary, nor has Ignatius any at chess. Ignatius wants to kill the Black Bishop, take his place next to the Queen, and seduce her (ll. 64–7). When Error reminds him that it is against the rules for chessmen to fight their own house, Ignatius replies that he would rule alone, 'not observe rule' (l. 71). The absolutist is no gamester at all, since he can only play a game alone (cf. l. 72).

Middleton had shown Error in the civic pageant *Triumphs of Truth*, 'Embolden'd by the privilege of Night | And her black faction' (Bullen, vii. 261). The black faction in *Game at Chess* too are on Error's side (cf. l. 43), and they begin the game aggressively, with the Black

---

[40] See Jane Sherman, 'The Pawns' Allegory in Middleton's *A Game at Chesse*', RES, NS 29 (1978), 150; and Gasper, *Dragon and the Dove*, 187. Gasper finds in the play links with Dekker's *Match Me in London*.

Queen's Pawn, a secular Jesuitess, and the Black Bishop's Pawn, a Jesuit *in voto*, scheming to corrupt the chaste White Queen's Pawn. The story of the White Queen's Pawn leans heavily on pamphlets against Spain and the Jesuits. Hawkish anti-Hispanism was not the official line before Charles's return from Spain in October 1623, and patriotic polemics before that date could also be veiled assaults on James's capitulation to Catholics at home and abroad. The anonymous pamphlet, *The Interpreter* (1622) thus attacks both 'Papist' and 'Protestant', branding one as an agent of Spain and Rome, and the other as a lackey of royal policy.[41] Even in the altered political climate following the prince's return, Middleton's sources continued to criticize the establishment. A pamphlet published in 1624 points out that if God had given a sign by striking Hunsdon House, his lightning did not spare St James's Palace, where a Catholic chapel was being designed for the Infanta by Inigo Jones.[42] Religious orthodoxy thus could easily contain deviant political interpretants.

Middleton's deviancy, however, reaches deeper than the brief truculence of partisan polemics. The innocence of the White Queen's Pawn, who is taken in by black theatre, is allied to a fatal ignorance. She is yet to learn that desire is transgressive at its root, and that it equivocates with one's reason more subtly than any Jesuit. The Pawn's forebears are the Duchess in *Dissemblers* and Bianca in *Women Beware*.

The Black Bishop's Pawn suggests a fast to cleanse the White Queen's Pawn's 'spotted righteousness' (1.1.88). He represents the penance as a 'courteous physic', 'Whose utmost cruelty should not exceed | The first fear of a bride to beat down frailty' (1.1.83–5). Despite the sexual hints, the White Queen's Pawn submits to the regimen, claiming that her desire, although at variance with her judgement, has always served virtue (cf. 1.1.94–5).

As a next step, the Black Bishop's Pawn encourages her to 'boldly | And safely let in the most secret sin' (1.1.99–100) into virtue's ear. Protestants suspected confession as a device used by the secret service of Catholic regimes,[43] and the Black Bishop's Pawn speaks in an aside of the 'special use' to which the confessional is put 'in all kingdoms' (1.1.109–10). Middleton further implies that the power of the confes-

---

[41] In Firth, *Stuart Tracts*, 233–46; see 243, 237, 235 respectively.

[42] [Thomas Scott], *Boanerges, or The Humble Supplication of the Ministers of Scotland, to the High Court of Parliament in England* (1624), D2ᵛ.

[43] See *An Impartiall Discouery of Iesuiticall Policie* (1619), B3ᵛ–4ᵛ; and Webster, *New and Choise Characters*, in Lucas (ed.), *Works*, iv. 42.

sional in sex and politics derives from its capacity to induce a self-recognition of desire by articulating the repressed.[44] Disclosing their subjects' 'most secret frailties' not only enables confessors, as the Black Bishop's Pawn says, 'to apt them . . . to our designs' (1.1.111, 115), it also liberates the subjects from the tyranny of self-censorship. It is the fear of a similar freedom that has prompted most attacks on the theatre since Plato.[45]

The White Queen's Pawn discloses that she was engaged to the White Bishop's Pawn until the Black Knight's Pawn gelded him.[46] She resents the suggestion that it was desire which steered her blood, since her 'desires | Dwell all in ignorance' (1.1.182, 171–2). This revelation from someone who seemed so certain that she had ever served virtue in her 'desire' is ironic, and it is more so given her later keenness on the Jesuit posing as her promised groom. Such ignorance makes her 'Boundless obedience' (2.1.38) a fatal political vice.[47] The White Queen's Pawn is an idealized figure of beleagured Protestant virtue, but her portrayal also suggests that what the polemicists saw as the quietism and prevarications of official policy may be linked to certain features of their own model of righteousness.

The stress on the sexual machinations of the Jesuits reflects popular anxiety about the political dangers of the Spanish match. 'This match tends only to bring in the Pope into our Churches,' Queen Elizabeth is made to say in *Vox Coeli* (1624), 'and the King of Spaine into our estate'. The queen continues: 'If he marry the *Infanta*, she may prove a false and vnsecret Secretary to the Prince her Husband, and a dangerous Princesse to the State'.[48] Marriage to the Infanta would make Charles guilty of a double betrayal, because, first, 'Princes are maried to the commonwealth; & the wife hath power of the husbands body, as the *husband* of hers',[49] and, secondly, in marrying a Catholic, he would be succumbing to idolatry as well as adultery: 'The Lord . . .

---

[44] On sex as a privileged theme of the confessional, see Foucault, *History of Sexuality: Introduction*, 58–65.

[45] The convergence of attitudes towards the confessional and the theatre is discussed in Mullaney, *Place of the Stage*, 100–15.

[46] Edgar C. Morris, 'The Allegory in Middleton's *A Game at Chesse*', *Englische Studien*, 38 (1907), 45–9, suggests that the gelding refers to Frederick's exclusion from the Bohemian crown.

[47] The translation of a French pamphlet notes that Jesuitical obedience demands '*the renunciation of all will, and all iudgement*'; see [Peter Gosselin], *The State-Mysteries of the Iesuites* (1623), D1.

[48] S.R.N.I. [John Reynolds], *Vox Coeli, or, Newes from Heaven* (1624), H4–11.

[49] [Scott], *Vox Regis*, B3.

keepe vs from ioyning with *Idolaters*: since wee see temporall fornication brings in spirituall'.[50]

A similar view of temporal and spiritual fornication as mutually
enabling conditions is urged by the Black Bishop's Pawn. When the
Black Knight derides his efforts to seduce the White Queen's Pawn as
a distraction from 'the main work' of political take-over, he sagely
replies, 'It goes on in this.' 'In this?' asks the Knight, 'I cannot see't.'
The Black Bishop's Pawn answers, alluding to a familiar proverb, that
one might just as well deny 'A dial's motion, 'cause you cannot see |
The hand move' (1.1.290–4).

Along with the entwined roots of sexual and political enterprise, the
text also disinters the secret collusion between the white actors' longings
and the black theatre's blandishments. The Black Queen's and the Black
Bishop's Pawns lead the White Queen's Pawn through a series of
theatrical shows in the first act: feigned tears, impressive costumes, false
salutations, simulated penance. The Black Bishop's Pawn is given the
lyrical set-pieces in the scene: the Jesuit loves spectacle and poetry as
much as Duke Francesco. That these drill a 'little passage' in the
seemingly 'impregnable' fort of her virtue (1.1.69, 184) betrays an
infirmity in the White House of which the plain hypocrisy of the White
King's Pawn is a more overt symptom: 'You see my outside, but you
know my heart, Knight, | Great difference in the colour' (1.1.313–14).
In a sermon preached in 1623, Robert Abbot likened the Church of
England to 'a beautifull woman, who standeth so for currant, except to
them who will say, White is blacke'.[51] The pawns' plot suggests that the
great difference between black and white could well be an optical
illusion bred in the self-deluding eyes of the gazer.

MIRROR OF DESIRE

The White Queen's Pawn finds herself locked 'unawares into sin's
servitude | With more desire of goodness' (2.1.83–4). The Black
Bishop's Pawn plays her spiritual father and courtly suitor at the same
time, speaking of 'blessing' and 'duty' on the one hand, and of
'courteous care', 'jealousy', 'pity', and 'honour's bubble' on the other
(2.1.65, 91, 96, 106, 130, 137). After his bid to force her chastity is foiled

---

[50] Scott, *Proiector*, C4^v.

[51] Robert Abbot, *A Hand of Fellowship, to Helpe Keepe Out Sinne and Antichrist* (1623), D5^v.

by the sudden appearance of a White Pawn, she threatens to expose him. The Black Bishop, identified with the Father General of the Jesuits (cf. 1.1.44–5), and Black Knight–Gondomar order the Black Bishop's Pawn to get away, after leaving antedated letters to serve as false alibi, since his fall would expose the more powerful pieces to danger. The rules of chess thus keep together what would otherwise split into main plot and sub-plot, Church and State, sex and politics.

In the next scene, the White Queen's Pawn complains to the 'King of integrity' (2.2.104) of the attempted rape. But the White King is duped by the forged letters, and leaves her to be punished by the Black House. His gullibility and desertion 'of a cause | So strong in truth and equity' (2.2.217–18) may be related to the war-party attacks on the concessions James made to Spain during the marriage talks, without being able to negotiate a political deal in favour of his deposed son-in-law. The matter was put with unusual bluntness in *Tom Tell-Troath*: 'every *Balaams* Asse, might easily forsee, that your Majesties Credulity was in the high Way to Perdition; and could not but bring you where the *Spaniard* would have you'.[52]

The White Knight steps in to assure the White Queen's Pawn that she is not lost, and, helped by the White Duke, he resolves to confront black intrigue with 'fair policy' (2.2.238). The enterprise of the White Knight and Duke is thus represented not as a romantic adventure, but as a defensive counter-manœuvre after the 'innocence' of the Queen's Pawn and the 'integrity' of the King have both proved disastrous for the White House.

Not much wiser after her recent experience, the White Queen's Pawn longs to see her promised groom in the 'magical glass' (3.1.330), although she believes her soul unchanged from the time she had pledged celibacy. Her self-division is not surprising, given her ignorance of desire. Middleton leaves us in no doubt about what the nature of this desire might be. He makes the White Queen's Pawn describe her fear and trembling with the image he had used for the moment of sexual capitulation in *Women Beware* and *Changeling*—that of the panting turtle under a stroking hand (3.3.6–7).

---

[52] *Tom Tell-Troath*, ii. 3E3ᵛ. The Venetian ambassador wrote on 20 Aug. 1624 to the Doge and the Senate about the play: 'The Spaniards are touched from their tricks being discovered, but the king's reputation is affected much more deeply by representing the case with which he was deceived.' See *CSP Ven.* xviii. 425. T. H. Howard-Hill, in 'Political Interpretations of Middleton's *A Game at Chess* (1624)', *YES* 21 (1991), 284, transcribes 'ease' in place of 'case'.

The Black Queen's Pawn is glad, 'for that trembling | Is always the first symptom of a bride' (3.3.8–9). She proceeds with the theatrical rituals—soft music, rhymed invocation, the fleeting shadow of the Jesuit in rich clothes. The White Queen's Pawn is torn apart by longing and self-reproach: 'It does require | A meeting 'twixt my fear and my desire' (3.3.69–70). A treacherous blush leaps to her cheek at the sight of the Jesuit. She finds celibate life 'too straight, too stubborn on the sudden' (4.1.52). However, she insists on a wedding when the Jesuitess tries to hustle the pair into bed. The Black Bishop's Pawn has a last-minute qualm about his vow of celibacy, but the Black Queen's Pawn, who enjoys pimping as thoroughly as did Livia, tells him that he can agree to a pre-contract 'without danger | Or any stain to your vow' (4.1.136–7). This equivocation works, and, after an intervening scene, a dumb show has the Black Queen's Pawn conduct the White Queen's and the Black Bishop's Pawns to separate rooms, and then snuff out the lights. The Black Queen's Pawn, who wants to get back at the Jesuit for having deported and robbed her, is later revealed as having used the darkness to take the White Queen's Pawn's place in his bed.

The White Queen's Pawn is saved from defloration, and she begins to see the imposture of the black pawns. Her lesson complete, she learns the difference between the common playhouse and the black theatre. The author of *Digitus Dei*, we may recall, thought that God had spared the Blackfriars playhouse because, unlike the Jesuits' theatre, it did not pretend to be other than what it was. The White Queen's Pawn brings against her seducers the same charge of false semiosis that the pamphlet had levelled against Jesuits:

> The world's a stage on which all parts are played:
> You'd count it strange to have a devil
> Presented there not in a devil's shape,
> Or, wanting one, to send him out in yours;
> You'd rail at that for an absurdity
> No college e'er committed. For decorum's sake then,
> For pity's cause, for sacred virtue's honour,
> If you'll persist still in your devil's part,
> Present him as you should do, and let one
> That carries up the goodness of the play
> Come in that habit, and I'll speak with him;
> Then will the parts be fitted and the spectators
> Know which is which. (5.2.19–31)

The extended conceit gives Middleton the opportunity to remind the crowd at the Globe that they too are spectators at a play, but one which uncovers lies by flaunting its fictionality. The White Queen's Pawn turns to the audience and claims for the performance the curative function of the stage:

> Nay, those you have seduced, if there be any
> In the assembly, when they see what manner
> You play your game with me, they cannot love you. (5.2.34-6)

The magic-mirror episode relies on the pamphlet allegations of bogus miracles and visions forged by Jesuits *'for the furtherance of their religion'.*[53] One pamphlet reported that a French Jesuit, Father Cotton, 'hath an Astrological Glasse, wherein he would let the King see verie perfectly, whatsoeuer his Maiestie was desirous to know'.[54] The motive for the bed-trick similarly draws on rumours of how English girls were smuggled out to Jesuit nunneries in Europe. The best-known of these sources, Thomas Robinson's *Anatomy of the English Nunnery at Lisbon*, tells the story of one Sister Anne, who accidentally spied an English Jesuit in 'a great Looking-glasse' seducing a confessee. The priest pleaded with her to keep her discovery secret, and, in return, promised absolution without penance if ever she needed one.[55] Middleton could fit these sources into the allusive frame provided by literary precedents such as Cambuscan's magic mirror in Chaucer's Squire's Tale, and Merlin's mirror, in which Britomart beholds Artegall's image, in Book 3 of Spenser's *Faerie Queene* (2.17–26). Magic glasses of all kinds had been used on the English stage as well, such as those in Greene's *Friar Bacon and Friar Bungay* (2.3, 4.3), Munday's *John a Kent and John a Cumber*, (ll. 1189–1329), and Beaumont and Fletcher's *Bloody Brother* (5.1), not to speak of the sequence in Rowley's *A Shoemaker, a Gentleman* (2.3), which was a likely source.[56] There were also rumours of actual astrological wonders. James Harrington's reported disclosure to Aubrey that a magician had shown the Earl of Denbigh the past and the future in a glass, and the story of the Earl of Surrey being shown the reflection of his mistress in a magic glass by

---

[53] Gee, *New Shreds of the Old Snare*, E1ᵛ.
[54] *Troubles in Bohemia*, D1ᵛ.
[55] [Thomas Robinson], *The Anatomy of the English Nunnery at Lisbon in Portugall* (1622), D2ᵛ–3.
[56] See Bald (ed.), *Game at Chesse*, 16, 150–1.

Cornelius Agrippa are good examples of the fund of popular mysteries Middleton could draw on.[57]

The traditional connotations of the mirror image make the magic glass serve also as an image of 'vanity', a word which combines shades of the Philautia, Superbia, and Vanitas of emblem literature.[58] 'Pride hath no other glass | To show itself but pride', Ulysses says in *Troilus and Cressida* (3.3.47–8), and the remark seems disturbingly true of the way the prognostic mirror shows the White Queen's Pawn the image of her own desire. Her self-flattery is unmistakable when she discovers a 'modest mind' in her dashing groom, and tells herself that 'in that virtue | Most worthily has fate provided for me' (5.2.2–3).

The association with vanity facilitated allusions to the political deployments of the mirror emblem. The 'enchaunted glasse' of Spenser (*Faerie Queene*, Bk. 4, 6.26.6) becomes the 'enchanted Glasse' of a flattering and deceiving court in *Bussy d'Ambois* (Q1, 1.1.84–104). The emblems of the false glass (*speculum fallax*) and the flattering mirror of others' eyes (*speculum oculorum alienorum*) were often conflated to denote the complementarity of self-love and the flattery of parasites.[59] In Shakespeare's *Richard II*, for instance, the king compares the 'flatt'ring glass' which hides his wrinkles to his 'followers in prosperity' (4.1.269–70).[60] Similar examples may be found in the Middleton canon.[61] The clearest association of the flattering glass with the court is made in his 1619 mayoral pageant, *The Triumphs of Love and Antiquity*. There Orpheus warns the Lord Mayor against 'flattering glasses, those false books | Made to set age back in great courtiers' looks' (Bullen, vii. 318).

Examples of the use of the false mirror to denote a sycophantic court are not difficult to find in the political tracts. *Tom Tell-Troath* has the following passage:

The great Spectatours of your Majesties Wisdome, whose dayly Exercise is to multiply the Object in the artificiall Glasses of Fraude, and Flattery, are so

---

[57] Harrington's disclosure is reported in John Aubrey, *Miscellanies* (1696; Franklin, NH, 1969), 53; and the story involving Surrey is mentioned by Drayton in *Englands Heroicall Epistles*; see *Works*, ii. 279.

[58] See Herbert Grabes, *The Mutable Glass: Mirror-Imagery in Titles and Texts of the Middle Ages and the English Renaissance*, trans. Gordon Collier (Cambridge, 1982), 153–6.

[59] See ibid. 80, 110.

[60] Cf. Marston, *Antonio's Revenge*, 1.2.18–19; and Webster, *New and Choise Characters*, in Lucas (ed.), *Works*, iv. 30.

[61] Cf. *Solomon*, Bullen, viii. 241–2, 256; *Family*, 1.2.64–5; *Timon*, 1.1.59; *No Wit*, 1.2.115–19; *Truth*, Bullen, vii. 244–5.

distracted with the infinite Faces in the Counterfayts, as they cannot discerne the Blemishes of the true.

Contrasted with this fraudulent mirror is the 'true Christall Fountaine' of Parliament, 'that will not onely present to your Majesties Vewe, as in a Mirrour, all the foule Spotts of the Commonweale, but serve you at the same Time with Waters . . . to wash them out'.[62] That the White Queen's Pawn, who reminds a critic of Lady England or Public Weal in estates moralities,[63] should be dazzled by the courtly habit of the Jesuit appears an indictment of the vanity and irresolution of the king, setting his looks by the flattering mirror of a mendacious court. Against all forged shadows, Middleton sets the most candid mirror—*speculum consuetudinis, imaginem veritatis*[64]—that of dramatic art.

FAIR POLICY

The Pawns' plot recalls many anxieties caused by the Spanish match. Fears of Charles's defection to Catholicism, of Spanish and Jesuit guile at home and abroad, of the sexual route to apostasy, of the defeat of the Protestant cause in Europe threatened by the early reverses in the Thirty Years War, of the suppression of Parliament—all these may be read into the trials of the White Queen's Pawn. The same issues underlie the story of the major chessmen. The rules of chess make the duplication natural: many plots, one game.

The representation of the prince's secret misadventure in Madrid as the White Knight's righteous counter-move may seem to recycle the apologetics of Buckingham's 1624 relation to Parliament. But its place in the plot also implies a rejection of the 'innocence' and 'integrity' of the White Queen's Pawn and her King. Although they seek to outplay black theatre with 'fair policy', the fairness of the White Knight and Duke still rests on dissimulation. Middleton's sources were unanimous in condemning Jesuit equivocation, which served Catholic princes 'in State-businesses to hide their plots',[65] and they never tired of warning that Spain did not keep faith with those they considered heretics.

[62] *Tom Tell-Troath*, ii. 3E2–2^v.

[63] See Sherman, 'Pawns' Allegory', 153.

[64] Aelius Donatus, *Commentum Terenti*, ed. Paul Wessner, 2 vols. (Leipzig, 1902–5), i. 22.

[65] Henry Mason, *The New Art of Lying, Covered by Iesuites vnder the Vaile of Equivocation* (1624), H4.

Protestants could not be seen to sponsor the same deviousness. They yet needed to plead for more sceptical diplomacy, since Jesuits and sectaries, like Milton's Comus, 'fight not with violence and professed enmity, but with plausible reasons, with smooth perswasions, and . . . glozing pretences'.[66] Moreover, James's apparent faint-heartedness had to be portrayed as plain-dealing so that its dangers might be listed. The dilemma was made more acute after James reneged on the marriage treaty, since militant Protestants had to applaud this turnaround involving a breach of international contract.[67] The resulting incoherence is evident in a passage such as the following:

> The more *sincerely* his Majesty hath dealt, the more *falsely* they; to let him see, *though there be faith to be kept with Heretiks, yet there is none to be giuen to them, nor expected from them.* Princes are to vse *plainesse*, and *perspicuity*, with their subjects, *policy*, and *reservednes*, with strangers . . .[68]

Middleton was not new to the dilemma posed by the passage. In *Hengist*, he had depicted a world in which amoral prowess worked and Christian probity did not. *Game at Chess* shows greater sophistication in handling a similar problem. The deviousness of the White Knight and Duke may ensure the triumph of the just, but the ludic and fictional discipline of the play-game also undermines their moral privilege and implies that they merely play the same game better.

The White Knight proposes to meet the Black House's guile 'With truth of cause and courage', but recognizes the regrettable need 'to feign a little' (4.4.3, 17). The rules of chess favour Middleton's irony here. Black or white, knights must change the colour of their square at every move. As Jerome Vida had explained: *Si nigrante prius campo exspectaverit, album | Mox petere, et sedis semper mutare colorem | Lex jubet.*[69]

The White Knight's arrival 'a Domo Candoris ad Domum Nigritudinis' (5.1.13–14) allows another display of black theatrical

[66] Hieron, *All the Sermons*, V5. The sermon was given in 1613.

[67] Spanish accounts accused Charles and Buckingham of double-dealing. See Fray Francisco de Jesus, *El Hecho de los Tratados del Matrimonio . . . Narrative of the Spanish Marriage Treaty*, trans. and ed. Samuel R. Gardiner, Camden Society, 101 (1869), 246.

[68] [Scott], *Vox Dei*, (n.d.), L1ᵛ.

[69] Mark Jerome Vida, *The Game at Chess*, trans. Richard Stanton Lambert (London, 1921), 14. The latest date for the work is 1513. Nicholas Breton writes of the knight's job of taking 'by sleight a traitrous foe' in 'The Chesse Play'; see Alexander B. Grosart (ed.) *The Works in Verse and Prose of Nicholas Breton*, 2 vols. (Edinburgh, 1879), i. sec. t, 5.

virtuosity: welcome speech,[70] lulling music,[71] self-lighting tapers on the altar, dancing statues. The White Knight remains unmoved by this 'erroneous relish' (5.1.35) of idolatry, although he plays along. In the last scene, he pretends to find his abstemious hosts too strict, and demands concessions to his vices before he can change sides. The Black Knight falls into the trap. He calls dissembling 'The only prime state-virtue' which 'picks ope princes' hearts' (5.3.150, 155) without stopping to consider that the White Knight has been using that same key to unlock the secrets of the Black House. The White Knight gives 'checkmate by | Discovery' (5.3.160–1),[72] and the black pieces are bagged.

One set of critics see the White Knight's story as a straightforward compliment paid to Charles and Buckingham, and even suggest that they sponsored the play as part of their campaign for war with Spain.[73] The strongest argument for the view is that Sir Henry Herbert would never have licensed the play if he were not certain of support for it from 'higher powers'.[74] Censorship after the prince's return may not have been as stiff as around 1621, the year in which the Calvinist theologian Samuel Ward, Master of Sidney Sussex College at Cambridge, was told by a correspondent that, in a book the latter had written, the publisher had press-corrected '*forbidden mariage with women popishly affected*' to '*vnfortunate mariages wth &cc*' because 'times . . . áre dangerous'.[75] Yet when Lady Elizabeth's provincial troupe announced in Norwich on 26 April 1624 that they would stage *The Spanish*

[70] On the real-life source of the speech, see G. R. Price, 'The Latin Oration in *A Game at Chesse*', *HLQ* 23 (1960), 389–93.

[71] False Spanish promises were sometimes compared to soft music. Cf. S.R.N.I. [John Reynolds], *Votivae Angliae, or, The Desires and Wishes of England* (1624), B4: 'Spayn recovered the *Valtolyne*, and deflowred the Fortes and passages of the Grisons, and whiles he (by his *Gondomar*) lull'd your Maiestie asleepe with the melodie of the Match, then hee finished the Conquest of the Pallatynat.' See also Cogswell, *Blessed Revolution*, 43.

[72] On the technical aspect of this kind of checkmate, see N. W. Bawcutt, 'New Light on Middleton's Knowledge of Chess', *N & Q* 232 (1987), 301–2.

[73] See Louis B. Wright, '*A Game at Chess*', *TLS*, 16 Feb. 1928, 112; and John Dover Wilson's review of Bald's edition, *Library*, 4th ser. 11 (1930), 110–11.

[74] John Woolley wrote to his master, the English agent in Brussels, on 20 Aug. 1624 that the play could not have got past the Master of the Revels 'without leave from the higher powers, I meane the Prince and Duke if not from the King'; see Cogswell, 'Middleton and the Court', 281. Sir John Holles wrote to Carr on 11 Aug. that the 'gamsters must haue a good retrayte' to be able 'to charge thus Princes actions . . . nay their intents'; see T. H. Howard-Hill, 'The Unique Eye-Witness Report of Middleton's *A Game at Chess*', *RES*, NS 42 (1991), 170.

[75] Bodleian, MS Tanner 73/1, fo. 29. The letter is dated May 26. On the change in censorship policy in 1624, see Cogswell, *Blessed Revolution*, 281–301.

Contract, a lost play presumably on the Spanish match, one of their members was prosecuted.[76]

On the other hand, Bald argued on the basis of the White Duke's reference to his own obesity and lechery (5.3.58–60, 121–3) that Middleton's allusions to Buckingham were not uniformly respectful.[77] Heinemann pleaded that the play's virulent anti-Catholicism could hardly have been designed to please Buckingham, who was at this time urging concessions to English Catholics as a step towards Charles's marriage to Henrietta Maria. One could add that Buckingham's wife came of a Catholic family, and that his mother was converted to Catholicism by Father Fisher, a Jesuit. Heinemann's guess is that the Earl of Pembroke, Buckingham's enemy and leader of the anti-Spanish group in the Privy Council, vetted the play and shielded his kinsman Sir Henry Herbert, especially since, as Lord Chamberlain, Pembroke was responsible for the control of the theatre.[78] On 27 August, Pembroke informed the President of the Privy Council of James's wish to let the King's Men resume playing provided they did not put on *Game at Chess*. This might mean that he had brokered their reprieve, but it does not imply that he had also sponsored the play. Howard-Hill and Cogswell point out that by 12 June 1624, when the play was licensed, and certainly by 5 August, when the first of its nine consecutive performances (except on 8 August, a Sunday) was given at the Globe, Pembroke had closed ranks with Buckingham, that the Spanish lobby was then defunct, and that the 'confessions' of the White Knight and Duke are in fact a compliment to the cunning of Charles and Buckingham in uncovering Spanish imperial designs.[79]

---

[76] G. E. Bentley, *The Jacobean and Caroline Stage*, 7 vols. (Oxford, 1941–68), v. 1455–6.

[77] R. C. Bald, ' "Assembled" Texts', *Library*, 4th ser. 12 (1932), 247–8. For a recent instance of the debate, see Martin Butler, 'William Prynne and the Allegory of Middleton's *Game at Chess*', *N & Q* 228 (1983), 153; and T. H. Howard-Hill, 'More on "William Prynne and the Allegory of Middleton's *Game at Chess*" ', *N & Q* 234 (1989), 350–1.

[78] Heinemann, *Puritanism and Theatre*, 165–9. Michael Brennan agrees in *Literary Patronage in the English Renaissance: The Pembroke Family* (London, 1988), 175.

[79] See T. H. Howard-Hill, 'The Origins of Middleton's *A Game at Chess*', *RORD* 28 (1985), 11; id., 'Political Interpretations', 281–5; and Cogswell, 'Middleton and the Court', 273–85. In a letter to Buckingham, dated 14 June 1624, Sir Edward Conway, Secretary of State, writes, 'The venom of the Spanish partie I trust is past'; see Bodleian, MS Tanner 73/2, fo. 447ᵛ. Evelyn May Albright, *Dramatic Publication in England, 1580–1640: A Study of Conditions Affecting Content and Form of Drama* (New York, 1927), 169, and Janet Clare, *'Art Made Tongue-Tied by Authority': Elizabethan and Jacobean Dramatic Censorship* (Manchester, 1990), 190–9, plausibly argue that the players were emboldened by the collapse of foreign policy rather than that of the Spanish party. The latter was always a soft and opportunistic clique; see Linda Levy Peck, *Court Patronage and Corruption in Early Stuart England* (Boston, 1990), 54.

In *The Triumphs of Integrity*, the mayoral pageant he wrote the previous year, Middleton had joined the chorus of thanksgiving which greeted Charles's return from Spain (cf. Bullen, vii. 395).[80] A soldier in the masque *The World Tossed at Tennis* (1619; with Rowley) joins the Protestant army of Prince Frederick to fight 'the most glorious wars | That e'er famed Christian kingdom' (ll. 875–6). But Middleton's support for party issues was more equivocal than that of most loyalists. I have argued that the metaphor of the chess game allowed him to displace the serious critique of sexual politics on to the Pawns' plot. The White Knight's story could thus be made to look politically innocuous, while it could be shown also as part of the same game the Pawns were playing. The White Queen's Pawn's vanity and desire complicate our response to the confessions of ambition and lust from her Knight and Duke, while the vulnerability of her innocence tempers our resistance to their dissembling. The allusion to Buckingham's love of food and women—contiguous vices, since 'gluttony is the forechamber of lust, and lust the inner rowme of gluttonie'[81]—is likewise infected by the more pungent portrayal of these vices in the Fat Bishop. Equally double-edged is the satire on Spanish abstemiousness (cf. 5.3.2–52). It reproduces the censorious reports of the prince's mingy reception in Madrid,[82] but when put beside the Fat Bishop's commendation of the White House 'For plenty and variety of victuals' (2.2.29), it begins to look like the hit at English extravagance which John Holles detected in it.[83] When reading the Black Knight's caricature of 'White House gormandisers' (5.3.39), it is necessary to remember that a cautionary play such as *A Larum for London* (1602) had depicted the Spanish conquest of Antwerp as divine punishment for its 'swilling Epicures' (A2), and that peacetime luxuries were being blamed at the time for the loss of heroic Elizabethan values.[84]

The riddle posed for critics by the equivocal handling of the White Knight's story is understandable when we see a comparable perplexity

---

[80] See M. C. Bradbrook, 'The Politics of Pageantry: Social Implications in Jacobean London', in Coleman and Hammond (eds.), *Poetry and Drama 1570–1700*, 71.

[81] Thomas Wright, *The Passions of the Minde* (1601), O6. The idea was a commonplace. See e.g. Hoccleve, *The Regement of Princes*, 137. Cf. *Widow*, 1.1.17–18: 'if gluttony be the meat, lechery is the porridge; they're both boiled together.'

[82] See Bullen, vii. 124–5; and Bald (ed.), *Game at Chesse*, 157.

[83] See Howard-Hill, 'Unique Eye-Witness Report', 169, 173–4.

[84] The Black Knight's speech bears comparison with Nashe's outburst against English gluttony in *Pierce Penilesse*; see McKerrow (ed.), *Works*, i. 200. See also Drayton, *Polyolbion*, 20. 35–40.

in Protestant pamphleteers, who were forced to picture Charles and Buckingham first as traitors and then as politic patriots.[85] The playwright was not as easily surprised, and he makes his point by giving victory to the White Knight precisely at the moment he comes closest to the 'souls' of the Black House, so that the Black Knight finds in his white counterpart a true 'brother' (5.3.157–8). 'Ambitious, covetous, luxurious falsehood' (5.3.163)—the assorted vices 'confessed' to by the White Knight and Duke are all included in Spanish dissembling (5.3.164), but so are all counter-measures. In *Triumphs of Integrity*, Integrity is so free of 'disguise or hypocritic veil' that we can literally see her 'thoughts' seated by her side (Bullen, vii. 392). The most powerful subjects of the 'King of integrity' are far from such crystalline transparence. On the chess-board stage of politics, the White House may wrest control only if they play the game: the play-game is the thing.

CHECKMATE BY DISCOVERY

The two major stories in the play are punctuated by variations on the turncoat theme. The White King's Pawn is exposed as a traitor, and the distressed White Queen is saved from the clutches of the fat prelate by the White Bishop. The second episode probably alludes to Queen Anne's conversion to Catholicism and her reported death-bed recantation to Archbishop Abbot.[86] It is possible that the White King's Pawn was initially meant to stand for Toby Matthew, the son of the Archbishop of York, who had converted to the Jesuit persuasion and who had counselled Charles and Buckingham in Madrid. In its revised form, the first episode is a satire on the Earls of Bristol and Middlesex. At the time when Middleton was writing or revising his play, both were battling hostile reprisals from Charles and Buckingham. John Digby, Earl of Bristol, was ambassador to Spain till May 1624. Despite his distinguished service as leader of English counter-espionage in Spain, Digby was put under house arrest on his return, and the blame for the ruinous terms of the marriage treaty was conveniently shifted to him. The Earl of Middlesex, Lionel Cranfield, resisted Bucking-

[85] See Cogswell, *Blessed Revolution*, 47–8, 291–4.
[86] See Bald (ed.), *Game at Chess*, 11. Queen Anne was one of Gondomar's sources of intelligence; see Garrett Mattingly, *Renaissance Diplomacy* (1956; Harmondsworth, 1965), 247.

ham's war plans as Lord Treasurer, and his impeachment on corruption charges began in April 1624.

There is also the lost, wandering figure of the Black Knight's Pawn, seeking absolution for gelding his white rival. He finds no comfort, since 'there is no precedent | Of any price or pardon' (4.3.122–3) for his offence in the *Taxae Poenitentiariae*, the mail-order catalogue for Roman pardons. The satire against the Catholic exchange rates of sins—two shillings for adultery, fivepence for fornication, sixpence for sodomy, nine pounds for simony, and thirteen pounds, four shillings, and sixpence for wilful murder (4.3.88–107)—could easily be turned against societies in which Castiza is auctioned off by her husband, Lethe hires his mother as bawd, Allwit leases out his wife, the doctor demands Jane's flesh for his fee, the Duke gives away a fort to silence his mistress's husband, and Beatrice offers a thousand florins to De Flores as hush-money. Sex and money level English court, city, and country as thoroughly as in the London comedies. 'The court has held the city by the horns | Whilst I have milked her,' says the Black Knight, and he has 'had good sops too | From country ladies for their liberties' (3.1.108–10).

The characters most skilled in trading conscience and changing colour are the two overreachers, the Black Knight and the Fat Bishop. The comic energy of the play is concentrated in this caricature of Count Gondomar's manipulation of Marco Antonio de Dominis, the apostate Archbishop of Spalatro, who defected from the Roman Church to the English, only to be lured back in 1622. Middleton returns to his favourite con man-conned plan in this encounter of Machiavel and Papist, the two exemplary masters of the play-game. The plan was conveniently laid out in the suggested source for the story, *Newes from Rome*:

It is an old saying, *Proditoris proditor*, one knave most commonly will finde out another . . . Right so it fared with *Spalato* and *Gundamar*, they alwaies fought one against another . . . [87]

The pamphlet accuses de Dominis of gluttony, lechery, and imposture—the sins 'confessed' to by the White Knight and Duke, and exercising all the episodes of the play. Even if it was not the play's source, the popular image of de Dominis the pamphlet recycles made it easy for Middleton to introduce the satire at a late stage without

---

[87] *Newes from Rome*, C4ᵛ. Bald (ed.), *Game at Chesse*, 147, suggested that the tract was a major source. But the tract possibly came after the play; see Howard Hill (ed.), *Game at Chess*, 33.

dislocating the original conception. The Archdall manuscript, judged by Bald to have been an earlier version of the text, lacks the character of the Fat Bishop, as also the lines indicating most strongly that the White King's Pawn stands for Middlesex (3.1.265–7).[88] These additions may have been designed to make the satire more sharply topical, but they also reinforce the basic comic design. The Black Knight does to the Fat Bishop what the White Knight does to him. Like Middleton's comic tricksters, the Black Knight succeeds only to be tripped up by someone better at his own game.

That the Fat Bishop is at home on either side has been rightly seen as destructive of 'any sense of distinction between the two houses'.[89] Middleton had partisan sympathies, and the portrayal of the Black House clearly exploits the 'black legend' of Hispanophobia.[90] Nevertheless, Middleton's insight into the tangled web of sexual, religious, and political conduct muddies the moral clarity of black and white. In earlier plays, he had used farce and bawdy to exaggerate such ambiguities. Here, their equivalent is one scene in which the Black Jesting Pawn and another black pawn capture a white one (3.2). It is inserted between the scene in which the White King's Pawn and the Fat Bishop change colour and that of the magic mirror, so that it may mediate our view of all this shape-shifting. The exchange between the Jesting Pawn and the White Pawn dissolves moral chromatics in carnal images and quibbles—the devil astride 'a nightmare | Made of a miller's daughter', 'a black-bird | In the great snow', the three looking 'like a birdspit, a white chick | Between two russet woodcocks' (3.2.7–10, 32–3). In a 1620 sermon, Thomas Scott had compared the hoarder, the monopolist, and the rack-renter to 'birds of a feather, who hang together of a string'.[91] The closing words of the Jesting Pawn, which must have been backed up by appropriate stage-action, employ a similar image of moral consanguinity, making a mockery of the

[88] See R. C. Bald, 'An Early Version of Middleton's *Game at Chesse*', *MLR* 38 (1943), 177–80. The attack on Cranfield could be an afterthought; see Howard-Hill, 'More on "William Prynne"', 349–50; and id., 'Political Interpretations', 277. Sir John Holles identified the Pawn with his friend, the Earl of Bristol; see A. R. Braunmuller, ' "To the Globe I rowed": John Holles Sees *A Game at Chess*', *ELR* 20 (1990), 351–4; and Howard-Hill, 'Unique Eye-Witness Report', 169, 173.

[89] Richard A. Davies and Alan R. Young, ' "Strange Cunning" in Thomas Middleton's *A Game at Chess*', *UTQ* 45 (1976), 240.

[90] See W. S. Maltby, *The Black Legend in England, 1558–1660* (Ann Arbor, Mich., 1968), 3.

[91] Thomas Scott, *The High-Waies of God and the King* (1623), K2ᵛ.

spiritual contention of black and white: 'We draw together now for all the world | Like three flies with one straw through their buttocks' (3.2.38–9).

Farce also dominates the final sequence when the black pieces are crammed into the bag, the point at which the Jesting Pawn makes a reappearance. He feels his 'verjuice' squeezed out of him by the Fat Bishop (5.3.189), who throws his weight about even inside the bag. The latter refuses to budge when the Black King is shoved in, but concedes that 'a queen may make a bishop stir' (5.3.203). Even when he can smell the Black Knight's fistula, the Fat Bishop, in a grotesque parody of Catholic opposition to Erastianism, insists on precedence 'Maugre king, queen, or politician' (5.3.215).

The White King and Knight see the chess-bag as 'hell' (5.3.179–80, 197), although it is not certain if it was shown as hell mouth on the stage. A dispatch from the Spanish ambassador Don Carlos Coloma to the Duke of Olivares says that the actor who played Charles 'heartily beat and kicked the "Count of Gondomar" into Hell, which consisted of a great hole and hideous figures'.[92] Identifying the chess-bag with hell was perhaps Middleton's idea.[93] The more traditional association had been with the grave. In the *Gesta Romanorum*, the jumbled pieces in the bag are a reminder of the levelling of social distinctions after death.[94] Similar uses have been spotted in medieval texts and Renaissance emblems.[95] Nearer Middleton's time, Marston's *Jack Drum's Entertainment* (Act 1, p. 185), and Sharpham's *Cupid's Whirligig* (1607; 4.1.24–8) had put the chess metaphor to the same use. In a 1608 sermon, Archbishop Abbot illustrated the emptiness of titles and rank with the same metaphor:

howsoever in the board they differ in their degree, yet when the game is ended, and they are swept all into the bagge, there is none better than the other, the meanest lieth above, and the greatest is underneath.[96]

---

[92] See Wilson and Turner, 'Spanish Protest', 480.

[93] See Paul Yachnin, '*A Game at Chess* and Chess Allegory', *SEL* 22 (1982), 325. On the change from 'pitt' to 'bag' in the printed quarto, see T. H. Howard-Hill, 'The Author as Scribe or Reviser? Middleton's Intentions in *A Game at Chess*', *Text*, 3 (1987), 314.

[94] See Sidney J. H. Herrtage (ed.), *The Early English Versions of the Gesta Romanorum*, EETS, extra ser. 33 (London, 1879), 71.

[95] See Davies and Young, ' "Strange Cunning" ', 236–7.

[96] George Abbot, *A Sermon Preached at Westminster May 26, 1608, at the Funerall Solemnities of Thomas Earle of Dorset* (1608), as quoted in R. W. Dent, *Proverbial Language in English Drama Exclusive of Shakespeare, 1495–1616* (Berkeley, Calif., 1984), 245–6.

In some instances, the metaphor of the world-as-chessboard merges with that of the world-as-stage, uniting the ludic and the fictional, game and play. When Don Quixote compares life to a play, at the end of which death strips the actors of the robes that distinguished them, Sancho replies:

'A fine comparison . . . although not so new that I haven't heard it on various occasions before—like the one of the game of chess, where each piece has its particular importance while the game lasts, but when it's over they're all mixed up, thrown together, jumbled, and shoved into a leather bag, which is much like shovelling life away into the grave.'[97]

In a verse letter to Sir Henry Wotton written in 1598, Donne disparagingly calls the court a playhouse. At the same moment, he is reminded of a game at chess:

> Beleeve mee Sir, in my youths giddiest dayes,
> When to be like the Court, was a playes praise,
> Playes were not so like Courts, as Courts'are like playes.
>
> Then let us at these mimicke antiques jeast,
> Whose deepest projects, and egregious gests
> Are but dull Moralls of a game at Chests.[98]

The equipollence of the metaphors seems to have become familiar by 1624. In that year, a quarto mourning the death of the Duke of Richmond uses the two figures almost interchangeably:

All, both good and bad are *Actors* on this stage of *Mortalitie*, euery one acting a part . . . some of lesse, some of greater dignitie; and the Play being ended *Exeunt omnes*, euery one goes off the stage, and as Chessemen without difference they are swept from the table of this World, wherein one was a *King*, another a *Queene*, a third a *Bishop* or *Knight* into Earths bagge; onely this distinction being betwixt good and bad, that the good are *Actors* of a *Comedie*; and howsoeuer they beginne, they end merrily: but the bad, are *Actors* of a *Tragedie*, and howsoeuer they beginne . . . their *Catastrophe* lamentable.[99]

Middleton's play, like the Jesuits' theatre superseded by God's at Lyons, ends as 'tragedy' for the black pieces and 'comedy' for the white. The black pieces are kicked into the bag, while the white stay

---

[97] Miguel de Cervantes Saavedra, *The Adventures of Don Quixote*, trans. J. M. Cohen (Harmondsworth, 1950), 539.

[98] Donne, 'To Sir Henry Wotton', in *Satires, Epigrams and Verse Letters*, 74.

[99] Iames Cleland, *A Monument of Mortalitie, vpon the Death and Funerals, of the Gracious Prince Lodovick, Late Duke of Richmond and Lenox* (1624), C1–1ᵛ.

on to lecture the audience. But the allied conceit of the playhouse permits the dramatist one final joke. After the White Queen's Pawn warns in an Epilogue that the friends of the Black House would 'be soon known' (l. 8), the pieces glide away to the tiring house to end the dream play. In *Solomon*, the adolescent Middleton had brooded on the impermanence of the difference made by birth and wealth—'Tell me the difference then of everything, | And who a subject was, and who a king' (Bullen, viii. 284). In his last work, the difference is conceived as fashioned by the play-game. White pieces strut briefly as champions of justice and helmsmen of national destiny, only to slip back into their status of chessmen and dream players. The superior claims of the White House are undermined for the same reason as that which saved the Blackfriars theatre from divine anger. The play, like the playhouse, parades its fictionality as an open pretence.

King James is supposed to have astutely dodged the anger of the Commons and that of Philip IV of Spain by banning the play not for its politics, but for violating the 'restraint giuen against the rep^rsentinge of anie modern Christian Kings in those Stage-playes'.[100] One wonders if staging royalty were not in itself a political offence serious enough to have had the performances stopped, the key players called before the Privy Council, and, possibly, the author arrested (a warrant was issued to the purpose on 18 August). *Game at Chess* seems to reverse the code which permitted the representation of royalty in spectacles such as the masque. The masque's way of validating royal authority was to erase the distance between the dance and the dancers, between the court as theatrical setting and the court as the source of existent power.[101] Middleton reverses this traffic between reality and fiction and, with it, the hierarchy idealized in the masque. His king is a chess piece, played more than player, with the bag as his eventual destination. What is worse, the whiteness of the White King is shown to signify nothing unless secured by the fine living and dissimulation of his Knight and Duke, by 'the crimes of the signifier'—Derrida's phrase for the abiding offences of players.[102] The king plays the player, and the player plays

[100] I am quoting from the transcript of Conway's letter, dated 12 Aug. 1624, to the Privy Council, in Bernard M. Wagner, 'New Allusions to *A Game at Chesse*', *PMLA* 44 (1929), 827–8.

[101] See Stephen Orgel, *The Illusion of Power: Political Theater in the English Renaissance* (Berkeley, Calif., 1975), 38–9.

[102] Jacques Derrida, *Of Grammatology*, trans. Gayatri Chakravorty Spivak (Baltimore, 1976), 304.

the king: the mainstay of order and degree swaps places with the most menacing symbol of Protean exorbitance.

For the Renaissance theatre, the world-as-stage metaphor was a familiar means of reflecting simultaneously on its own artifice and on that of social and political identities.[103] No other dramatic text reflects on such artifice as steadfastly as Middleton's last play. Theatre and game conspire to give rulers 'checkmate', in the sense that they equate princely histrionics with that of lowly players. It was in the sense of an equal that Nashe had used the word in *Pierce Penilesse*, when he lamented that upstarts were being 'raised from the plough to be checkmate with Princes'.[104] The word's duplicity joins that of the overall dramatic conceit in desacralizing the myths of authority. If our experience of such matters in today's world is anything to judge by, power dreads the art which is unimpressed by its mystique more than that which simply objects to its decisions. In casting the divinely ordained king and his son as counters and players on a chessboard-stage, Middleton overstepped the limits of the theatre's licensed marginality, and pulled the wrath of earthly gods down on his head. But he had made sure of the only triumph that a 'vulgar pasquin'[105] may score over lordly players—a checkmate by theatrical discovery.

[103] See Louis A. Montrose, 'The Purpose of Playing: Reflections on a Shakespearean Anthropology', *Helios*, NS 7 (1980), 57.
[104] McKerrow (ed.), *Works*, i. 173.
[105] The phrase was used for the play by Holles. See Howard-Hill, 'Unique Eye-Witness Report', 168.

Afterword

A recent survey of drama and society in the English Renaissance ends with applauding Middleton as 'a master' who 'will take no contemporary value for granted, no reality as unchanging'.[1] The encomium is as fair an indication as any of the source of Middleton's appeal for our times. His promiscuous texts are proven material for postmodern theatre and pedagogy, constantly assaulting our tidy notions of high and low, genre and counter-genre. More important, they share our suspicion of culture's habitual representation of values, institutions, and relationships, implying that these are never quite the things we are taught to see them as, but are productions of the contingent discourses of power. What saves this reflection from trite cynicism is his insight into the complicit premises of such discourses, and of their expressions in sex and economics, market-place and lawcourt, civil society and State.

It is not surprising that academic criticism should have managed to find in Middleton the extremes of both committed didacticism and detached irony. One reason it still finds him so difficult to place is the suggestion in his plays that desires, morals, society, and politics, as also the ways we usually talk about these things, are subject to rules which can operate only by misrepresenting themselves to our consciousness. The suggestion makes Middleton an important waymark in our emergence out of cognitive innocence. Paul Ricoeur wrote that while Descartes had taught the West to doubt everything but consciousness, Marx, Nietzsche, and Freud took away that consolation, destroying the certain coincidence of meaning and its presumed self-evidence. Ricoeur proposed a useful maxim for post-Freudian generations: 'Consciousness is not a given but a *task*.'[2] For the writer committed to art as a truth-event, what Heidegger called 'happening of truth',[3] consciousness has always been a task, and art has always presupposed the possibility of such radical scepticism. Consciousness is a task for Middleton's protagonists, and their passage from innocence to

---

[1] Michael Hattaway, 'Drama and Society', in A. R. Braunmuller and Michael Hattaway (eds.), *The Cambridge Companion to English Renaissance Drama* (Cambridge, 1990), 124.

[2] Paul Ricoeur, *The Conflict of Interpretations: Essays in Hermeneutics*, ed. Don Ihde (Evanston, Ill., 1974), 108.

[3] Heidegger, *Poetry, Language, Thought*, 71.

experience is its analogue. The process is mediated by the theatre, and Middleton, as I have tried to show, was a pioneer of the theatre which is aware of the ruses of its own language, and, consequently, of its subversive potencies. The moralist and 'Puritan' versions of Middleton leave one dissatisfied because these underplay the secular stress of his work, and its concern with the perilous indeterminacy of the theatre's technique and social place.

The consciousness which Middleton's theatre mediates, I have also argued, derives its vitality from a broad and popular social base. This is not to say that it echoes the partisan prejudices of the populace. The psycho-sexual depth sounded by even a commercial success such as *Game at Chess* is not conducive to the maintenance of mob antipathies. Freud compares the person who refuses to accept that more goes on inside his mind than he is aware of to 'an absolute ruler who is content with the information supplied him by his highest officials and never goes among the people to hear their voice'.[4] The collusion of political, ideological, and psychosexual self-evasion glimpsed in Freud's comparison was one of Middleton's discoveries as well. His suspicion of the pretences of Stuart absolutism was thus inseparable from his suspicion of the ethical and psychological subterfuge of late feudal society. Middleton's theatre, like Shakespeare's, took the part of the 'people' by articulating the silenced implications behind socially acknowledged rules of reasoning.

Middleton, in many ways, answers to Walter Benjamin's Apollonian version of the 'destructive character', who desecrates inherited mysteries, thereby giving them a new social utility. In Benjamin's metaphor, he reduces 'the existing to rubble' for the sake of 'the path that extends through it'.[5] Unlike Benjamin's 'destructive character', Middleton had a stake in being understood, but he has remained the most misunderstood playwright among Shakespeare's contemporaries. The distracting quest for his 'personality' and 'views' has produced the predictable misreadings which persist in very recent criticism.[6] One of

---

[4] Freud, 'A Difficulty in the Path of Psycho-Analysis', in Strachey (ed.), *Standard Edition*, xvii. 143.

[5] See Irving Wohlfarth, 'No-Man's Land: On Walter Benjamin's "Destructive Character" ', *Diacritics*, 8 (1978), 47–65, which gives a translation of the German text in Walter Benjamin, *Gesammelte Schriften*, ed. Rolf Tiedemann and Hermann Schweppenhäuser, 6 vols. (Frankfurt, 1972–88), vi. 1. 396–8.

[6] An instance is the recently revived charge of misogyny. See David Holbrook, *Images of Woman in Literature* (New York, 1989), 131–2; and Anne M. Haselkorn, 'Sin and the Politics of Penitence: Three Jacobean Adulteresses', in Anne M. Haselkorn and Betty S. Travitsky (eds.), *The Renaissance Englishwoman in Print: Counterbalancing the Canon* (Amherst, Mass., 1990), 126–30.

the aims of this book has been to shun the reductive routes to Middleton's 'beliefs' and, instead, to trace in the plays' reinvention of anterior forms the encounter of ideological self-conditioning and historical experience. This is not, as I hope I make clear, to deny Middleton partisan sympathies, but to rescue them from easy abstractions.

As doctrinaire historicism and ahistorical formalism appear to be losing their political briefs, the time seems exactly right for a revaluation of Middleton's status. The labour of textual scholars from Oliphant to Holdsworth has come to its promised fruition in the modern-spelling Oxford edition of his works. I should like to hope that it will install Middleton in the foreground of our cultural consciousness. That will be the appropriate tribute for a great chronicler of modern culture's loss of innocence.

Bibliography

I. MIDDLETON'S WORKS

1. Source Texts for References

The Changeling, ed. N. W. Bawcutt, Revels Plays (London, 1958).

A Chaste Maid in Cheapside, ed. R. B. Parker, Revels Plays (London, 1969).

A Fair Quarrel, ed. R. V. Holdsworth, New Mermaids (London, 1974).

A Game at Chess, ed. T. H. Howard-Hill, Revels Plays (Manchester, 1993).

The Ghost of Lucrece, ed. J. Q. Adams (New York, 1937).

Hengist, King of Kent, or The Mayor of Queenborough, ed. R. C. Bald (New York, 1938).

The Honest Whore, Part I, in *The Dramatic Works of Thomas Dekker*, ed. Fredson Bowers, 4 vols. (Cambridge, 1953–61), ii.

[*The Lady's Tragedy*] *The Second Maiden's Tragedy*, ed. Anne Lancashire, Revels Plays (Manchester, 1978).

A Mad World, My Masters, ed. Standish Henning, Regents Renaissance Drama (London, 1965).

The Meeting of Gallants at an Ordinary, in *The Plague Pamphlets of Thomas Dekker*, ed. F. P. Wilson (Oxford, 1925).

Michaelamas Term, ed. Richard Levin, Regents Renaissance Drama (London, 1967).

The Nice Valour, or, The Passionate Mad-Man, ed. George Walton Williams, in Fredson Bowers (gen. ed.), *The Dramatic Works in the Beaumont and Fletcher Canon*, 9 vols. published (Cambridge, 1966–93), vii.

No Wit, No Help Like a Woman's, ed. Lowell Johnson, Regents Renaissance Drama (Lincoln, Neb., 1976).

The Owles Almanacke. Prognosticating Many Strange Accidents, ed. D. C. Allen (Baltimore, 1943).

The Penniless Parliament of Threadbare Poets, in *Iacke of Dover, his Quest of Inquirie, or his Priuy Search for the Veriest Foole in England* (1604).

Platoes Cap Cast at this Yeare 1604 (1604).

The Puritan, in *The Shakespeare Apocrypha: Being a Collection of Fourteen Plays which have been Ascribed to Shakespeare*, ed. C. F. Tucker Brooke (Oxford, 1908).

The Revenger's Tragedy, ed. R. A. Foakes, Revels Plays (London, 1966).

The Roaring Girl, ed. Paul A. Mulholland, Revels Plays (Manchester, 1987).

A Trick to Catch the Old One, ed. G. J. Watson, New Mermaids (London, 1968).

The Two Gates of Salvation, Set Wide Open: or, The Mariage of the Old and New Testament (1609).

Wit at Several Weapons, ed. R. K. Turner, in *Dramatic Works in the Beaumont and Fletcher Canon*, vii.

The Witch, in *Three Jacobean Witchcraft Plays: The Tragedy of Sophonisba. The Witch. The Witch of Edmonton*, ed. Peter Corbin and Douglas Sedge, Revels Plays Companion Library (Manchester, 1986).

Women Beware Women, ed. J. R. Mulryne, Revels Plays (London, 1975).

A Yorkshire Tragedy, in *Shakespeare Apocrypha*, ed. Brooke.

For the remaining works, the references are to *The Works of Thomas Middleton*, ed. A. H. Bullen, 8 vols. (London, 1885–7).

2. *Other Editions of Middleton's Works Cited*

BALD, R. C. (ed.), *A Game at Chesse* (Cambridge, 1929).

BROOKS, JOHN B. (ed.), The Phoenix *by Thomas Middleton: A Critical Edition* (New York, 1980).

CAWLEY, A. C., and GAINES, BARRY (eds.), *A Yorkshire Tragedy*, Revels Plays (Manchester, 1986).

COLEGROVE, C. LEE (ed.), *A Critical Edition of Thomas Middleton's* Your Five Gallants (New York, 1979).

DAALDER, JOOST (ed.), *The Changeling*, New Mermaids (re-edited, London, 1990).

LEVINE, ROBERT T. (ed.), *A Critical Edition of Thomas Middleton's* The Widow (Salzburg, 1975).

LOUGHREY, BRIAN, and TAYLOR, NEIL (eds.), *Thomas Middleton: Five Plays*, Penguin Classics (London, 1988).

PRICE, G. R. (ed.), Michaelmas Term *and* A Trick to Catch the Old One: *A Critical Edition* (The Hague, 1976).

—— (ed.), *A Fair Quarrel*, Regents Renaissance Drama (London, 1977).

SHAW, CATHERINE M. (ed.), *The Old Law*, Garland English Texts (New York, 1982).

SHEPHERD, SIMON (ed.), *The Family of Love*, Nottingham Drama Texts (Nottingham, 1979).

II. OTHER PLAYWRIGHTS

1. *Source Texts for References*

Anonymous Plays

BROOKE, C. F. TUCKER (ed.), *Shakespeare Apocrypha* [for *The London Prodigal* and *The Birth of Merlin*].

CANON, CHARLES DALE (ed.), A Warning for Fair Women: *A Critical Edition* (The Hague, 1975).

DE VOCHT, H. (ed.), *A Knack to Know an Honest Man*, MSR (Oxford, 1910).

GREG, W. W. (ed.), *A Larum for London*, MSR (Oxford, 1913).

—— (ed.), *The Contention between Liberality and Prodigality*, MSR (Oxford, 1913).

PROUDFOOT, G. R. (ed.), *A Knack to Know a Knave*, MSR (Oxford, 1963 [1964]).

SMITH, G. C. MOORE (ed.), Club Law: *A Comedy Acted in Clare Hall, Cambridge about 1599–1600* (Cambridge, 1907).

Plays by Known Authors

BARRY, LORDING, *Ram Alley*, ed. Peter Corbin and Douglas Sedge, Nottingham Drama Texts (Nottingham, 1981).

BEAUMONT, FRANCIS, and FLETCHER, JOHN, *The Dramatic Works in the Beaumont and Fletcher Canon*, gen. ed. Fredson Bowers, 9 vols. published (Cambridge, 1966–93).

—— *The Bloody Brother, or Rollo, A Tragedy*, in A. Glover and A. R. Waller (eds.), *The Works of Francis Beaumont and John Fletcher*, 10 vols. (Cambridge, 1905–12), iv.

BEHN, APHRA, *The City Heiress*, in Montague Summers (ed.), *The Works of Aphra Behn*, 6 vols. (London, 1915), ii.

BURTON, ROBERT, *Robert Burton's* Philosophaster *with an English Translation of the Same. Together with his Other Minor Writings in Prose and Verse*, trans. and ed. Paul Jordan-Smith (Stanford, Calif., 1931).

[CARY, ELIZABETH], *The Tragedy of Mariam*, ed. A. C. Dunstan, MSR (Oxford, 1914).

CHAPMAN, GEORGE, *The Plays of George Chapman: The Comedies. A Critical Edition*, ed. Allan Holaday (Urbana, Ill., 1970).

—— *The Plays of George Chapman: The Tragedies with* Sir Gyles Goosecappe. *A Critical Edition*, ed. Allan Holaday (Cambridge, 1987).

DANIEL, SAMUEL, *The Tragedy of Philotas*, ed. Laurence Michel (New Haven, Conn., 1949).

DAY, JOHN, *Humour out of Breath*, in Herbert P. Horne, *et al.*, (eds.), *Nero and Other Plays* (London, 1888).

—— *Law Tricks*, ed. John Crow, MSR (Oxford, 1949 [1950]).

DEKKER, THOMAS, *The Dramatic Works of Thomas Dekker*, ed. Fredson Bowers, 4 vols. (Cambridge, 1953–61) [for references to all Dekker plays, including collaborations, except *The Roaring Girl*].

FIELD, NATHAN, *Amends for Ladies*, in William Perry (ed.), *The Plays of Nathan Field* (Austin, Tex., 1950).

FORD, JOHN, *The Broken Heart*, ed. T. J. B. Spencer, Revels Plays (Manchester, 1980).

GARNIER, R., *Antonius*, in *A Discourse of Life and Death . . . by Phil. Mornay . . . Antonius, A Tragoedie by R. Garnier. Both Done in English by the Countesse of Pembroke* (1592).

GAGER, WILLIAM, *Vlysses Redvx* (Oxford, 1592).

GREENE, ROBERT, *The Plays and Poems of Robert Greene*, ed. J. Churton Collins, 2 vols. (Oxford, 1905).

GREVILLE, FULKE, *Poems and Dramas of Fulke Greville First Lord Brooke*, ed. Geoffrey Bullough, 2 vols. (Edinburgh, 1939).

HEYWOOD, THOMAS, *A Woman Killed with Kindness*, ed. R. W. Van Fossen, Revels Plays (London, 1961).

—— *The Fair Maid of the West*, Parts 1 and 2, ed. R. K. Turner, Regents Renaissance Drama (London, 1968).

—— *The Dramatic Works of Thomas Heywood Now First Collected with Illustrative Notes and Memoirs of the Author*, ed. R. H. Shepherd, 6 vols. (London, 1874) [for references to remaining Heywood plays].

JONSON, BEN, *Ben Jonson*, ed. C. H. Herford, Percy and Evelyn Simpson, 11 vols. (Oxford, 1925–52) [for references to all Jonson's works, including collaborations].

KYD, THOMAS, *The Works of Thomas Kyd*, ed. Frederick S. Boas (Oxford, 1901).

LYLY, JOHN, *The Complete Works of John Lyly*, ed. R. Warwick Bond, 3 vols. (Oxford, 1902).

MARLOWE, CHRISTOPHER, *The Works of Christopher Marlowe*, ed. C. F. Tucker Brooke (Oxford, 1910).

MARSTON, JOHN, *The Dutch Courtesan*, ed. M. L. Wine, Regents Renaissance Drama (London, 1965).

—— *Antonio's Revenge*, ed. W. Reavley Gair, Revels Plays (Manchester, 1978).

—— *Parasitaster, or The Fawn*, ed. David A. Blostein, Revels Plays (Manchester, 1978).

—— *The Plays of John Marston*, ed. H. Harvey Wood, 3 vols. (Edinburgh, 1934–9) [for remaining Marston plays, including *Histriomastix*].

——, *et al.*, *The Insatiate Countess*, ed. Giorgio Melchiori, Revels Plays (Manchester, 1984).

MASON, JOHN, *The Turke*, ed. Joseph Q. Adams, Materialen zur Kunde des älteren Englischen Dramas, 37 (Louvain, 1913).

MASSINGER, PHILIP, *The Plays and Poems of Philip Massinger*, ed. Philip Edwards and Colin Gibson, 5 vols. (Oxford, 1976).

MEDWALL, HENRY, *The Plays of Henry Medwall*, ed. Alan H. Nelson (Cambridge, 1980).

[MUNDAY, ANTHONY], *John a Kent and John a Cumber*, ed. Muriel St Clare Byrne, MSR (Oxford, 1923).

PRESTON, THOMAS, *Cambyses King of Persia*, Tudor Facsimile Texts (London, 1910).

ROWLEY, WILLIAM, *All's Lost by Lust; A Shoemaker, a Gentleman*, ed. C. W. Stork (Philadelphia, 1910).

—— *A Critical Old-Spelling Edition of* A New Wonder, a Woman Never Vexed, ed. Trudi Laura Darby (New York, 1988).

SHAKESPEARE, WILLIAM, *The Complete Works: Compact Edition*, ed. Stanley Wells and Gary Taylor (Oxford, 1988).
SHARPHAM, EDWARD, *The Fleire*, ed. Hunold Nibbe, Materialen zur Kunde des älteren Englischen Dramas, 36 (Louvain, 1912).
—— *Cupid's Whirligig*, ed. Allardyce Nicoll (Waltham St Lawrence, 1926).
SHIRLEY, JAMES, *The Dramatic Works and Poems of James Shirley*, ed. Alexander Dyce and William Gifford, 6 vols. (London, 1833).
STRINDBERG, AUGUST, *Eight Famous Plays*, trans. Edwin Björkman and N. Erichsen (New York, 1949).
WEBSTER, JOHN, *The Complete Works of John Webster*, ed. F. L. Lucas, 4 vols. (London, 1927).

III. PRIMARY SOURCES CITED

1. Manuscripts

Bodleian Library, MS Tanner 73/1, 73/2.

2. Pre-1800 Imprints

Place of publication is London unless otherwise stated. Dates are new-style.

Anonymous Works

A Discovery of the Most Secret and Subtile Practises of the Iesvites (1610).
The Holy Fast of Lent Defended against All its Prophaners (1677).
The Iesvites Comedie Acted at Lyons in France, the Seuenth and Eight Dayes of August Last Past 1607 (1607).
Newes from Rome, Spalato's Doome, or An Epitome of the Life and Behaviour of M. Antonius de Dominis (1624).
The Terrible and Deserued Death of Francis Rauilliack . . . for the Murther of the French King, Henry the Fourth (1610).
Tom Tell-Troath: or, A Free Discourse Touching the Manners of the Time, repr. in *The Harleian Miscellany: or A Collection of . . . Pamphlets and Tracts found in the Late Earl of Oxford's Library*, 8 vols. (1744–6), ii. 3D4ᵛ–3G1ᵛ.
Troubles in Bohemia, and Diuers Other Kingdomes. Procured by the Diuellish Practises of State-Medling Iesuites (1619).
Vox Graculi, or Iacke Dawes Prognostication . . . for this Yeere 1623 (1622).

Works of Known Authors

ABBOT, ROBERT, *A Hand of Fellowship, to Helpe Keepe Out Sinne and Antichrist* (1623).
BACON, FRANCIS, *The Charge of Sir Francis Bacon Knight . . . touching Duells* (1614).

BARGRAVE, ISAAC, *A Sermon Preached before the Honorable Assembly of Knights, Citizens and Burgesses of the Lower House of Parliament, February the Last 1623* (1624).

—— *A Sermon against Selfe Policy, Preached in Whitehall in Lent, 1621* (1624).

—— (trans.), *An Impartiall Discouery, of Iesuticall Policie* (1619).

BÉTHUNE, MAXIMILIEN DE, *Memoirs of Maximilian de Bethune, Duke of Sully, Prime Minister to Henry the Great,* trans. Charlotte Lennox, 3 vols. (1756).

BODIN I[EAN], *The Six Bookes of a Commonweale,* trans. Richard Knolles (1606).

BOWNDE, NICOLAS, *The Doctrine of the Sabbath, Plainely Layde Forth* (1595).

BURGES, C[ORNELIUS], *The Fire of the Sanctuarie Newly Vncouered, or, A Compleat Tract of Zeale* (1625).

CHEEK, IOHN, *The Hurt of Sedition, how Greeuous it is to a Common Welth* (1549; 4th edn., 1576).

CLELAND, IAMES, *A Monument of Mortalitie, vpon the Death and Funerals, of the Gracious Prince Lodovick, Late Duke of Richmond and Lenox* (1624).

CORNWALLIS, CHARLES, *A Discourse of the Most Illustrious Prince, Henry, Late Prince of Wales* (1641).

COWELL, IOHN, *The Interpreter, or Booke Containing the Signification of Words* (Cambridge, 1607).

DYKE, DANIELL, *The Mystery of Selfe-Deceiving, or, A Discovrse and Discouery of the Deceitfulnesse of Mans Heart* (1614).

GEE, IOHN, *The Foot out of the Snare, with a Detection of Sundry Late Practices and Impostures of the Priests and Iesuits in England* (1624).

—— *New Shreds of the Old Snare* (1624).

[GOSSELIN, PETER], *The State-Mysteries of the Iesuites, by Way of Questions and Answers* (1623).

GOUGE, WILLIAM, *Of Domesticall Duties: Eight Treatises* (1622).

G[REEN], I[OHN], *A Refutation of the Apology for Actors* (1615).

H., J., *A True and Perfect Relation of that Most Horrid and Hellish Conspiracy of the Gunpowder Treason . . . Collected Out of the Best and Most Authentique Writers* (1662).

HALL, IOSEPH, *Holy Obseruations: Lib. I* (1607).

—— *Qvo Vadis? A Iust Censvre of Travell as It is Commonly Undertaken by the Gentlemen of Our Nation* (1617).

H[EALE], W[ILLIAM], *An Apologie for Women* (Oxford, 1609).

HEYWOOD, THOMAS, *An Apology for Actors* (1612).

[——]*A Curtaine Lecture* (1637).

HIERON, SAMUEL, *All the Sermons of Samuel Hieron, Minister of Gods Word, at Modbury in Deuon* (Cambridge, 1614).

HIGGONS, THEOPHILUS, *Mysticall Babylon, or Papall Rome* (1624).

[KENNETT, W.], *A Complete History of England, with the Lives of All the Kings and Queens thereof,* 3 vols. (1706).

[KNOX, JOHN], *The First Blast of the Trumpet against the Monstrous Regiment of Women* (Geneva, 1558).

LA PRIMAUDAYE, PETER DE, *The French Academie*, trans. T. B[owes] (1586).

LAVENDER, THEOPHILUS (ed.), *The Travels of Certaine Englishmen into Africa, Asia . . . and to Sundry Other Places* (1609).

LOK, HENRY, *Ecclesiastes, Otherwise Called the Preacher* (1597).

M., I., *A Health to the Gentlemanly Profession of Seruing-men, or, The Seruingmans Comfort* (1598).

MASON, HENRY, *The New Art of Lying, Covered by Iesuites vnder the Vaile of Equivocation* (1624).

MORTON, THOMAS, *New English Canaan or New Canaan* (Amsterdam, 1637).

NIXON, ANTHONY, *The Blacke Yeare* (1606).

OVERBURY, THOMAS, *A Wife, Now a Widowe* (1614).

PERKINS, WILLIAM, *A Discourse of the Damned Art of Witchcraft* (Cambridge, 1608).

[RAINOLDS, IOHN], *Th'Overthrow of Stage-Playes, by the Way of Controversie betwixt D. Gager and D. Rainoldes* (n.p., 1599).

[ROBINSON, THOMAS], *The Anatomy of the English Nunnery at Lisbon in Portugall* (1622).

ROMEI, HANIBALL, *The Courtiers Academie*, trans. I[ohn] K[epers] (1598).

SANDYS, GEORGE, *A Relation of a Iourney Begun An. Dom: 1610* (1615; 2nd edn., 1615).

SAVIOLO, VINCENTIO, *Vincentio Saviolo his Practise* (1595).

SCOT[T], THOMAS, *The Workes of the Most Famovs and Reverend Divine Mr. Thomas Scot. Batcheler of Diuinite, Sometimes Preacher in Norwich* (Utrecht, 1624). [Individual works by Scott and S.R.N.I. (John Reynolds) cited, including *Digitus Dei*, are bound into this collection with separate title-pages and pagination.]

SKORY, EDMUND, *An Extract out of the Historie of the Last French King Henry 4. of Famous Memory* (1610).

SMEL-KNAUE, SIMON, *Fearefull and Lamentable Effects of Two Dangerous Comets* (1591).

SPRINT, IOHN, *Propositions, Tending to Proove the Necessarie Vse of the Christian Sabbaoth, or Lords Day* (1607).

STUBBES, PHILLIP, *The Anatomie of Abuses* (1583).

T[OFTE], R., *Of Mariage and Wiuing, An Excellent, Pleasant, and Philosophicall Controuersie, betweene the Two Famous Tassi* (1599).

VICARS, IOHN, *Babels Balm, or The Honey-Combe of Romes Religion* (1624).

W[RIGHT], T[HOMAS], *The Passions of the Minde* (1601).

3. Primary Sources in Modern Editions

ANDREWES, LANCELOT, *Sermons*, ed. G. M. Story (Oxford, 1967).

ANONYMOUS, *Two Books of Homilies Appointed to be Read in Churches* (Oxford, 1859).

—— *The Early English Versions of the Gesta Romanorum*, ed. Sidney J. H. Heritage, EETS, extra ser. 33 (London, 1879; repr. 1962).

—— *The Interpreter*, in C. H. Firth (ed.), *Stuart Tracts 1603–1693* (Westminster, 1903), 233–46.

ASCHAM, ROGER, *The Whole Works of Roger Ascham*, ed. Revd. Dr Giles, 4 vols. (London, 1864–5).

AUBREY, JOHN, *Miscellanies* (Franklin, NH, 1969).

ST AUGUSTINE, *The City of God against the Pagans*, trans. and ed. George E. McCracken, 7 vols., Loeb Classics (London, 1957).

BACON, FRANCIS, *The Works of Francis Bacon*, ed. J. Spedding *et al.*, 14 vols. (London, 1857–74).

BRETON, NICHOLAS, *The Works in Verse and Prose of Nicholas Breton*, ed. Alexander B. Grosart, 2 vols. (1879; New York, 1966).

BROWN, RAWDON, and HINDS, ALLEN B. (eds.), *Calender of State Papers and Manuscripts Relating to English Affairs Existing in the Archives and Collections of Venice and Other Libraries of Northern Italy, 1202–1675*, 38 vols. (London, 1864–1947).

BURNE, S. A. H. (ed.), *The Staffordshire Quarter Sessions Rolls, v. 1603–1606, Collections for a History of Staffordshire*, ed. Staffordshire Record Society (Kendal, 1940).

BURTON, ROBERT, *The Anatomy of Melancholy*, ed. Holbrook Jackson (1932; repr. London, 1978).

CAPELLANUS, ANDREAS, *Andreas Capellanus on Love*, trans. and ed. P. G. Walsh (London, 1982).

CERVANTES SAAVEDRA, MIGUEL DE, *The Adventures of Don Quixote*, trans. J. M. Cohen (Harmondsworth, 1950).

CESSOLES, JACQUES DE, *Game and Playe of the Chesse*, trans. William Caxton, ed. William E. A. Axon (London, 1883).

CHAMBERLAIN, JOHN, *The Letters of John Chamberlain*, ed. Norman Egbert McClure, 2 vols. (Philadelphia, 1939).

CHAUCER, GEOFFREY, *Complete Works*, ed. Walter W. Skeat (London, 1912).

CORYAT, THOMAS, *Coryat's Crudities Hastily Gobled Up in Five Moneths Travells*, 2 vols. (Glasgow, 1905).

DEKKER, THOMAS, *The Non-Dramatic Works of Thomas Dekker*, ed. Alexander B. Grosart, 5 vols. (1884–6; New York, 1963).

—— *The Plague Pamphlets of Thomas Dekker*, ed. F. P. Wilson (Oxford, 1925).

DELONEY, THOMAS, *The Works of Thomas Deloney*, ed. Francis Oscar Mann (Oxford, 1912).

DONATUS, AELIUS, *Commentum Terenti*, ed. Paul Wessner, 2 vols. (Leipzig, 1902–5).

DONNE, JOHN, *The Sermons of John Donne*, ed. Evelyn M. Simpson and George R. Potter, 10 vols. (Berkeley, Calif., 1953–62).
—— *The Satires, Epigrams and Verse Letters*, ed. W. Milgate (Oxford, 1967).
—— *Ignatius his Conclave*, ed. T. S. Healy (Oxford, 1969).
DRAYTON, MICHAEL, *The Works of Michael Drayton*, ed. J. William Hebel, 5 vols. (Oxford, 1961).
FORD, JOHN, *The Works of John Ford*, ed. William Gifford and Alexander Dyce, 3 vols. (London, 1869).
FOXE, JOHN, *The Acts and Monuments of John Foxe*, ed. Josiah Pratt, 8 vols. (1853–70; repr. London, 1877).
FULLER, THOMAS, *The Church History of Britain*, ed. J. S. Brewer, 6 vols. (Oxford, 1845).
GREENE, ROBERT, *The Life and Complete Works in Prose and Verse of Robert Greene*, 15 vols., Huth Library (n.p., 1881–6).
GUAZZO, STEEVEN, *The Civile Conversation* (1581–6), trans. George Pettie and Bartholomew Young, 2 vols., Tudor Translations, 2nd ser. 8 (London, 1925).
HAKLUYT, RICHARD, *Principal Navigations, Voyages, Traffiques and Discoveries of the English Nation*, 12 vols. (Glasgow, 1903–5).
HALES, JOHN, 'Of Duels', in John Chandos (ed.), *In God's Name: Examples of Preaching in England from the Act of Supremacy to the Act of Uniformity* (London, 1971), 212–16.
HALL, JOSEPH, *Virgidemiarum: Satires* (London, 1825).
HEMMINGE, WILLIAM, *Elegy on Randolph's Finger Containing Well-Known Lines 'On the Time-Poets'*, ed. G. C. Moore Smith (Oxford, 1923).
HENSLOWE, PHILIP, *Henslowe's Diary*, ed. R. A. Foakes and R. T. Rickert (Cambridge, 1961).
HIGGINS, JOHN, and BLENERHASSET, THOMAS, *Parts Added to* The Mirror for Magistrates, ed. Lily B. Campbell (Cambridge, 1946).
HOCCLEVE, THOMAS, *Hoccleve's Works, iii. The Regement of Princes . . . and Fourteen of Hoccleve's Minor Poems*, ed. Frederick J. Furnivall, EETS, extra ser. 72 (London, 1897).
HOLLES, GERVASE, *Memorials of the Holles Family 1493–1656*, ed. A. C. Wood, Camden Society, 3rd ser. 55 (1937).
HOWELL, T. B., and HOWELL, T. J. (eds.), *A Complete Collection of State Trials*, 33 vols. (London, 1809–26).
HUME, DAVID, *The History of England from the Invasion of Julius Caesar to the Revolution in 1688*, abridged and ed. Rodney W. Kilcup (Chicago, 1975).
HUTCHINSON, LUCY, *Memoirs of the Life of Colonel Hutchinson with the Fragment of an Autobiography of Mrs Hutchinson*, ed. James Sutherland (Oxford, 1973).
JAMES I, KING OF ENGLAND, *The Political Works of James I*, ed. Charles Howard McIlwain (1918; New York, 1965).
—— *The Poems of James VI of Scotland*, ed. James Craigie, 2 vols., Scottish Text Society (Edinburgh, 1955–8).

[—— et al.], *The Gunpowder Treason. Trials of the Conspirators . . . Also History of the Gunpowder Plot, Written by King James* (1867), repr. in *Tracts (Chiefly Rare and Curious Reprints), Relating to Northamptonshire* (Northampton, 1870), 26–38.

JESUS, FRAY FRANCISCO DE, *El Hecho de los Tratados del Matrimonio . . . Narrative of the Spanish Marriage Treaty*, trans. and ed. Samuel R. Gardiner, Camden Society, 101 (1869).

JOHN OF SALISBURY, *The Statesman's Book of John of Salisbury. Being the Fourth, Fifth, and Sixth Books, and Selections from the Seventh and Eighth Books of the* Policraticus, trans. John Dickinson (New York, 1927).

KOHL, BENJAMIN G., and WITT, RONALD G., (eds.), *The Earthly Republic: Italian Humanists on Government and Society* (Manchester, 1978).

Le STRANGE, NICHOLAS, *'Merry Passages and Jeastes': A Manuscript Jestbook of Sir Nicholas Le Strange (1603–1655)*, ed. H. F. Lippincott (Salzburg, 1974).

LEMON, ROBERT, and GREEN, MARY ANNE EVERETT (eds.), *Calendar of State Papers, Domestic Series, of the Reigns of Edward VI, Mary, Elizabeth I, and James I, 1547–1625*, 12 vols. (London, 1856–72).

LOOMIE, ALBERT J. (ed.), *Spain and the Jacobean Catholics*, 2 vols., Catholic Record Society (Records Series), 64 and 68 (n.p., 1973, 1978).

MACHYN, HENRY, *The Diary of Henry Machyn, Citizen and Merchant-Taylor of London from A.D. 1550 to A.D. 1563*, ed. J. G. Nichols, Camden Society, 42 (1848).

MILTON, JOHN, *The Poems of John Milton*, ed. Helen Darbishire (Oxford, 1961).
—— *Political Writings*, ed. Martin Dzelzainis (Cambridge, 1991).

MORYSON, FYNES, *An Itinerary Containing his Ten Yeeres Travell*, 4 vols. (Glasgow, 1907).
—— *Shakespeare's Europe: Unpublished Chapters of Fynes Moryson's* Itinerary, ed. Charles Hughes (London, 1903).

NASHE, THOMAS, *The Works of Thomas Nashe*, ed. Ronald B. McKerrow, 5 vols. (1904–10; repr. with corrections and supplementary notes by F. P. Wilson, Oxford, 1958).

PAINTER, WILLIAM, *The Palace of Pleasure*, ed. Joseph Jacobs, 3 vols. (London, 1890).

PEACHAM, HENRY, *The Complete Gentleman, The Truth of our Times* and *The Art of Living in London*, ed. Virgil B. Heltzel (Ithaca, NY, 1962).

PERKINS, WILLIAM, *William Perkins 1558–1602: English Puritanist. His Pioneer Works on Casuistry*, ed. Thomas F. Merrill (The Hague, 1966).

PISAN, CHRISTINE DE, *Epître d'Othea à Hector*, trans. Stephen Scrope, ed. Curt F. Bühler, EETS 264 (London, 1970).

PLATTER, THOMAS, *Thomas Platter's Travels in England, 1599*, trans. Clare Williams (London, 1937).

RALEGH, WALTER, *The History of the World*, abridged and ed. C. A. Patrides (Philadelphia, 1971).

ROLLINS, HYDER E. (ed.), *Old English Ballads 1553–1625: Chiefly from Manuscripts* (Cambridge, 1920).

ROSEN, BARBARA (ed.), *Witchcraft* (London, 1969).

ROSS, E. DENISON, (ed.), *Sir Anthony Sherley and his Persian Adventure* (London, 1933).

SCOT, REGINALD, *The Discoverie of Witchcraft*, ed. Brinsley Nicholson (London, 1886).

SCOTT, WALTER (ed.), *Secret History of the Court of James the First*, 2 vols. (Edinburgh, 1811).

SENECA, Moral Essays, trans. and ed. John W. Basore, 3 vols., Loeb Classics (London, 1935).

—— *Ad Lucilium epistulae morales*, trans. and ed. Richard M. Gummere, 3 vols., Loeb Classics (London, 1917–25; rev. edn. 1943).

SIDNEY, PHILIP, *The Prose Works of Sir Philip Sidney*, ed. Albert Feuillerat, 4 vols. (Cambridge, 1912).

—— *The Countess of Pembroke's Arcadia (The Old Arcadia)*, ed. Jean Robertson (Oxford, 1973).

SPENSER, EDMUND, *The Works of Edmund Spenser: A Variorum Edition*, ed. Edwin Greenlaw *et al.*, 11 vols. (Baltimore, 1932–57).

TAYLOR, JOHN, *Works of John Taylor, the Water Poet*, ed. Charles Hindley (London, 1876).

VIDA, MARK JEROME, *The Game of Chess*, trans. Richard Stanton Lambert (London, 1921).

VIRGIL, *Eclogues, Georgics, Aeneid*, ed. H. Rushton Fairclough, 2 vols., Loeb Classics (1916; rev. edn., London, 1935).

WILSON, THOMAS, *The State of England Anno Dom. 1600*, ed. F. J. Fisher, Camden Miscellany, 16 (1936), 1–43.

YONGE, WALTER, *Diary of Walter Yonge, Esq. Justice of the Peace, and M.P. for Honiton. Written . . . from 1604 to 1628*, ed. George Roberts, Camden Society, 41 (1848).

IV. SECONDARY SOURCES

Select List of Works Cited

AKRIGG, G. P. V., *Jacobean Pageant or The Court of King James I* (London, 1962).

ALBRIGHT, EVELYN MAY, *Dramatic Publication in England, 1580–1640: A Study of the Conditions Affecting Content and Form of Drama* (New York, 1927).

ALTHUSSER, LOUIS, *For Marx*, trans. Ben Brewster (1969; London, 1979).

—— *Lenin and Philosophy and Other Essays*, trans. Ben Brewster (London, 1971).

ALTIERI, JOANNE, 'Against Moralizing Jacobean Comedy: Middleton's *Chaste Maid*', *Criticism*, 30 (1988), 171–87.

—— 'Pregnant Puns and Sectarian Rhetoric: Middleton's *Family of Love*', *Mosaic*, 22 (1989), 45–57.

ARMSTRONG, WILLIAM A., 'The Elizabethan Conception of the Tyrant', *RES* 22 (1946), 161–81.

ARTAUD, ANTONIN, *The Theatre and its Double*, trans. Victor Corti (London, 1970).

ASP, CAROLYN, *A Study of Thomas Middleton's Tragicomedies* (Salzburg, 1974).

AYERS, PHILIP J., 'Parallel Action and Reductive Technique in *The Revenger's Tragedy*', *ELN* 8 (1970), 103–7.

AYERS, P. K., 'Plot, Subplot, and the Uses of Dramatic Discord in *A Mad World, My Masters* and *A Trick to Catch the Old One*', *MLQ* 47 (1986), 3–18.

BALD, R. C., ' "Assembled" Texts', *Library*, 4th ser. 12 (1932), 243–8.

—— 'Middleton's Civic Employments', *MP* 31 (1933), 65–78.

—— 'The Sources of Middleton's City Comedies', *JEGP* 33 (1934), 373–87.

—— 'An Early Version of Middleton's *Game at Chesse*', *MLR* 38 (1943), 177–80.

BARISH, JONAS, *The Antitheatrical Prejudice* (Berkeley, Calif., 1981).

BARKER, RICHARD HINDRY, *Thomas Middleton* (New York, 1958).

BAWCUTT, N. W., '*The Changeling*: A Source for the Sub-Plot', *N & Q* 200 (1955), 233.

—— 'Middleton's *The Phoenix* as a Royal Play', *N & Q* 201 (1956), 287–8.

—— '*The Revenger's Tragedy* and the Medici Family', *N & Q* 202 (1957), 192–3.

—— 'New Light on Middleton's Knowledge of Chess', *N & Q* 232 (1987), 301–2.

BECK, ERVIN, 'Terence Improved: The Paradigm of the Prodigal Son in English Renaissance Comedy', *RD* 6 (1973), 107–22.

BEIER, A. L., *Masterless Men: The Vagrancy Problem in England 1560–1640* (London, 1985).

BELSEY, CATHERINE, *The Subject of Tragedy: Identity and Difference in Renaissance Drama* (London, 1985).

BENJAMIN, WALTER, *The Origin of German Tragic Drama*, trans. John Osborne (London, 1977).

BENTLEY, G. E., *The Jacobean and Caroline Stage*, 7 vols. (Oxford, 1941–68).

—— *The Profession of Player in Shakespeare's Time 1590–1642* (Princeton, NJ, 1984).

BERGERON, DAVID, 'Art within *The Second Maiden's Tragedy*', *MRDE* 1 (1984), 173–86.

BERGGREN, PAULA S., ' "A Prodigious Thing": The Jacobean Heroine in Male Disguise', *PQ* 62 (1983), 383–402.

BERLIN, NORMAND, 'The "Finger" Image and Relationship of Character in *The Changeling*', *English Studies in Africa*, 12 (1969), 162–6.

BLAU, HERBERT, 'The Absolved Riddle: Sovereign Pleasure and the Baroque Subject in the Tragicomedies of John Fletcher', *NLH* 17 (1986), 539–54.

BOWERS, FREDSON, 'Middleton's *Fair Quarrel* and the Duelling Code', *JEGP* 36 (1937), 40–65.

BOWERS, RICK, 'Middleton's *A Trick to Catch the Old One*', *Explicator*, 51 (1993), 211–14.

BRADBROOK, M. C., *Themes and Conventions of Elizabethan Tragedy* (Cambridge, 1935).

—— *The Growth and Structure of Elizabethan Comedy* (1955; Harmondsworth, 1963).

—— *The Rise of the Common Player: A Study of Actor and Society in Shakespeare's England* (London, 1962).

—— *English Dramatic Form: A History of its Development* (London, 1965).

BRADLEY, E. T., *Life of Lady Arabella Stuart*, 2 vols. (London, 1889).

BRAUNMULLER, A. R., ' "To the Globe I rowed": John Holles Sees *A Game at Chess*', *ELR* 20 (1990), 340–56.

BREIGHT, CURT, ' "Treason Doth Never Prosper": *The Tempest* and the Discourse of Treason', *SQ* 41 (1990), 1–28.

BRIGGS, JULIA, 'Middleton's Forgotten Tragedy *Hengist King of Kent*', *RES*, NS 41 (1990), 479–95.

BRODWIN, LEONORA LEET, *Elizabethan Love Tragedy 1587–1625* (London, 1972).

BROMHAM, A. A., 'The Date of *The Witch* and the Essex Divorce Case', *N & Q* 225 (1980), 149–52.

—— 'Thomas Middleton's *Hengist, King of Kent* and John Ponet's *Shorte Treatise of Politike Power*', *N & Q* 227 (1982), 143–5.

—— 'The Contemporary Significance of *The Old Law*', *SEL* 24 (1984), 327–39.

—— 'The Tragedy of Peace: Political Meaning in *Women Beware Women*', *SEL* 26 (1986), 309–29.

—— and BRUZZI, ZARA, The Changeling *and the Years of Crisis, 1619–1624: A Hieroglyph of Britain* (London, 1990).

BROMLEY, LAURA G., 'The Lost Lucrece: Middleton's *The Ghost of Lucrece*', *PLL* 21 (1985), 258–74.

BROOKE, NICHOLAS, *Horrid Laughter in Jacobean Tragedy* (New York, 1979).

BROOKS, JOHN B., 'Middleton's Stepfather and the Captain of *The Phoenix*', *N & Q* 206 (1961), 382–4.

BRUSTEIN, ROBERT, *Seasons of Discontent: Dramatic Opinions 1959–1965* (London 1966).

BRUSTER, DOUGLAS, *Drama and the Market in the Age of Shakespeare* (Cambridge, 1992).

—— '*The Changeling* and Thomas Watson's *Hecatompathia*', *N & Q* 238 (1993), 222–4.

BUCKINGHAM, E. L., 'Campion's *Art of English Poesie* and Middleton's *Chaste Maid in Cheapside*', *PMLA* 43 (1928), 784–92.

BULLOUGH, GEOFFREY, ' "The Game at Chesse": How it Struck a Contemporary', *MLR* 49 (1954), 156–63.

BUSHNELL, REBECCA, *Tragedies of Tyrants: Political Thought and Theater in the English Renaissance* (Ithaca, NY, 1990).

BUTLER, MARTIN, 'William Prynne and the Allegory of Middleton's *Game at Chess*', *N & Q* 228 (1983), 153–4.

CAMPBELL, OSCAR JAMES, *Comicall Satyre and Shakespeare's* Troilus and Cressida (1938; repr. San Marino, Calif., 1970).

CAWLEY, ROBERT RALSTON, *The Voyagers and Elizabethan Drama* (Boston, 1938).

CHAKRAVORTY, SWAPAN, 'Medwall's *Fulgens and Lucres* as a Probable Source for Middleton and Rowley's *A Fair Quarrel*', *N & Q* 238 (1993), 214–15.

—— 'Middleton's *Michaelmas Term*, Inductio 13–19', *Explicator*, 51 (1993), 209–11.

CHAMBERS, E. K., *The Elizabethan Stage*, 4 vols. (Oxford, 1923).

CHATTERJI, RUBY, 'Theme, Imagery, and Unity in *A Chaste Maid in Cheapside*', *RD* 8 (1965), 105–26.

—— 'Unity and Disparity in *Michaelmas Term*', *SEL* 8 (1968), 349–63.

CHENEY, PATRICK, 'Moll Cutpurse as Hermaphrodite in Dekker and Middleton's *The Roaring Girl*', *Ren. & Ref.* 19 (1983), 120–34.

CHEW, SAMUEL C., *The Crescent and the Rose: Islam and England during the Renaissance* (New York, 1937).

CHIAPELLI, FREDI (ed.), *First Images of America: The Impact of the New World on the Old*, 2 vols. (Berkeley, Calif., 1976).

CHRISTIAN, M. G., 'Middleton's Acquaintance with the *Merrie Conceited Jests of George Peele*', *PMLA* 50 (1935), 753–60.

—— 'An Autobiographical Note by Thomas Middleton', *N & Q* 175 (1938), 259–60.

—— 'Middleton's Residence at Oxford', *MLN* 61 (1946), 90–1.

—— 'A Sidelight on the Family History of Thomas Middleton', *SP* 44 (1947), 490–6.

CLARE, JANET, *'Art Made Tongue-Tied by Authority': Elizabethan and Jacobean Dramatic Censorship* (Manchester, 1990).

COGSWELL, THOMAS, 'Thomas Middleton and the Court, 1624: *A Game at Chess* in Context', *HLQ* 47 (1984), 273–88.

—— *The Blessed Revolution: English Politics and the Coming of War* (Cambridge, 1989).

COLEMAN, ANTONY and HAMMOND, ANTONY (eds.), *Poetry and Drama 1570–1700: Essays in Honour of Harold F. Brooks* (London, 1981).

COLLINSON, PATRICK, *The Elizabethan Puritan Movement* (1967; repr. Oxford, 1990).

—— *Godly People: Essays in English Protestantism and Puritanism* (London, 1983).

COMENSOLI, VIVIANA, 'Play-Making, Domestic Conduct, and the Multiple Plot in *The Roaring Girl*', *SEL* 27 (1987), 249–66.

COVATTA, ANTHONY, *Thomas Middleton's City Comedies* (Lewisburg, Pa., 1973).

CRUPI, CHARLES W., 'The Transformation of De Flores in *The Changeling*', *Neophilologus*, 68 (1984), 142–9.

DAALDER, JOOST, 'Folly and Madness in *The Changeling*', *EC* 38 (1988), 1–21.

DAVIES, RICHARD A., and YOUNG, ALAN R., ' "Strange Cunning" in Thomas Middleton's *Game at Chess*', *UTQ* 45 (1976), 236–45.

DAWSON, ANTHONY B., '*Women Beware Women* and the Economy of Rape', *SEL* 27 (1987), 303–20.

—— 'Mistris Hic & Haec: Representations of Moll Frith', *SEL* 33 (1993), 385–404.

DE SOUSA, GERALDO U., 'Thomas Middleton: Criticism Since T. S. Eliot', *RORD* 28 (1985), 73–85.

DESSEN, ALAN C., 'Middleton's *The Phoenix* and the Allegorical Tradition', *SEL* 6 (1966), 291–308.

DEVEREUX, E. J., 'The Naming of Sir Oliver Kix', *N & Q* 232 (1987), 297–8.

DODSON, DANIEL, 'King James and *The Phoenix*—Again', *N & Q* 203 (1958), 434–7.

DOLLIMORE, JONATHAN, *Radical Tragedy: Religion, Ideology and Power in the Drama of Shakespeare and his Contemporaries* (1984; 2nd edn., Hemel Hempstead, 1989).

—— *Sexual Dissidence: Augustine to Wilde, Freud to Foucault* (Oxford, 1991).

DOOB, PENELOPE B. R., 'A Reading of *The Changeling*', *ELR* 3 (1973), 183–206.

DORAN, MADELEINE, *Endeavors of Art: A Study of Form in Elizabethan Drama* (Madison, Wis., 1954).

DUNKEL, W. D., 'The Authorship of *The Revenger's Tragedy*', *PMLA* 46 (1931), 781–5.

DUNLAP, R., 'James I, Bacon, Middleton, and the Making of *The Peacemaker*', in J. W. Bennett et al. (eds.), *Studies in the English Renaissance Drama in Memory of Karl Julius Holzknecht* (New York, 1959), 82–94.

DYNES, WILLIAM R., 'The Trickster-Figure in Jacobean City Comedy', *SEL* 33 (1993), 365–84.

ECCLES, MARK, 'Middleton's Birth and Education', *RES* 7 (1931), 431–41.

—— 'Thomas Middleton: A Poett', *SP* 54 (1957), 516–36.

—— 'Middleton's Comedy *The Almanac*, or *No Wit, No Help Like a Woman's*', *N & Q* 232 (1987), 296–7.

ELIOT, T. S., *Selected Essays 1917–1932* (London, 1932).

ELLIS-FERMOR, UNA, *The Jacobean Drama: An Interpretation* (London, 1936).

EMPSON, WILLIAM, *Some Versions of Pastoral* (London, 1935).

EWBANK [EKEBLAD], INGA-STINA, 'A Note on *The Revenger's Tragedy*', *N & Q* 200 (1955), 98–9.

—— 'On the Authorship of *The Revenger's Tragedy*', *ES* 41 (1960), 225–40.

—— 'Realism and Morality in *Women Beware Women*', *E & S* 22 (1969), 57–70.

FALK, SIGNI, 'Plautus' *Persa* and Middleton's *A Trick to Catch the Old One*', *MLN* 66 (1951), 19–21.

FARLEY-HILLS, DAVID, *The Comic in Renaissance Comedy* (London, 1981).

—— *Jacobean Drama: A Critical Study of the Professional Drama, 1600–25* (London, 1988).

—— 'How Often did the Eyases Fly?', *N & Q* 236 (1991), 461–6.

FARR, DOROTHY, *Thomas Middleton and the Drama of Realism: A Study of Some Representative Plays* (Edinburgh, 1973).

FERGUSON, MARGARET W. *et al.* (eds.), *Rewriting the Renaissance: The Discourses of Sexual Difference in Early Modern Europe* (Chicago, 1986).

FINLAYSON, MICHAEL G., *Historians, Puritanism, and the English Revolution: The Religious Factor in English Politics before and after the Interregnum* (Toronto, 1983).

FISHER, MARGERY, 'Notes on the Sources of Some Incidents in Middleton's London Plays', *RES* 15 (1939), 283–93.

FOAKES, R. A., 'The Art of Cruelty: Hamlet and Vindice', *SS* 26 (1973), 21–31.

FOUCAULT, MICHEL, *Discipline and Punish: The Birth of the Prison*, trans. Alan Sheridan (1977; Harmondsworth, 1979).

—— *The History of Sexuality, i. An Introduction*, trans. Robert Hurley (1978; Harmondsworth, 1984).

FREUD, SIGMUND, *The Standard Edition of the Complete Psychological Works of Sigmund Freud*, ed. James Strachey, 24 vols. (London, 1953–74).

FRIEDENREICH, KENNETH (ed.), *'Accompaninge the Players': Essays Celebrating Thomas Middleton, 1580–1980* (New York, 1983).

FROST, DAVID L., *The School of Shakespeare: The Influence of Shakespeare on English Drama 1600–42* (Cambridge, 1968).

GADAMER, HANS-GEORG, *Philosophical Hermeneutics*, trans. and ed. David E. Linge (Berkeley, Calif., 1976).

GAIR, REAVLEY, *The Children of Paul's: The Story of a Theatre Company 1553–1608* (Cambridge, 1982).

GANSHOF, F. L., *Feudalism*, trans. Philip Grierson (1952; 3rd edn., London, 1964).

GARDINER, SAMUEL R., *History of England from the Accession of James I to the Outbreak of the Civil War 1603–1642*, 10 vols. (London, 1864–1903).

GARDNER, HELEN, 'Milton's "Satan" and the Theme of Damnation in Elizabethan Tragedy', *E & S* 1 (1948), 46–66.

GASPER, JULIA, *The Dragon and the Dove: The Plays of Thomas Dekker* (Oxford, 1990).

GEERTZ, CLIFFORD, *Local Knowledge: Further Essays in Interpretive Anthropology* (New York, 1983).

GEORGE, DAVID, 'Weather-Wise's Almanac and the Date of Middleton's *No Wit No Help Like a Woman's*', *N & Q* 211 (1966), 297–301.

—— 'Thomas Middleton at Oxford', *MLR* 65 (1970), 734–6.

—— 'Thomas Middleton's Sources: A Survey', *N & Q* 216 (1971), 17–24.

GIBBONS, BRIAN, *Jacobean City Comedy* (1968; 2nd edn., London, 1980).

GOFFMAN, ERVING, *Interaction Ritual: Essays on Face-to-Face Behaviour* (London, 1972).

GOLDBERG, JONATHAN, *James I and the Politics of Literature: Jonson, Shakespeare, Donne and their Contemporaries* (Baltimore, 1983).

GORDON, D. J., 'Middleton's *No Wit, No Help Like a Woman's* and Della Porta's *La Sorella*', *RES* 17 (1941), 400–14.

GOSSETT, SUZANNE, ' "Best Men are Molded out of Faults": Marrying the Rapist in Jacobean Drama', *ELR* 14 (1984), 305–27.

GRABES, HERBERT, *The Mutable Glass: Mirror-Imagery in Titles and Texts of the Middle Ages and the English Renaissance*, trans. Gordon Collier (Cambridge, 1982).

GREENBLATT, STEPHEN J., *Shakespearean Negotiations: The Circulation of Social Energy in Renaissance England* (Oxford, 1988).

—— *Learning to Curse: Essays in Early Modern Culture* (New York, 1990).

—— *Marvelous Possessions: The Wonder of the New World* (Oxford, 1991).

GURR, ANDREW, *Playgoing in Shakespeare's London* (Cambridge, 1987).

HALLETT, CHARLES A., *Middleton's Cynics: A Study of Middleton's Insight into the Moral Psychology of the Mediocre Mind* (Salzburg, 1975).

HARRIS, ANTHONY, *Night's Black Agents: Witchcraft and Magic in Seventeenth-Century English Drama* (Manchester, 1980).

HASELKORN, ANNE M., 'Sin and the Politics of Penitence: Three Jacobean Adulteresses', in Anne M. Haselkorn and Betty S. Travitsky (eds.), *The Renaissance Englishwoman in Print: Counterbalancing the Canon* (Amherst, Mass., 1990), 119–36.

HAYDN, HIRAM, *The Counter-Renaissance* (New York, 1935).

HEIDEGGER, MARTIN, *Poetry, Language, Thought*, trans. Albert Hofstadter (New York, 1971).

HEINEMANN, MARGOT, *Puritanism and Theatre: Thomas Middleton and Opposition Drama under the Early Stuarts* (Cambridge, 1980).

—— 'Rebel Lords, Popular Playwrights, and Political Culture: Notes on the Jacobean Patronage of the Earl of Southampton', *YES* 21 (1991), 63–86.

HELMS, LORRAINE, 'Roaring Girls and Silent Women: The Politics of Androgyny on the Jacobean Stage', *Themes in Drama*, 11 (1989), 59–73.

HENKE, JAMES T., *Renaissance Dramatic Bawdy (Exclusive of Shakespeare): An Annotated Glossary and Critical Essays*, 2 vols. (Salzburg, 1974).

HIBBARD, G. R., 'The Tragedies of Thomas Middleton and the Decadence of Drama', *Renaissance and Modern Studies*, 1 (1957), 35–64.

HILL, CHRISTOPHER, *Society and Puritanism in Pre-Revolutionary England* (1964; Harmondsworth, 1986).

—— *The World Turned Upside Down: Radical Ideas during the English Revolution* (London, 1972).

—— *A Nation of Change and Novelty: Radical Politics, Religion and Literature in Seventeenth-Century England* (London, 1990).

HILLEBRAND, HAROLD N., 'Thomas Middleton's *The Viper's Brood*', *MLN* 42 (1927), 35–8.

HOLDEN, WILLIAM P., *Anti-Puritan Satire 1572–1642* (New Haven, Conn., 1954).

HOLDSWORTH, R. V., 'Middleton and *The Tragedy of Mariam*', *N & Q* 231 (1986), 379–80.

—— 'Notes on *The Changeling*', *N & Q* 234 (1989), 344–6.

—— (ed.), *Three Jacobean Revenge Tragedies: A Casebook* (Basingstoke, 1990).

—— '*Measure for Measure*, Middleton and "Brakes of Ice" ', *N & Q* 236 (1991), 64–7.

—— 'The Date of *Hengist, King of Kent*', *N & Q* 236 (1991), 516–19.

—— 'Notes on *Women Beware Women*', *N & Q* 238 (1993), 215–22.

HOLMES, DAVID M., *The Art of Thomas Middleton: A Critical Study* (Oxford, 1970).

HOLZKNECHT, K. J., 'The Dramatic Structure of *The Changeling*', *Renaissance Papers* (1954; repr. Ann Arbor, Mich., 1961), 77–87.

HOTINE, MARGARET, '*Richard III* and *Macbeth*: Studies in Tudor Tyranny?', *N & Q* 236 (1991), 480–6.

HOWARD, CLARE, *English Travellers of the Renaissance* (London, 1914).

HOWARD, JEAN E., 'Renaissance Antitheatricality and the Politics of Gender and Rank in *Much Ado About Nothing*', in Jean E. Howard and Marion F. O'Connor (eds.), *Shakespeare Reproduced: The Text in History and Ideology* (New York, 1987), 163–87.

—— 'Crossdressing, the Theatre, and Gender Struggle in Early Modern England', *SQ* 39 (1988), 418–40.

HOWARD-HILL, T. H., 'The Origins of Middleton's *A Game at Chess*', *RORD* 28 (1985), 3–14.

—— 'The Author as Scribe or Reviser? Middleton's Intentions in *A Game at Chess*', *Text*, 3 (1987), 305–18.

—— 'More on "William Prynne and the Allegory of Middleton's *Game at Chess*" ', *N & Q* 234 (1989), 349–51.

—— 'Political Interpretations of Middleton's *A Game at Chess*', *YES* 21 (1991), 274–85.

—— 'The Unique Eye-Witness Report of Middleton's *A Game at Chess*', *RES* NS 42 (1991), 168–78.

HOY, CYRUS, 'The Shares of Fletcher and his Collaborators in the Beaumont and Fletcher Canon (V)', *SB* 13 (1960), 77–108.

—— *Introductions, Notes, and Commentaries to Texts in* The Dramatic Works of Thomas Dekker *Edited by Fredson Bowers*, 4 vols. (Cambridge, 1980).

HUEBERT, RONALD, 'Middleton's Nameless Art', *SR* 95 (1987), 591–609.

JACKSON, MACD. P., *Studies in Attribution: Middleton and Shakespeare* (Salzburg, 1979).

JAMESON, FREDRIC, *The Political Unconscious: Narrative as a Socially Symbolic Act* (London, 1981).

JARDINE, LISA, *Still Harping on Daughters: Women and Drama in the Age of Shakespeare* (Brighton, 1983).

JOHANSSON, BERTIL, *Religion and Superstition in the Plays of Ben Jonson and Thomas Middleton* (Uppsala, 1950).

JORDAN, ROBERT, 'Myth and Psychology in *The Changeling*', *RD* 3 (1970), 157–65.

KEEN, MAURICE, *Chivalry* (New Haven, Conn., 1984).

KERNAN, ALVIN, *The Cankered Muse: Satire of the English Renaissance* (New Haven, Conn., 1959).

KIERNAN, V. G., *The Duel in European History: Honour and the Reign of Aristocracy* (Oxford, 1986).

KNIGHTS, L. C., *Drama and Society in the Age of Jonson* (London, 1937).

KROOK, DOROTHEA, *Elements of Tragedy* (New Haven, Conn., 1969).

LAKE, DAVID J., *The Canon of Thomas Middleton's Plays: Internal Evidence for the Major Problems of Authorship* (Cambridge, 1975).

LAMB, CHARLES, *Specimens of English Dramatic Poets who Lived about the Time of Shakespeare* (1808; London, 1854).

LANCASHIRE, ANNE, '*The Second Maiden's Tragedy*: A Jacobean Saint's Life', *RES*, NS 25 (1974), 267–79.

—— 'The Emblematic Castle in Shakespeare and Middleton', in J. C. Gray (ed.), *Mirror up to Shakespeare: Essays in Honour of G. R. Hibbard* (Toronto, 1984), 223–41.

LEGGATT, ALEXANDER, *Citizen Comedy in the Age of Shakespeare* (Toronto, 1973).

LEINWAND, THEODORE B., *The City Staged: Jacobean Comedy, 1603–1613* (Madison, Wis., 1986).

—— 'Spongy Plebs, Mighty Lords, and the Dynamics of the Alehouse', *JMRS* 19 (1989), 159–84.

LEPAGE, RAYMOND, 'A Study in Dramatic Transposition and Invention: Della Porta's *La Sorella*, Rotrou's *La Sœur*, and Middleton's *No Wit, No Help Like a Woman's*', *Comparative Literature Studies*, 24 (1987), 335–52.

LEVIN, RICHARD, *The Multiple Plot in English Renaissance Drama* (Chicago, 1971).

—— 'Quomodo's Name in *Michaelmas Term*', *N & Q* 218 (1973), 460–1.

LIMON, JERZY, *Dangerous Matter: English Drama and Politics in 1623/4* (Cambridge, 1986).

LLOYD, BERTRAM, 'A Minor Source of *The Changeling*', *MLR* 19 (1924), 101–2.

LOMAX, MARION, *Stage-Images and Traditions: Shakespeare to Ford* (Cambridge, 1987).

LOOMBA, ANIA, *Gender, Race, Renaissance Drama* (1989; Delhi, 1992).

MCALINDON, T., *English Renaissance Tragedy* (London, 1986).

MCELROY, JOHN F., *Parody and Burlesque in the Tragicomedies of Thomas Middleton* (Salzburg, 1972).

MCFARLANE, K. B., ' "Bastard Feudalism" ', *Bulletin of the Institute of Historical Research*, 20 (1945), 161–80.

MCLUSKIE, KATHLEEN, *Renaissance Dramatists* (Atlantic Highlands, NJ, 1989).

MCMILLIN, SCOTT, 'Acting and Violence: *The Revenger's Tragedy* and its Departures from *Hamlet*', *SEL* 24 (1984), 275–91.

MALCOLMSON, CRISTINA, ' "As Tame as the Ladies": Politics and Gender in *The Changeling*', *ELR* 20 (1990), 320–39.

MARCUS, LEAH S., *The Politics of Mirth: Jonson, Herrick, Milton, Marvell, and the Defense of Old Holiday Pastimes* (Chicago, 1986).

—— *Puzzling Shakespeare: Local Reading and its Discontents* (Berkeley, Calif., 1988).

MAROTTI, ARTHUR F., 'The Method in the Madness of *A Mad World, My Masters*', *Tennessee Studies in Literature*, 15 (1970), 99–108.

—— 'The Purgations of Middleton's *The Family of Love*', *PLL* 7 (1971), 80–4.

MARTIN, LYNNEWOOD F., 'The Family of Love in England: Conforming Millenarians', *Sixteenth Century Journal*, 3 (1972), 99–108.

MATHEWS, ERNST G., 'The Murdered Substitute Tale', *MLQ* 6 (1945), 187–95.

MAXWELL, BALDWIN, *Studies in Beaumont, Fletcher, and Massinger* (Chapel Hill, NC 1939).

—— *Studies in the Shakespeare Apocrypha* (New York, 1956).

MONTROSE, LOUIS A., 'The Purpose of Playing: Reflections on a Shakespearean Anthropology', *Helios*, NS 7 (1980), 51–74.

MOONEY, MICHAEL E., ' "The Common Sight" and Dramatic Form: Rowley's Embedded Jig in *A Faire Quarrel*', *SEL* 20 (1980), 305–23.

MOORE, JOHN ROBERT, 'The Contemporary Significance of Middleton's *Game at Chesse*', *PMLA* 50 (1935), 761–8.

MORETTI, FRANCO, *Signs Taken for Wonders: Essays in the Sociology of Literary Forms*, trans. Susan Fischer et al. (1983; rev. edn., London, 1988).

MORGAN, JOHN, *Godly Learning: Puritan Attitudes towards Reason, Learning, and Education, 1560–1640* (Cambridge, 1986).

MORRIS, EDGAR C., 'The Allegory in Middleton's *A Game at Chesse*', *Englische Studien*, 38 (1907), 39–52.

MOSS, JEAN DIETZ, 'The Family of Love and English Critics', *Sixteenth Century Journal*, 6 (1975), 35–52.

MOUNT, DAVID B., 'The "[Un]reclaymed forme" of Middleton's *A Trick to Catch the Old One*', *SEL* 31 (1991), 259–72.

MULHOLLAND, PAUL A., 'The Date of *The Roaring Girl*', *RES*, NS 28 (1977), 18–31.

—— 'Let Her Roar Again: *The Roaring Girl* Revived', *RORD* 28 (1985), 15–27.

MULLANEY, STEVEN, *The Place of the Stage: License, Play, and Power in Renaissance England* (Chicago, 1988).

OLIPHANT, E. H. C., *The Plays of Beaumont and Fletcher: An Attempt to Determine their Respective Shares and the Shares of Others* (New Haven, Conn., 1927).

ORGEL, STEPHEN, *The Illusion of Power: Political Theater in the English Renaissance* (Berkeley, Calif., 1975).

ORNSTEIN, ROBERT, *The Moral Vision of Jacobean Tragedy* (Madison, Wis., 1960).

OSMOND, ROSALIE, *Mutual Accusation: Seventeenth-Century Body and Soul Dialogues in their Literary and Theological Context* (Toronto, 1990).

PARKER, R. B., 'Middleton's Experiments with Comedy and Judgment', in John Russell Brown and Bernard Harris (eds.), *Jacobean Theatre* (London, 1960), 178–99.

PASTER, GAIL, *The Idea of the City in the Age of Shakespeare* (Athens, Ga., 1985).

—— 'Quomodo, Sir Giles, and Triangular Desire: Social Aspiration in Middleton and Massinger', in A. R. Braunmuller and J. C. Bulman (eds.), *Comedy from Shakespeare to Sheridan: Change and Continuity in the English and European Dramatic Tradition: Essays in Honor of Eugene M. Waith* (Newark, NJ, 1986), 165–78.

—— 'Leaky Vessels: The Incontinent Women of City Comedy", *RD* 18 (1987), 43–65.

PENDLETON, THOMAS A., 'Shakespeare's Disguised Duke Play: Middleton, Marston, and the Sources of *Measure for Measure*', in John W. Mahon and Thomas A. Pendleton (eds.), *'Fanned and Winnowed Opinions': Shakespearean Essays Presented to Harold Jenkins* (London, 1987), 77–98.

PENTZELL, RAYMOND J., '*The Changeling*: Notes on Mannerism in Dramatic Form', *CD* 9 (1975), 3–28.

PHIALAS, P. G., 'Middleton's Early Contact with the Law', *SP* 52 (1955), 186–94.

POTTER, JOHN, ' "In Time of Sports": Masques and Masking in Middleton's *Women Beware Women*', *PLL* 18 (1982), 368–83.

POWER, W., 'Thomas Middleton vs. King James I', *N & Q* 202 (1957), 526–34.
—— '*The Phoenix*, Raleigh, and King James', *N & Q* 203 (1958), 57–61.
—— 'Double, Double', *N & Q* 204 (1959), 4–8.
PRICE, G. R., 'The Shares of Middleton and Dekker in a Collaborated Play', *Papers of the Michigan Academy of Science, Arts and Letters*, 30 (1944), 601–15.
—— 'The Early Editions of *The Ant and the Nightingale*', *PBSA* 43 (1949), 179–90.
—— 'The First Edition of *A Faire Quarrell*', *Library*, 5th ser. 4 (1949), 137–41.
—— 'The Latin Oration in *A Game at Chesse*', *HLQ* 23 (1960), 389–93.
—— 'The Early Editions of *A Trick to Catch the Old One*', *Library*, 5th ser. 22 (1967), 205–27.
RABKIN, NORMAN, 'Problems in the Study of Collaboration', *RORD* 19 (1976), 7–13.
RACKIN, PHYLLIS, 'Androgyny, Mimesis, and the Marriage of the Boy Heroine on the English Renaissance Stage', *PMLA* 102 (1987), 29–41.
RANDALL, DALE B. J., 'Some Observations on the Theme of Chastity in *The Changeling*', *ELR* 14 (1984), 347–66.
RASMUSSEN, ERIC, 'Shakespeare's Hand in *The Second Maiden's Tragedy*', *SQ* 40 (1989), 1–26.
RHODES, NEIL, *Elizabethan Grotesque* (London, 1980).
RIBNER, IRVING, *Jacobean Tragedy: The Quest for Moral Order* (London, 1962).
RICKS, CHRISTOPHER, 'The Moral and Poetic Structure of *The Changeling*', *EC* 10 (1960), 290–306.
—— 'Word-Play in *Women Beware Women*', *RES*, NS 12 (1961), 238–50.
RICOEUR, PAUL, *The Conflict of Interpretations: Essays in Hermeneutics*, ed. Don Ihde (Evanston, Ill., 1974).
RORTY, RICHARD, *Consequences of Pragmatism: Essays: 1972–1980* (Minneapolis, 1982).
ROSE, MARY BETH, *The Expense of Spirit: Love and Sexuality in English Renaissance Drama* (Ithaca, NY, 1988).
ROWE, JR., GEORGE E., *Thomas Middleton and the New Comedy Tradition* (Lincoln, Neb., 1979).
ROWSE, A. L., *The Elizabethans and America* (London, 1959).
—— *Sex and Society in Shakespeare's Age: Simon Forman the Astrologer* (New York, 1974).
RUIGH, ROBERT E., *The Parliament of 1624: Politics and Foreign Policy* (Cambridge, Mass., 1971).
SAID, EDWARD W., *Orientalism* (1978; Harmondsworth, 1985).
SALINGAR, L. G., '*The Revenger's Tragedy* and the Morality Tradition', *Scrutiny*, 6 (1938), 402–22.
—— '*The Revenger's Tragedy*: Some Possible Sources', *MLR* 60 (1965), 3–12.
—— '*The Changeling* and the Drama of Domestic Life', *E & S* 32 (1979), 80–96.

SARTRE, JEAN-PAUL, *What is Literature?*, trans. Bernard Frechtman (London, 1950).

SCHOENBAUM, SAMUEL, *Middleton's Tragedies: A Critical Study* (New York, 1955).

—— 'Middleton's Tragicomedies', *MP* 54 (1956), 1–19.

—— 'A New Middleton Record', *MLR* 55 (1960), 82–4.

—— *Internal Evidence and Elizabethan Dramatic Authorship: An Essay in Literary History and Method* (London, 1966).

—— *Shakespeare and Others* (Washington, DC, 1985).

SELIGMANN, RAPHAEL, 'A Probable Early Borrowing from Middleton and Dekker's *The Roaring Girl*', *N & Q* 238 (1993), 229–31.

SHAND, G. B., 'The Two Editions of Thomas Middleton's *The Blacke Booke*', *PBSA* 71 (1977), 325–8.

—— 'The Naming of Sir Walter Whorehound', *N & Q* 227 (1982), 136–7.

—— 'Source and Intent in Middleton's *Sir Robert Sherley*', *Ren. & Ref.* 19 (1983), 257–64.

SHAPIRO, MICHAEL, *Children of the Revels: The Boy Companies of Shakespeare's Time and their Plays* (New York, 1977).

SHEPHERD, SIMON, *Amazons and Warrior Women: Varieties of Feminism in Seventeenth-Century Drama* (Brighton, 1981).

SHERMAN, JANE, 'The Pawns' Allegory in Middleton's *A Game at Chesse*', *RES*, NS 29 (1978), 147–59.

SHERSHOW, SCOTT CUTLER, 'The Pit of Wit: Subplot and Unity in Middleton's *A Trick to Catch the Old One*', *SP* 88 (1991), 363–81.

SHUGER, DEBORA KULLER, *Habits of Thought in the English Renaissance: Religion, Politics, and the Dominant Culture* (Berkeley, Calif., 1990).

SIMMONS, J. L., 'The Tongue and its Office in *The Revenger's Tragedy*', *PMLA* 92 (1977), 56–68.

—— 'Diabolical Realism in Middleton and Rowley's *The Changeling*', *RD* 11 (1980), 135–70.

SISSON, C. J., *Lost Plays of Shakespeare's Age* (Cambridge, 1936).

SLATER, ANN PASTERNAK, 'Hypallage, Barley-Break, and *The Changeling*', *RES*, NS 34 (1983), 429–40.

SOMMERVILLE, J. P., *Politics and Ideology in England, 1603–1640* (London, 1986).

STALLYBRASS, PETER, 'Reading the Body: *The Revenger's Tragedy* and the Jacobean Theater of Consumption', *RD* 18 (1987), 121–48.

STEEN, SARA JAYNE, 'The Response to Middleton: His Own Time to Eliot', *RORD* 28 (1985), 63–71.

—— *Ambrosia in an Earthen Vessel: Three Centuries of Audience and Reader Response to the Works of Thomas Middleton* (New York, 1993).

STEVENSON, LAURA CAROLINE, *Praise and Paradox: Merchants and Craftsmen in Elizabethan Popular Literature* (Cambridge, 1984).

SUTHERLAND, SARAH, *Masques in Jacobean Tragedy* (New York, 1983).

SWINBURNE, ALGERNON CHARLES, *The Age of Shakespeare* (London, 1908).

TAYLOR, GARY and JOWETT, JOHN, *Shakespeare Reshaped 1606–1623* (Oxford, 1993).

TAYLOR, NEIL and LOUGHREY, BRYAN, 'Middleton's Chess Strategies in *Women Beware Women*', *SEL* 24 (1984), 341–54.

TENNENHOUSE, LEONARD, *Power on Display: The Politics of Shakespeare's Genres* (New York, 1986).

THOMAS, KEITH, *Religion and the Decline of Magic: Studies in Popular Belief in Sixteenth and Seventeenth Century England* (London, 1971).

—— 'The Puritans and Adultery: The Act of 1650 Reconsidered', in Donald Pennington and Keith Thomas (eds.), *Puritans and Revolutionaries: Essays in Seventeenth-Century History Presented to Christopher Hill* (Oxford, 1978), 257–82.

—— *Man and the Natural World: Changing Attitudes in England 1500–1800* (London, 1983).

THOMPSON, ELBERT N. S., *The Controversy between the Puritans and the Stage* (New York, 1903).

TOMLINSON, T. B., *A Study of Elizabethan and Jacobean Tragedy* (Cambridge, 1964).

TRICOMI, ALBERT H., *Anticourt Drama in England 1603–1642* (Charlottesville, Va., 1989).

TYACKE, NICHOLAS, 'Puritanism, Arminianism and Counter-Revolution', in Conrad Russell (ed.), *The Origin of the English Civil War* (London, 1973), 119–43.

UNDERDOWN, DAVID, *Revel, Riot, and Rebellion: Popular Politics and Culture in England 1603–1660* (Oxford, 1985).

WAGNER, BERNARD M., 'New Allusions to *A Game at Chesse*', *PMLA* 44 (1929), 827–34.

WELLS, STANLEY and TAYLOR, GARY, *William Shakespeare: A Textual Companion* (Oxford, 1987).

WHIGHAM, FRANK, *Ambition and Privilege: The Social Tropes of Elizabethan Courtesy Theory* (Berkeley, Calif., 1984).

WHITE, BEATRICE, *Cast of Ravens: The Strange Case of Sir Thomas Overbury* (London, 1965).

WHITE, MARTIN, *Middleton and Tourneur* (Basingstoke, 1992).

WICKHAM, GLYNNE, *Early English Stages 1300 to 1660*, 3 vols. (London, 1959–81).

WIGGINS, MARTIN, *Journeymen in Murder: The Assassin in English Renaissance Drama* (Oxford, 1991).

WIGLER, STEPHEN, 'Penitent Brothel Reconsidered: The Place of the Grotesque in Middleton's *A Mad World, My Masters*', *L & P* 25 (1975), 17–26.

—— ' "Tis Well He Died, He Was a Witch": A Note on *The Revenger's Tragedy*, V. iii. 17', *ELN* 14 (1976), 17–20.

WILLIAMS, RAYMOND, *The Country and the City* (New York, 1973).

WILLIAMS, ROBERT I., 'Machiavelli's *Mandragola*, Touchwood Senior, and the Comedy of Middleton's *A Chaste Maid in Cheapside*', *SEL* 10 (1970), 385–96.

WILLIAMSON, MARILYN L., '*The Phoenix*: Middleton's Comedy *de Regimine Principum*', *Renaissance News*, 10 (1957), 183–7.

WILSON, EDWARD M. and TURNER, OLGA, 'The Spanish Protest against *A Game at Chesse*', *MLR* 44 (1949), 476–82.

WILSON, F. P., *The Plague in Shakespeare's London* (1927; repr. London, 1963).

—— *Shakespearian and Other Studies*, ed. Helen Gardner (Oxford, 1969).

W[ILSON], J. D., Review of R. C. Bald (ed.), *A Game at Chesse, Library*, 4th ser. 11 (1930), 105–16.

WOHLFARTH, IRVING, 'No-Man's Land: On Walter Benjamin's "Destructive Character" ', *Diacritics*, 8 (1978), 47–65.

WRIGHT, LOUIS, B., '*A Game at Chess*', *TLS* 16 Feb. 1928, 112.

—— *Middle-Class Culture in Elizabethan England* (Chapel Hill, NC, 1935).

YACHNIN, PAUL, '*A Game at Chess* and Chess Allegory', *SEL* 22 (1982), 317–30.

—— 'The Significance of Two Allusions in Middleton's *The Phoenix*', *N & Q* 231 (1986), 375–7.

—— '*A Game at Chess*: Thomas Middleton's "Praise of Folly" ', *MLQ* 48 (1987), 105–23.

—— 'The Powerless Theater', *ELR* 21 (1991), 49–74.

—— 'The Politics of Theatrical Mirth: *A Midsummer Night's Dream, A Mad World, My Masters*, and *Measure for Measure*', *SQ* 43 (1992), 51–66.

YOUNG, ALAN R., *The English Prodigal Son Plays: A Theatrical Fashion of the Sixteenth and Seventeenth Centuries* (Salzburg, 1979).

ZIMMERMAN, SUSAN (ed.), *Erotic Politics: Desire on the Renaissance Stage* (New York, 1992).

Index

The index refers to the main text only, although footnotes which contain new or additional information, or refer to the texts of Middleton and his contemporaries are also referred to. Reference is limited to the first mention on a page, i.e. subsequent mention in a footnote on the same page is not listed separately.

All mentions of a work or its dramatis personae are treated as references to the author, with the exception of anonymous works and the works of Thomas Middleton. Detailed treatment of Thomas Middleton's works is indicated by the use of italicized page numbers.